Pastor and Professor

Pastor and Professor

A Public Faith

Donald Blosser

Anne
may your own faith
be a public expression
of love for all people

Don Blosser

WIPF & STOCK · Eugene, Oregon

Wipf & Stock
An Imprint of Wipf and Stock Publishers
199 W. 8th Ave., Suite 3
Eugene, OR 97401

www.wipfandstock.com

ISBN 13: 978-1-62032-134-8

Manufactured in the U.S.A.

Contents

Preface: Five Miles Out on a Dirt Road | vii

Introduction: Following Jesus in the Prophetic Tradition | xv

1   More Than a Good Idea | 1

2   Theological Earthquake | 38

3   What Really Matters? | 67

4   Same Book, Different Message | 97

5   Finding God without Even Looking | 129

6   Making Friends with God | 162

7   Follow Your Heart | 189

Epilogue: Back to the Home Place | 221

Bibliography | 233

Preface

Five Miles Out on a Dirt Road

From the cowardice that shrinks from new truth,
From the laziness that is content with half truths,
From the arrogance that thinks it knows all truth,
O God of Truth, deliver us.

—Anonymous
Ancient Prayer

You will know the truth, and the truth will make you free.

—Jesus
John 8:32

Let the children come to me.
You must never stop them from coming.
The kingdom of God belongs to little children like this.
This is how all of us must be if we want to enter the kingdom of God.

—Jesus
Luke 18:16

For those who do not know what "God" means,
LOOK AT JESUS![1]

—John Dominic Crossan

---

1. Crossan, *God and Empire: Jesus Against Rome, Then and Now.*

Five Miles Out on a Dirt Road

"Time to get up, Donny. Cleveland won last night three to one." That was how Mom (Edith) started the day for me. In the 1940s the Cleveland Indians were not winning many games. Even so, those were the days of Bob Feller, Dale Mitchell, Luke Easter, and my personal favorite, Lou Boudreau. Mom was quite a sports fan, although I don't know that she ever saw a big league baseball game in her life.

Memories of the past are often like this. They have a disjointed quality that somehow, upon reflection, assembles into a cohesive narrative. And it is the process of recalling select memories and creating such a narrative that reveals who we are today, and allows us to consider who we might become.

I came into this world near the end of the Great Depression as the youngest of nine children. Our family was highly competitive. It was a situation that had its drawbacks. I suppose it all depends on how you look at it. However, I understand now that the memories of my daily struggles are reflections on my place as the youngest child. I wanted to win at everything I did; to have the last word even if only to myself on my way out the door; and yet I doubted my winning abilities because maybe everyone was just "letting me win" since I was, after all, "little Donny."

As a child of the depression, I later shared John Denver's sentiments expressed in "Thank God I'm a Country Boy." Our forty-four acre farm provided food. It also gave us an appreciation of simple things and a strong work ethic. At the time, I wondered why we didn't have the nice things that other people had, like an indoor toilet, a nice car, something other than hand-me-down clothes, or even ten cents for ice cream at the Dairy Queen. But we siblings knew we were loved. Even so, I don't remember ever hearing Dad say "I love you" to Mom. But every day when he came home from work, he went to the kitchen and kissed her. We kids knew what was coming, so we scattered because we didn't want to see that.

The kitchen was the warm, family gathering place for us kids. We had a big kitchen table where we did our homework. We could sit at the table and talk with Mom about anything, even though it usually meant listening to *her*, because she loved to talk and tell stories.

Cooking was not easy for Mom. We had an old coal-burning stove that, when the fire got too hot, would burn supper. By contrast, when the fire was not hot enough we had to wait for supper. When I was in high school, Dad bought a used electric stove, and we all discovered that Mom really was a good cook. We had plenty of fresh vegetables from the garden, but I also ate enough corn meal mush, liver, and oatmeal to last a lifetime.

Dad was a house painter with an excellent reputation. He had work lined up months in advance, sometimes even a year or more if it was a big project, like a barn. Other painters would come out to the farm and ask Dad if he could use extra help. Sometimes Dad would hire them for a few days to finish painting a barn or shed, but he was never eager to do that because he had very high standards. For six years I worked with Dad each summer to pay my way through college. I can't begin to count the number of times I heard "it takes less time to do it right than it does to do it over" when my work was not up to his high standards.

After supper, if we'd done our obligatory daily hoeing and weeding in the garden, Dad would hit fly balls to us in the front yard. Even that activity had a bit of competition to it. Dad tried to hit the ball over my head, and I tried to throw it all the way back on the fly. There was no such thing as calling "I got it" during these "fly ball" sessions. I learned to push and shove, even knock my sisters Doris or Lois down to earn my right to catch it—regardless of where the ball was headed.

Having sisters was a good thing. I never got tired of having Velma, Doris, or Lois read stories. My favorites were *Tales About Timothy* and *Curious George*. Velma and Lois went on to be elementary school teachers. I like to think that some of the inspiration for this career choice came from the times they sat me down on the stair steps and played teacher with me, their little brother Donny, as the only pupil. It was inevitable that I could easily read at a second grade level before I ever entered Miss Albright's first grade class. We had no kindergarten at our school because that was an unheard of luxury reserved for "rich city kids." Even so, because of my family I had an excellent preschool education in both reading and counting.

Mom helped us create childhood dramas using stories she read from Egermeier's Bible Story Book. For some reason I have never understood, I was always given a nonspeaking animal part. But I got a part nonetheless, and these Bible story dramas became another building block of my education. We never thought to question whether the stories really happened the way they said. We simply play acted them the way they were written. Mom gave us empty boxes to build the walls of Jericho, and we marched around them making all the noise we could. But I was never patient enough to march all seven times around this make-believe city. After one trip around the city wall, I was ready for the fun of knocking down the boxes. I especially liked the Jonah story because, lacking the traditional whale, Mom gave us an old blue blanket that we tied across the backs of several chairs. I would crawl under the blanket for the proverbial "three days." I often fell asleep in the belly of our make-believe whale. Only years later did my sisters tell me that they liked playing "Jonah and the Whale," because it got me under the blanket and out of their way so they could do what they wanted to do without little brother pestering them.

Our old farmhouse was a warm, friendly house with enough rooms to make for fun games of hide and seek. My favorite place to hide was a scary place called the "dark room." In reality, it was a huge hall closet at the top of the stairs that had no windows and no electric light. My older brothers and sisters knew that was where I liked to hide, so finding little brother Donny was never a problem. It also meant that Donny was "it" most of the time. I still have strong memories of being terribly afraid while hiding behind a box in the dark room. Knowing that there were people out there (granted, they were my brothers and sisters) trying to find me was almost more than I could handle. My vivid imagination created monsters, bad guys, or even wild animals who were trying to "get me."

This fear of mine that goes with hiding from others has persisted in strange ways throughout my life. For example, even to this day, I do not like the feeling of being alone in a dark house. I will turn on extra lights and turn up the television to keep me company, even though I am not watching it. This same fear has also reappeared in most unusual ways. For example, in the summer of 1977 my wife, Carolyn, and I, with our five children, were on a camping trip in Europe. During this trip, we stopped in Amsterdam to visit the Anne Frank house, which was high on our "must do" list. We went through the bookcase door and into the attic where the Frank family and their friends had hidden for several years. As we shut the door behind us, I felt a cold shiver of fear go through me as I imagined what they must have felt knowing that German soldiers might burst through the door at any time.

Our household had few rules while I was a boy, and they were not rigidly enforced. Instead, our daily life was built around routines and expectations. At suppertime we were all expected to be at the table, and we had to wait for Mom to read a few verses from the Bible. Then Dad led in a standard, memorized prayer. Mom was not into discipline, although one day when I was caught taking a dime from her purse (so I could buy candy that afternoon), Mom sat down and told me very firmly to go to the kitchen and bring her the yardstick. I knew what that meant, so I hid the yardstick under the table and told her that I couldn't find it. That warranted two extra "strokes" for telling a lie. I remember that it hurt, but that Mom cried more than I did. If we did something really bad, Mom deferred to Dad, telling us: "Your father will deal with this when he gets home." That was bad news because with Dad punishment was a very serious matter.

Living on the farm meant that there was always work to do, even if sometimes it felt "made up," like hoeing field corn on a hot August afternoon. But this sort of labor did make me eager for school to start in September. The farm also meant that we had huge gardens with row after row of corn, potatoes, beans, tomatoes, peas, and carrots. Even in the worst years of World War II, we always had plenty of food. Every Saturday morning, Dad took the paint cans and smelly turpentine rags out of our old 1935 Plymouth. He and Mom filled the back seat with the best of the garden vegetables, plus dozens of fresh eggs, for their regular produce route in Youngstown, Ohio.

Taking care of these gardens taught me more than just how to work. People from town would come out to our farm asking for food. We lived on a dirt road about five miles from town, and such a visit represented quite a journey for them. Mom was quite generous, giving away fresh vegetables, a few eggs, and occasionally a pint of milk. Dad was not happy with the way Mom gave away garden produce. "That could have been sold on the route," he would say. But Mom simply felt the people looked hungry, and she kept giving away food. As an adult, I see both Mom and Dad in myself. I am far too quick to give something away (that's Mom) and then I wish later that I still had it (that's Dad). Mom's generosity seems to be the dominant factor in me. Even today, when our daughter Kathy calls asking if we can help with something, I tend to say, "Sure, we can do that," only to have her say, "Dad, can I talk to Mom first?" The flip side of my Mom's generosity also became deeply embedded into my psyche: "The Blossers help others, but we don't ask others to help us." I know I should ask for help sometimes. But I don't ask for help, or at least I don't want to ask.

One Saturday evening, when I was about twelve or thirteen years old, I recall doing all those things that we had to do to be ready for Sunday church: taking a bath, shining our shoes, memorizing Bible verses for Sunday school. But on that particular evening, Mom asked if I had thought about joining the church. I hadn't given it much thought. In many ways it felt like I was already a member of the church, because we participated in everything the church did. Mom told me she thought I was old enough to join and that it was time for me to be baptized. This was not a request. It was a directive.

A month or so later, the bishop was our visiting preacher. At the end of his sermon, he gave a traditional invitation: "Anyone who wanted to accept Christ as their savior should raise their hand." I was sitting with Dad that morning, and his instructions were the usual "every eye closed, and every head bowed." But I sneaked a peek over at Mom, and she nodded her head, so I raised my hand. After the benediction, I was told to come forward to meet with the bishop. I was surprised to see that he had tears in his eyes. I wondered why, because I was simply doing what Mom told me to do.

I have looked back on that decision many times. In retrospect, I wish I had been a bit older in order that I could have had a better understanding of what this meant. Fifteen years later, when I was a young pastor, a few parents were upset with me because I did not want to pressure their pre-teenaged children to join the church just because the parents thought it was the right time. This early teenage experience of mine to join the church was one of those events that, unknown to me at the time, had shaped my faith in a particular direction.

As I reflect back on that experience, I know I took faith seriously. But my understanding of what a faith commitment was, and what it meant to be an adult, has changed significantly over the years. As a boy, my immaturity led me to feel that I had to make a new faith commitment every time I learned something new about God and about myself. I felt that I had to publicly update who I was by responding every time an invitation to accept Christ was given. This, of course, raises profound questions about what it means to exhibit a public faith. For now, let me say it is no coincidence that this concept is expressly stated in the subtitle of this book.

In our family, going to school every day and having our homework done was a matter of pride. We joked about it sometimes. Mom's standard was: "If you are breathing, you are well enough to be in school." Mom and Dad had only a few years of elementary school education, but they both believed in the benefits of education. There was never any doubt in their minds: the Blosser children were going to college. That meant we had to get good grades in junior high school, so we would do well in high school, so we could get into college. One year I. E. Burkhart, of Goshen College, came to see my sisters about going to Goshen College. He promised me that Goshen would have a room ready for me when I was ready for college. I was really impressed that a college would do that, just for me. Mom and Dad's devotion to education paid off. Seven of their nine children went to college, six graduated, two earned master's degrees, and two of us have PhDs. Mom was justifiably proud of her children.

But our family did more than emphasize education and provide food to those who travelled down the dirt road to knock on our door. My home congregation (Midway Mennonite Church) helped organize a city mission outreach in the steel mill district of Youngstown, Ohio. The church leadership asked me, as a high school senior, to be part of the mission team that drove to Youngstown each Sunday morning. We would set up the temporary church meeting space, then fan out through the streets in order to invite children to come to Sunday school.

Living on the farm did not prepare me for what I experienced in the steel mill district of Youngstown. We had no inside plumbing other than the kitchen sink. But here families were living in houses with no front door, no plumbing whatever, and with half of the windows broken. The thick sulfur soot from the steel mills was everywhere, and by 10 a.m. on an August morning, the heat and smells were stifling. As a teenager, I thought I knew a lot about life. In school I had read about slavery. But here I was confronted with disrupted family structures, nauseous smells, and poverty conditions that seemed unlivable and were, to me, unbelievable.

For nearly a year I went back each Sunday to the steel mill district of Youngstown. Parents began to call me by name, and often I would shoot hoops with an older brother while a younger child was being dressed for Sunday school. I knew nothing about teaching, but I faked it as best I could by either telling a Bible story, or getting the four or five students to talk about their week and what they wanted to do. I felt guilty most of the time because I didn't think I was teaching them anything. Most weeks I could hardly wait to get back to the farm where I could at least get a breath of fresh air and a drink of cold water.

But it was in this setting of hard poverty that I first began to wonder over some key concerns that are with me to this day. At the time, my thinking went like this: "I know Bible stories are important, but what these families need is decent housing, clean water to drink, a toilet, and air that is breathable. Was there more that I should be doing, other than just telling them a Bible story about Moses? Maybe these people need a Moses to liberate them as badly as did Israel in Egypt!"

One Sunday afternoon in my senior year of high school, my pastor, Ernest Martin, invited me to go with him to visit a patient at the Cleveland hospital. We planned to meet with the I-W (alternate service) unit there. On that trip Ernest talked with me about what a pastor does, about the importance of caring for people, and about the centrality of the way of peace in following Jesus. I watched as he visited with the patient and then interacted with the young men who were fulfilling their alternative to military service by working as hospital orderlies. This was all quite new for me. I knew that pastors preached sermons, but here I was learning about other important pastoral work.

I look back now and see the nurturing impact of my mother, the cross-cultural experience of teaching Sunday school in Youngstown, and the quiet mentoring of a good pastor. Perhaps my decision to become a pastor, and to express my faith publicly, wasn't totally my own decision after all.

Introduction

Following Jesus in the Prophetic Tradition

I was playing golf at Black Squirrel, our local golf club. I was alone, so the starter put me with a man whom I had never met before. On the first hole, the man pushed his first shot into the lake to the right of the fairway. He slammed his club on the ground and let fly with the proverbial blue streak of vivid, colorful language. On the third hole, he pushed his drive out of bounds on the right, and unleashed another volley of vehement, colorful expletives that included God, Jesus, and a few other religious terms that I was less familiar with. As we were walking down the fourth fairway, he politely asked me, "What do you do for a living?" How was I supposed to answer that?

Pastors and professors are, by nature, very public in what they do. We regularly stand before groups of people to introduce new concepts. We invite a classroom of students or a congregation of parishioners to wrestle with new ideas. Usually, introducing new ideas works better in the classroom than it does in the congregation. Students expect to learn, to explore the edges of their knowledge, and to be challenged to think. Tell them what they already know and they quickly get bored, or even stop coming to class. By contrast, in the congregational setting if too many new ideas are heard from the pulpit, members of the congregation may stop coming to church. Thus pastors and professors are continually confronted with how best to present information to their audience. Can one individual be pastoral, prophetic, and professional all at the same time? The biblical record tells us that doing so can pose significant challenges. Bible professors know the truth of these challenges, and current pastors are very careful about how they introduce new faith concepts in their Sunday morning sermons.

Congregational preaching and classroom teaching is much more than simply delivering a twenty minute sermon or a fifty minute lecture. Sermons and lectures are conceived and prepared; and each comes to life through the faith, the vision, and the convictions of the pastor/professor. Most people in the congregation are not aware of the intentionality that goes into sermon preparation. It is rare for a parishioner ask, "Why did the pastor preach that sermon this morning?" Wouldn't it be exciting if a congregation could see behind the sermon to discover the rationale and the thinking process that goes into developing a sermon?

Homiletics classes in our seminaries teach the dramatic power of the spoken word from the pulpit. But I don't remember much discussion of what we should expect the sermon to do. Should a sermon educate and inform, thus improving biblical knowledge for the church members? Should it inspire and issue a challenge to action among listeners, thus creating new behaviors and new activities for community witness or mission? Should the Sunday morning sermon dare to challenge the established beliefs of the congregation by introducing new theological concepts? Likewise, do we really expect the Bible professor to ignore the latest discoveries in serious biblical study simply because these ideas might force students to rethink some of their own beliefs? Would it be right for the pastor or the professor to believe that we already know everything there is to know about the Bible, meaning that all we can do is reinforce the accepted truths of the last generation?

These are important questions. And it is from this perspective that this book invites pastors to preach with more intentionality and purpose, and to have the courage to express a public faith that will educate, inform, inspire, and challenge others—and themselves. This same challenge faces the Bible professor as he or she seeks to nurture a growing faith that has integrity for students. These are not easy tasks: both pastors and professors recognize that in creative preaching from the pulpit and divergent teaching from the lectern, they are exposed to criticism that could have dramatic negative impacts upon their professional careers and future.

And so, it is my hope that this book will do several things:

a) Encourage the reader to allow me to walk with them in discovering changes that are unfolding as their faith develops

b) Encourage the reader to see how the message of scripture challenges us to explore new ways of living that are faithful to what Jesus taught and did

c) Encourage congregations to expect to learn new ideas from sermons, much as students expect to hear new concepts in the classroom

d) Encourage pastors and professors to discover new confidence in the potential that preaching and teaching offers as they share both the biblical story and their own story in the congregation and in the classroom, so that all those who hear are more comfortable sharing their own faith stories with each other.

This book is offered not in the belief that it contains wonderful truth never before stated. Rather, it is offered in the hope that its readers will identify with my personal experiences and struggles with faith so that they too will find courage to keep walking into their own future. If readers are inspired to reach out in new ways to people around them, if they are challenged to consider new understandings of faithfulness to the biblical text, and if they discover a new freedom to accept themselves as God accepts them while recognizing the constant potential for growth in their own lives, then the risks of my sharing my story in this way will be well worth it.

If the reader has questions, or has a different way of reading a specific story from scripture, or is troubled by what I share here, I would welcome the opportunity to listen and talk with you so that we might both grow in our faith. I would also be glad to hear from you if something from my life story was helpful to you in your own journey.

—Don Blosser
Goshen, Indiana

1

More Than a Good Idea

I know that you have been told:
"You shall love your neighbor and hate your enemy."
But I am telling you, love your enemies
and pray for those who persecute you
so that you may be children of your father in heaven.
—Jesus
Matthew 5:43–45

When I was a child, I thought, and talked, and felt like a little child.
But now that I have become an adult
my childish speech and feelings and ways of thinking
are no longer adequate for how I live my life.
—Paul
1 Corinthians 13:11

Conflict is an opportunity to know.
Struggling through conflict can make us vulnerable,
sharpen our senses, help us see our inadequacy
and open us to God and to others in new ways.[1]
—Carolyn Schrock-Shenk

We are truly one people, and as compassionate community
we need to find ways to be more intentional with each other.
We need to discover how to share our narratives
in compassionate friendship with those who are different from ourselves.
—Tony Brown
"We Must Be The Change"
Commencement Address, Hesston College
May 2010

---

1. Schrock-Shenk and Ressler, *Making Peace with Conflict*, p. 2.

More Than a Good Idea

A big brother can be a very good influence. My big brother, Carl, is ten years older than me. Growing up, we shared a large drafty bedroom in the old farmhouse. Carl was my hero. He was good at virtually everything he did. The Columbiana Park officials in town even moved the right field fence back fifteen feet to keep Carl from hitting so many home runs. He led our high school basketball team to two very successful winning seasons. When I was a freshman, I made the varsity basketball team. And even though not as a starter more than one person said, "Oh good, that's Carl Blosser's little brother, Donny." Carl was a tough act to follow.

One Christmas, when I was about eight or nine years old, Carl gave me a basketball. He put up a basketball hoop over the garage and began regular drills with me on dribbling and shooting. After school I shot baskets for hours, even when there was snow on the ground. Carl was a good teacher, but he was merciless. I had to make ten free throws in a row before we could quit. More than once we skipped supper because I kept missing the ninth or tenth free throw. When you are ten years old, hungry, and have been shooting free throws for an hour, that's pressure. Six years later Carl's tenacity paid off. When a game was on the line, my high school coach wanted the ball in my hands so that I would get fouled and be the one shooting free throws.

But, as a basketball player, I had developed other habits that Carl felt he needed to correct. I was a serious player. Or, at least, I took seriously the challenge of being a freshman on the varsity team. It's worth noting that my high school, Fairfield High School, had fewer than 100 students. So when I say that I made varsity as a freshman, it sounds more impressive than it really was. Regardless, in my first year on the varsity team I frequently had a different opinion than did the referees when they called a foul on me. I would mutter a few well chosen words just loud enough for the officials to hear. The results were predictable. Several times I was called for a technical foul or was even ejected from the game. My mother, who was always in the stands and could out-cheer any high school student sitting near her, was mortified by my embarrassing behavior. Once, after quietly expressing an alternative opinion, I was sent to an early shower. Carl left his seat in the stands, came down to the locker room, backed me up against the wall, and tore into me with a lecture that would have made a drill sergeant proud. He had some choice words of his own. Carl was older and no longer lived at home, so he could use words I was not supposed to even know. He told me I was of absolutely no use to the team taking a shower when they were still playing, and that if I didn't clean up my language and stop swearing, he'd give me a beating I'd never forget. He was bigger than me, and I believed him. His bluff worked. I stopped swearing, finished the season, played three more years in high school and several years of college basketball without ever being ejected from another game. This experience with Carl taught me the importance of being a team member, of taking charge of my own behavior, and of establishing priorities in my life.

Years earlier, in 1944, Carl had joined the army. Mom and Dad were devastated. I can still see Carl waving goodbye to me as he went out the door the morning dad took him to the train station to report for military service at Fort Bragg, North Carolina. I was only seven years old, but I knew something really terrible had happened at our house. Mom cried off and on for weeks. Something changed on that day. I didn't know it then, but that event changed the way my parents raised me. Mom and Dad were determined that they would not make the same mistakes with me that they believed they had made with Carl. They found stories about peace in the church library. They gave me stories and texts from the Bible to read. One of my favorite books was *Wings of Decision* by Eunice Shellenberger. It is the story of two friends: one joined the Air Force, while the other went into alternative service. Mom and Dad made sure I understood that our family followed Jesus in the way of peace. There were obvious comparisons within our own family. While Carl was in the army (stationed in the Panama Canal Zone as a company clerk), two of my other older brothers, Howard and Paul, were in Civilian Public Service (CPS); and my sister Laura was in voluntary service as a CPS camp cook.

We followed the war closely because Carl was in it. Every evening we listened to Walter Cronkite. We prayed for Carl every day, but we also prayed for people who lived in Germany and Japan. As a boy, I sat at the kitchen table and wondered what God did with our prayers. Did the German people also pray? Would God hear them too? How would God know whose prayers to answer? Those prayers helped me begin to understand that God loves all people—even our enemies—and that war is a sin against God.

People knew my Dad as a quiet man, but as we hoed potatoes in the garden, he would talk with me about how awful war is, what it does to innocent people, and how war does not solve national problems. When the United States dropped an atomic bomb on Hiroshima in August 1945, the town of Columbiana celebrated. The war would soon be over. Our sons and brothers would be coming home. But that evening at the supper table Dad broke from his standard recited prayer and prayed for forgiveness for what we had done to the innocent people of that city in Japan. In his own simple way, Dad taught me that we had done more than destroy a city; we had killed thousands of innocent people who did not deserve to die. I was learning that following Jesus might, on occasion, put us at odds with national values.

As a sophomore I played first chair clarinet in the high school band, but Mom and Dad never let me march in the annual Memorial Day parade. The band director was not sympathetic. Every year I had to make an "I will not be marching with you on Memorial Day . . ." speech to the band. It was not well received by some band members. I learned to accept the name-calling and subtle insults suggesting that I was anti-American and significantly lacking in courage.

We never went to town to watch the parade. We started the day working on the farm, then at noon we would go to Firestone Park for a family reunion with all our aunts and uncles and cousins. Most of them had been at the parade and wanted to talk about the floats and the bands. More than once they asked, "I thought you played in the band. Where were you this morning?"

These experiences instilled in me the beginning of a lifelong understanding that following Jesus is about more than just avoiding war; it means being an active peacemaker. Peace is much more than just a good idea; it is one of the faith pillars on which we build our lives as followers of Jesus.

Years later, as pastor of the Freeport, Illinois, Mennonite Church, I preached sermons on peace. I talked about peace with the local service clubs, churches, and schools. I also wrote an occasional letter to the *Freeport Journal Standard*. Carolyn, my wife, and I were active tax resisters. This was not as glamorous as it sounds because at that time I was a part-time pastor with four children and our income was well below the IRS taxable level. These acts were a matter of faith for us. We deducted the forty-cent tax on our phone bill that was clearly designated as a war tax. Each month we received a letter reminding us of our obligation to pay this tax, so we began attaching a letter of explanation with our monthly payment. The telephone company kept adding the tax, but they stopped sending the stern letter. To their credit, they never disrupted our phone service. I wonder whether we still have an outstanding tax bill in the archives of the Freeport phone company.

When we moved to Akron, Pennsylvania, in 1969, I had a growing conviction that, as a pastor, I should do more than simply preach sermons on peace. Being passively critical of the Vietnam War from the pulpit of a peace church is not taking much of a risk. One week the Akron congregation took out a full-page ad in the Lancaster *Intelligencer Journal* opposing the war. Three days later two IRS agents from Washington, DC, walked into my office in downtown Akron. They saw the ad portrayed as a political act that jeopardized the tax exempt status of the church. They made it perfectly clear that our church was a target for IRS scrutiny. I didn't know whether I should be intimidated or be glad that at least somebody had read the ad. We sought counsel from lawyers within the congregation who urged us to run a second ad. Only this time we removed the church name and listed only individual names, including persons from other churches who shared our concerns for peace. We heard nothing more from the IRS, but their threat made some members of the congregation very nervous. This started me thinking about what I was willing to do, and how much risk I was willing to take, as an active peacemaker on a public stage.

These two ads opened another opportunity for me. Phil and Dan Berrigan were Catholic peace activists who were often in the news with their antiwar demonstrations. They also had seen the two ads. They invited me to join them at Jonah House in Baltimore for prayer and creative planning as they wrestled with ways to call attention to the public dangers of nuclear war. In our discussions, we focused on the obvious result of nuclear war—people die. How does one prepare for one's own death? We decided to protest the development of nuclear weapons by digging our own graves in symbolic preparation for our inevitable death. We decided that the White House lawn was the best location for these graves because this would ensure broad TV coverage.

The day began at Jonah House with several hours of prayer and quiet meditation in preparation. Several priests, two nuns, and one retired general in full military uniform were members of our core group. These five persons took the standard White House tour. As they exited the White House and walked down the front drive, we handed them foxhole shovels through the fence, and they began to dig a grave in the White House lawn with network TV cameras and a sizeable crowd looking on.

The White House security was efficient and swift. Phil and Dan Berrigan were well known for their direct political actions. As soon as one shovel was stuck in the ground, the police began making arrests. Sister Liz McAllister was our spokesperson who explained our actions to the national network news. Phil Berrigan used his penetrating wit to report, "The city of Washington was so pleased with what we had done, they invited us to be their guests at a city facility where they have promised us a free meal and a bed for the night." I was not included in the city's invitation for "bed and breakfast in jail" because I was outside the fence, but I felt that I had participated in a legitimate witness on a very important issue.

It was inevitable that as I was taking this public stand, our children would get the message. One evening, I went with our oldest daughter, Lois, to an Ephrata Junior High School program. I casually stood to my feet as everyone began singing the national anthem. Lois was an eighth grade student. She yanked on my sleeve, saying, "Dad, what are you doing—sit down!" This presented an interesting dilemma. Should I offend my own daughter (I could deal with that later at home) or should I offend the rest of the town who were singing with obvious enthusiasm? As quietly and unobtrusively as possible I sat down, hoping no one would notice. But people did see it, and I heard about it for weeks. Several Ephrata pastors were quite sharp in their criticism that my action had turned a local celebration into a political demonstration. They did not believe this was appropriate spiritual leadership for a pastor.

As was often the case, friends helped me think through what I was doing. David Kovach was pastor of the Akron Lutheran Church. We were very close friends, and we met almost daily for coffee at The Akron Restaurant. Both of us were unhappy with the war, but we had slightly different ideas about how to respond to it. He pushed hard, forcing me to think through the implications of my more direct political actions. Because I claimed to be a theological pacifist, I had to resolve within myself what level of passive or indirect violence was legitimate. Does the nonlethal violence of Jesus in cleansing the temple validate our attempts to disrupt a military system that makes lethal violence an accepted way of life for the nation? Must one be a purist who avoids violence in all its forms? Is disruptive, nonlethal violence legitimate for the committed follower of Jesus? I knew the depth of my own commitment to theological pacifism, but I was being challenged by those who felt my peace activist actions were not always legitimate. Would being arrested for my beliefs make any difference in the grand scheme of American military policy? I kept debating within myself whether peace is just a good theological idea or if it is an active way of life.

Our family moved to Scotland in 1976, where I began my PhD studies at the University of St Andrews. My peace activism had always been directed at specific American issues, usually military spending or national policies, that too quickly used war for problem solving. I had never thought much about how war and faith and government practices might intersect in a different political system.

On our second Sunday in Scotland, we worshipped with the local Church of Scotland congregation. I was not prepared for what I saw as I walked into church that morning. A British Union Jack was draped over the pulpit; an airplane tire was on the communion table; a small shock of rifles was standing to the right of the pulpit; and a huge Royal Air Force (RAF) emblem was hanging on the cross. It was all very impressive, and it certainly got my attention. The church was observing Battle of Britain Sunday, celebrating a major air battle over the south of England that is credited with turning the tide of World War II in favor of Britain. The sermon praised the brave RAF pilots who "flew into the face of the devil himself" to defend God and country. Near the end of the sermon, the pastor told the congregation, "If I had known that we would have American visitors with us here this morning, I would have added an American flag because it was their tax dollars that paid for our salvation." Suddenly, war, peace, and following Jesus took on a whole new dimension.

Over the next three years, this pastor and I became good friends. We talked several times about his life as an RAF pilot during those intense German bombing raids over London. As I compared his experiences to mine (a farm boy in Ohio who thought our imposed blackouts were really exciting), it occurred to me that I had a lot of listening to do before I dared to lecture anyone on how they should follow Jesus.

But listening did not come easy for me. I was an experienced pastor who was doing graduate work on a PhD. I had to fight the temptation to interrupt others. I had academic answers for all false statements before anyone was even finished making them. I am older now, and I hope I am more considerate. But I still slide far too quickly into an attack mode, wanting to argue my biblical or theological points without allowing others to complete their own thoughts, or even their first sentence.

Dr. Matthew Black was my academic advisor at St Andrews. He challenged me in a different way, drawing from his own experience in

World War II as a British soldier fighting in France. During an intense firefight, he dove into a culvert for safety. At that same instant, a German soldier crawled in the other end. Matthew quietly said, "I got to my gun first and I killed him. I had no reason to do that except he was the enemy. I knew immediately that I had done something terribly wrong. I had sinned against God. But I did not know there were any other options. I had never heard the Jesus message of peace in the congregation where I grew up." He then singled me out in class, "Don, where have the Mennonites been? Why did you not tell us that Jesus teaches us to love our enemies, and he actually means it? How can you know that and assume that God won't care if you keep quiet?"

How does one answer that kind of question? Can one connect non-judgmental empathy for those who fought in the war with Jesus' prophetic call to love our enemies? How do we respond to the soldiers who fought in the war because their pastors and their churches never told them to do or believe anything different than that? What if these soldiers honestly believe that killing other people is a valid Christian response for protecting God and the church because that is all they have ever been taught? As I talked with Rev. Charles Miller and Dr. Matthew Black, I began to see that my issue is not with the soldier who actually fights in the battlefields of war. These soldiers believed they were serving God. My argument was with the church, with our colleges and seminaries, for accepting and then preaching a gospel that did not capture the essence of Jesus and his message. Can Christian people actually love Jesus and yet kill other people to protect their right to love Jesus? I could not agree with that for myself. But in the same breath I cannot condemn soldiers for doing what their church and their country (both of whom claim to be following Jesus) demand that they do. This condemnation is reserved for the church and for the nation, not the individual soldier. Indeed, to what extent can we remain silent and still claim to be faithful followers of Jesus?

When I returned to the United States and joined the faculty at Goshen College in 1979, I wanted students to understand that believing in peace involves much more than simply having right theological ideas. Do we really believe something if it has no impact on how we live? In my Jesus and the Gospels class, the subject one evening was peace in the teachings of Jesus. To illustrate what would otherwise be an intellectual discussion, I decided to go back to my days with Phil and Dan Berrigan and use political theater to stage my own arrest for tax evasion, plus aiding nonregistrants. Because our son John was a nonregistrant, and we were engaged in symbolic tax resistance, the charges had some legitimacy. A friend, who was unknown to the students, interrupted the class with an official looking warrant, confirmed my identity, and then read the charges against me. He politely informed me that I was under arrest and that I should come with him. I asked a student to take my books and notes back to my office, and I left the classroom with no further comment.

This created a serious existential teaching moment. The class responded quickly. Several students went to our home to be with Carolyn. A few students tried to visit me in the local jail. Others spread the word across campus and spontaneous prayer groups sprang up. (I was actually on my way to Bluffton University in Ohio, where I was to speak at a peace conference the next morning.) At Goshen College many students were up half the night trying to determine exactly what had happened. President Burkholder was supportive of what I had done, but was concerned that I had not informed anyone about this dramatic teaching experience. Two days later a meeting was arranged for me to meet with students to explain and discuss my actions.

Is it valid to use radical peace protests that force people out of their comfort zone? Is it appropriate to disrupt a social system, even nonviolently, to make a theological point? Jesus did this several times, and his actions were usually not well received by those who were impacted by what he did. Does that make it appropriate to assume that similar nonviolent actions are valid, or even helpful in our own day?

Am I really a child of God if I ask the state, in my name and with my tax money, to dispose of those who the state says are a threat to me? Is that something a follower of Jesus should do? Throughout history the institutional church has tended to reject those who preach a radical message of God's love for enemies because that message threatens the church's acceptance within the nation. The church is even more hostile toward those who express that message in public demonstrations or radical actions. If the church agrees to be silent about what the state does so that the state will not threaten our right to worship Jesus, the Christ, haven't we crucified Jesus again for our own comfort and safety? The result is a retreat into a spiritual gospel that abdicates moral decision making to the state. Where is the good news of the gospel in that message?

Not everyone shares this commitment to an active peace witness. Many fine Christian people argue that peace is a good theological idea, but it is just that—a theological idea, nothing more. How do you talk about Jesus while ignoring the peace and justice concerns of the Sermon on the Mount? Is it appropriate to make peace a critical priority in our Anabaptist conversations with other Christian groups? But before we take on this ecumenical Christian dialogue, we need to think more carefully about our own commitment to peace. As individuals, when our personal wealth increases we very casually accept the social/economic values of that prosperity, and in doing that we severely domesticate the gospel. We passively accept national wars that claim to protect our wealth and defend our faith without realizing that when we do this we are turning our back on Jesus. This act of acceptance in fact rejects the very faith we think we are defending.

I still wrestle with accepting persons who feel differently about the importance of peace in the teachings of Jesus. I find it hard to reconcile within myself how a person can take Jesus seriously and yet reject his call to be a peacemaker and a healer of human relationships. I am well aware that this attitude is not consistent with my commitment to accept all people. This struggle goes on within me on an almost daily basis.

What is the value of having church succeed (whatever that means) if it sacrifices the teachings of Jesus in order to gain that success? How can I share Jesus' message of peace without appearing to believe that I am spiritually superior to those who read the message of Jesus in a different way? I often feel caught in the tension between wanting to be a follower of Jesus while also wanting to be pastoral for anyone who claims Jesus as Lord. I pray for courage that I might be faithful in how I read the Bible and follow Jesus. But I also pray that I might be as loving and merciful with others as Jesus is with me. Believing that Jesus calls us to be people of peace is not simply a good theological idea, it resides at the heart of the gospel that Jesus preached and was central in the life he lived. Certainly this should be our good news as well.

But Daddy: A Conversation with a Child about Peace

Jesus frequently used persons or events happening around him as the springboard for a parable or an important teaching moment. "See that man over there sowing his field? That's how it is in the Kingdom of God." "Do you see that shepherd with his sheep? That is how God is." "See that Pharisee standing on the corner saying his prayers? If you really want God to hear you . . ." Teachable moments! No wonder we remember them so well.

In the Old Testament, parents were encouraged to use every event in daily life to teach their children the commandments of God. They were to do this when they were sitting at home, when they were walking along the road, in the morning when they got up, and in the evening before going to bed. They were to have them hanging on the walls around the house.

Carolyn and I tried to use this biblical model with our own family. I cherish the memory of those teachable moments with our own children. Often, we recognize these moments only after they have passed. For example, in the autumn of 1971, Carolyn and I were living in Akron, Pennsylvania. We had gone to Virginia for several days to visit my older brother Carl. I had been a history major in college, so we took our children on a tour of two Civil War battlefields. As an ardent theological pacifist, I had some concern about what message our children would get from this experience, because both battlefields present a rather glorified image of war. Plus, our nation was at war again, this time in Vietnam— a war we did not support—and it was considered unpatriotic and even unchristian by many people to not support this war.

Our children brought their own childlike curiosity and probing questions to these old battlefields. And, along the way, my children gave me an opportunity to answer their questions and talk with them about our own values in following Jesus. Sometimes the best teachable moments simply happen.

> These commandments that I give you are to be written on your heart. Impress them upon your children. Talk about them when you sit at home and when you walk along the road, when you lie down and when you get up. (Deuteronomy 6:6–7)

* * *

But Daddy: A Conversation with a Child about Peace

It was one of those rare October days. We were in Virginia visiting relatives when we took our children on the tour of the Wilderness and Chancellorsville battlefields. The air was crisp and clear, the leaves were beautiful, and the sun was shining in a cloudless sky. As we followed the self-guided tour, stopping to read the signs, looking at the canons, and answering questions from our children, I noticed that Kathy (she's six) would not move until she had hold of my hand.

"Daddy," she said, "I'm afraid. Are we in enemy land?"

"No," I assured her, "we are not in enemy land."

John, he's eight and thinks he knows a lot more, jumped out of a depression in the ground that had a sign saying it had once been a bunker for Confederate troops, and informed Kathy that this war was fought only by Americans. To use his words, "It was just us fighting each other, there weren't really any enemies."

Kathy stopped, looked up at me and said, "Daddy, I don't understand. If there weren't any enemies, why did they fight each other?" I wasn't sure how to answer that one. So we sat down in that Confederate bunker and talked about war, about hatred, about enemies, why people fight, and what we should do because we want to follow Jesus.

That's a good assignment. You should try it sometime. Explain to your six, eight, and eleven year old children why war is wrong, yet people fight them. Explain what Jesus said about killing people and then answer them when they ask why Christian people kill each other. Explain what it means to give your whole life to Jesus and then justify sitting back and doing nothing to stop wars. Children can ask hard questions, as I found out!

"But Daddy, if everybody knew about Jesus, they wouldn't go to war and kill other people, would they?"

Where do you go with that one? It makes such simple sense—to an eleven year old. How do you explain that Christians have, in the name of Christian faith, fought more wars, destroyed more homes, and killed more people than any other people in history? How do you tell her that some people preach that God is a God of love and yet completely support a war that kills and destroys the very people God is trying to love?

I remembered that just last week she came home from elementary school asking about the sign one of her classmates had on his desk: *Kill a commie for Christ*. She had wondered why anybody would want to do that!

Somehow we have taken the words of Jesus and have messed them up pretty badly. We look back in history and see the Crusades; bloody, destructive, dehumanizing campaigns carried out in the name of Christ to save Jerusalem from the infidels. But then, we don't really have to look back. Look around today and you will discover that we are still fighting crusades. Only the Turks are now the Communists, and the Holy City of Jerusalem is now Washington, DC. The reasons behind today's crusades are grotesquely familiar.

"We must protect God and our homeland from the pagans." We don't understanding that by going to war we are joining the ranks of paganism, and that in so doing we are rejecting the call of Christ to live in the way of peace.

There was a time in our own history when we, the church, were the quiet in the land. Because of persecution for being outspoken for our faith, the church faced extinction, and so it went underground and became silent. Now, once again, we have become the quiet in the land, accepting a popular, spiritual gospel that does not include calling our nation to repent for its acceptance of militarism in the name of Jesus.

We have decided to remain silent and permit the killing and destroying of whole countries, believing that because we don't go ourselves, we do not share in their guilt. We are quiet. Is it because we are afraid to risk houses or brothers or sisters or faith or children or fields for my sake and the gospel? (Mark 10:29). We have sold our birthright for a mess of pottage. Only by now the pottage goes down so smoothly because it is well flavored with high profits, good wages, comfortable homes, and prosperous businesses. We forget that, in God's sight, pottage is still pottage no matter how delicately you flavor it.

Do we really believe that peace is only a condition of the mind? Is it just something that Jesus taught, that we are glad we have, but something we do not really need to work for on behalf of all humanity? How can I sit comfortably by, enjoying the peace of God that I have in my heart, while my country is dropping more than eighty-five thousand tons of bombs every day on somebody else's homeland? What am I to do when the people of my nation brazenly pray for God's help and protection as our nation, in our name, bombs railroad lines and mines harbors?

A verse from the book of James keeps running through my mind: "You need to prove to me that you can have faith without living it out in daily activity." (James 2:18). Are my actions living proof of the content of my faith? Believing without doing anything about what I believe is worthless.

It isn't faith at all—even the devil believes (and it scares him half to death). And yet we sit, comfortable in our spiritual peace with God.

"But Daddy, they tell us in school that if we live in this country, we have to do what the government says."

Yes, I know. I've heard that one too. Only now they say, "Love it or leave it." But those of us who love God and follow the teachings of Jesus believe that when our government fights a war, we have to refuse to participate in it. We are people of a new kingdom, and Jesus is the head of this kingdom, so we do what he taught. And Jesus taught us that it is wrong to kill another person.

How do you explain to your daughter that Jesus told us the war is over? How do you help her see that this huge, beautiful country that has been so good to her, is bombing another country until it soon will be unable to grow enough food to feed its own people? How do you explain that those leaders who tell us how they are bringing peace are actually bringing more destruction to the world? You don't—and her next question points out your failure.

"But Daddy, how can they say that? Don't they tell the truth?"

Perhaps, like me, you hear the voice of Isaiah rattling around in your mind:

> No, the hand of Yahweh is not too short to save, nor His ear too dull to hear. But your iniquities have made a gulf between you and your God. Your sins have made him veil his face so as not to hear you, since your hands are stained with blood, your fingers with crime. Your lips utter lies, your tongues murmur treachery. No one speaks the truth, or pleads sincerely. Their plans are sinful plots, violence is their only method. Their feet run to do evil, and are quick to shed innocent blood. Their thoughts are sinful thoughts, wherever they go there is havoc and ruin. They know nothing of the way of peace, there is no fairness in their paths. They build crooked roads, and those who follow down them never find peace. Justice is far removed from us and integrity keeps its distance. We look for light and all is darkness. (Isa 59:1–4, 6–9)

We live in a country where war has become a way of life. It has become a dominant theme that controls the way our nation does business. We are told to go to war, to hate, to kill, and to destroy. But Jesus told us to love and to share. Sometimes we have to say to the government: "No! We are committed to following Jesus. We cannot and will not do what you ask of us." In order to stand firm to this conviction, a person must understand the actual teachings of Jesus—and then put those teachings into action.

"But Daddy, if you think war is wrong, what are you doing about it?" (Sometimes children can be dreadfully personal!) "Well, I pray that God will change people's minds about war, and that God will use me to help them see that the way of Jesus is the way of peace. I try to convince other people that they should believe in Jesus and follow what he teaches."

"But Daddy, is that enough?" (Children just don't know when to quit!) "No, Lois, it is not enough. I believe that Jesus taught it is wrong to kill another person. I believe it is also wrong to be part of the whole military machine. It is wrong to build guns that people use to kill other people, just as it is wrong to use that gun yourself. For many of us, it also means that we cannot provide the money to pay someone else to build the gun, or buy the steel that is used to make it, or the bullets that it shoots.

"Sixteen years ago, the government told me I had to join the army and help them fight a war. I told them that I was a Christian and I could not do that. Now, the government tells me I must give it money so it can pay other people to fight and kill. Once again, I have to say that I cannot do that, because I am a Christian. A lot of the taxes we pay, as well as a number of special taxes, go directly to help fight this war. I have told the government that because Jesus said I should not kill, I cannot give them that tax money. Instead, I give that money to the church to help those people who don't have anything to eat or any place to live because we are destroying their land."

I had the feeling it was time to stop, so I looked up and saw that our eleven-year-old was crying. She explained: "I was just thinking about how Jesus must feel when he sees what we are doing to people in Vietnam. Do you think He understands? Daddy, you said you pray. Could we pray, now?"

When I nodded, she started: "Dear God, I'm sorry our country kills so many people. I'm sorry more people don't listen to what you said. I pray that You would forgive us. And God, I pray that you would stop this war before anybody else gets killed. Amen."

Amen—and amen.

Who Speaks for God?

During the summer of 2000, the United States was entering the final months before a national election that was polarized over the war in Iraq. Pundits were predicting a very close election, and God-language was widely used in the media and political campaigns to justify the war. This war was positioned as a modern religious crusade that defended Christian America against a terrible, heathen enemy. As a follower of Jesus who believes that war defies the teachings of Jesus on how Christians should live, this was a difficult summer for me. I saw many Christians who were sucked into this partisan, divisive, religious climate without stopping to think about what was happening.

There is a common assumption that politics have no place in the pulpit, and that preachers should stay away from mentioning political subjects in their sermons. Sermons should be based on biblical or theological themes. But does that mean a pastor dare never address issues of justice, war and peace, hunger, or human rights? Those subjects do have political content, but they were also of great concern to biblical prophets like Amos, Isaiah, and Jeremiah. These concerns show up in the message of Jesus. Paul spoke about hunger, poverty, and other church-state issues as he wrote to congregations. Is it possible to separate the gospel from the daily activities of our lives? Should the church speak up when government twists religion to support its own political gain?

I was a member of the Board of Elders in the congregation when the worship committee asked me to preach on the assigned lectionary texts for that specific Sunday. I had over a month to prepare the sermon, and so I began reading these texts every day in the hope of discovering a common theme within them. This became an exciting exercise as the themes of war, peace, and obedience to God began to stand out in these texts.

Knowing that our congregation had members who were active in both political parties, yet believing that what I was seeing in these texts was a faithful understanding of the message, I shared with the pastor an outline of what I was finding. He agreed that I should proceed, but cautioned me to avoid blatant, partisan political language. Whether I succeeded is a matter of personal opinion!

The response to the sermon was quite mixed. Several persons were very critical of the lead pastor for allowing partisan politics in the pulpit. Others gave effusive praise that someone finally had the courage to speak the truth. *Mennonite Weekly Review* (a national church newspaper) reported on the sermon, but printed only a brief outline. The *Mennonite* (the official denominational paper) carried a shortened version as a lead article, but weeks after the election. *Christianity Today* refused to carry it, saying it was too political.

Jesus regularly confronted the Roman imperial theology that used religion to validate wars that were supposedly fought to bring peace. His message that justice and righteousness brings peace is a central part of what it means to be a follower of "the way."

Every pastor has to wrestle with what, and with how much, is appropriate to say in his or her own congregation. It does little good to waste twenty minutes in worship by saying things that no one will hear. It is good to remind ourselves that change usually happens within relationships, and seldom by just hearing a sermon that tells people that they are wrong. Pastors who do their pastoral work well, and build relationships within the congregation, will usually experience a freedom to speak more openly. Perhaps we need to remind ourselves that the biblical prophets were not always heralded as spokespersons of God's truth when they challenged Israel to rethink its own response to God. But if the church is silent, national political organizations seize upon that silence and fill it with their own self-serving explanations of how what they are doing is actually the will of God. By then, the tone has been set. If the church does not speak for God, who will?

What follows is the sermon I preached on those assigned lectionary texts, four years after September 11, 2001.

* * *

Who Speaks for God?[2]

These are tense times. Our country is sharply divided because of a heated political election that is being dominated by the language of fear, war, and terror. Meanwhile the message of Jesus calls us to a commitment of justice, peace, and hope. That language is not very popular right now. But when the church is silent, the world fills that silence with its own explanation of God. That language then shapes how we see the world. This morning, I challenge the church to speak out with its ancient, yet

2. The biblical foundation for this sermon are Psalms 79:1–13; Jeremiah 8:19; 9:1; and 1 Timothy 2:1–4.

very modern biblical message. What is the message of God that needs to be heard in the world today?

Psalm 79 was written as a lament over the destruction of the temple in the days of Jeremiah (about 2,600 years ago). Babylon seemed intent on taking over the whole world. The temple, central symbol of Jewish worship and life, lay smoking in ruins. Israel was in shock and disbelief, and was living in daily terror as the impossible had just happened. An army of pagan enemies had literally struck at the heart of the city, and life would never be the same again.

We understand those feelings. When central symbols of American life were attacked, when lives were lost, the nation felt violated. How do people survive in times of tragedy and enormous grief? The response of Israel was so typical, so human, so much like us. Facing an imminent threat from Babylon, Israel cried out to God for mercy and help:

> How long O Lord?
> Will you be angry forever?
> Don't hold against us the sins of our fathers.
> May your mercy come quickly, for we are in desperate need.
> (Ps 79:5, 8)

Now this is not a bad response; it's actually a pretty good human response. But wait a minute. Tucked into the middle of those four verses is something else in Pslams 79:6: "Pour out your wrath on the nations that do not acknowledge you, on people who do not call on your name"; and a few verses later in Psalms 79:12: "Pay back on them seven times the reproach that they have hurled at you, O Lord!" These verses remind us again that the Psalms do not always give us clear godly instruction. Sometimes they reflect human responses to life. We learn from those ancient and all-too-human responses even though they are not very godlike.

Do you see what is happening? Pay them back for what they have done, not to us, but *to you O Lord*. Suddenly God is being dragged into the middle of a military struggle between two nations. It sounds more than just vaguely familiar, doesn't it? It is almost as if the Psalmist was looking over our shoulder, whispering in our ear: "Lord, don't hold us responsible for our sins—show mercy because we righteous people are in need. You are obliged to defend us, O God. You have to show the world that you are on *our* side—you must protect your good name by saving us."

In case you haven't noticed and I am sure that you have, there is a lot of God talk in the nation these days. Often this talk has very little to do with God. But maybe we shouldn't blame the Psalmist for these misguided pleas. Maybe we shouldn't blame our politicians for fanning the flames of war in the name of God. Maybe we should blame the church.

Traditionally, we believe that God is about healing and mercy, forgiveness and redemption, reconciliation and salvation—at least for us! In Jeremiah's day they would have said almost exactly the same thing. But when the nation went to war under Jehoiakim, the king began to use the name of God to rally support for the national military mission against the enemy. And the religious leadership rather quickly fell into step in support of the king.

But Jeremiah didn't see it that way. The religious leaders said (Jer 8:8–9): "We are wise, for we have the law of the Lord." Let me rephrase that: We know we are right, and we can quote scripture to prove it. Jeremiah's response? "How can you say that . . . when the lying pens of the scribes have twisted it so badly. . . . What kind of wisdom is that?"

How do you turn truth into a lie? It takes time, but it can be done. Let's look at the progression of our own ideas in six small, simple steps:

1. God is about salvation, redemption, and healing, calling people to live together in peace.

2. Peace is something special that you teach as an ideal after you get people saved. It is a second step for Christians who have a special calling; people like pastors, priests, and nuns.

3. Peace is an optional extra for Christians. Some do it, some don't. You are free to decide for yourself because it is not central for salvation. It is an optional, ethical choice.

4. Peace has nothing to do with the gospel, because the message of Jesus is internal and spiritual, dealing with your future heavenly home. Peace, on the other hand, is an external political issue that won't work in times like today when the stakes are so high and the enemy is so evil. War is justified because the enemy is so demonic.

5. War is the way to deal with evil in the world. But since we are godly people, we fight in the name of God against those pagan infidels whom God also hates.

6. Because we Christians have God on our side, we regularly ask God to bless us as we fight this war. If you object to this war, you are either not godly or not patriotic, for we know that God is with us, not with them.

Somewhere in that six step process, the biblical train left the tracks. While claiming to be God's people we put ourselves in direct defiance of what Jesus taught. Is it any wonder that the nations of this world increasingly hate us, and retaliate by claiming God is actually on their side? I wonder how God feels about the way we, in the United States, abuse, deny, and violate what Jesus taught.

There is a story in the Jewish Talmud about the angels in heaven as they watch the children of Israel who were trapped at the Red Sea. The Egyptian army was coming right up behind them. Suddenly the sea opened, and the children of Israel ran through to safety on the other side. The Egyptian army came charging into the sea after them, but the walls of water collapsed and they were drowned. The angels burst into songs of joy, celebrating Israel's miraculous escape. They invited God to join in their celebration, but God responded, "How can I sing when my children are dying?" "Oh, no," the angels said. "Come look, they aren't dying, they are safe on the other side." To which God solemnly answers: "the Egyptians are also my children, and they are dying . . . how can I sing songs of joy?"

It is so easy to get swept up in the narrow nationalism of wartime enthusiasm. It is so easy to forget that Yahweh never intended to be a warring, nationalistic deity for Israel (although Israel tried hard to do that to God). Nor is God a nationalistic deity for America in the twentieth century (even though we try just as hard as Israel did). Jesus teaches us that God is God over all nations, and that God's love and mercy extends to all people, even those who do not yet name the name of Jesus.

If we are children of God, how can we choose to hate and support the killing of people whom God our Father loves? Is it not the height of hypocrisy for us to presume to tell God whom God must love (us), and whom God must hate (them)? Is it not audacious to expect God to bless *us* while we try to kill *them*? We are right back in Psalm 79, telling God that God must protect God's own name by defending us.

That brings us to 1 Timothy 2, where in verses 1–4 we are told to pray for our leaders. But note carefully how these verses instruct us to pray. We are not to pray for military success on the battlefield. We are to pray for kings and presidents so that they might lead us into peace because God wants all people to know the truth and to be saved. The sequence in 1 Timothy 2:1–4 suggests that in times of war God knows the truth is not proclaimed, and people are not being saved. Thus, war is a violation of God's intentions for humanity. This presents a logical, theological impossibility. We cannot proclaim the gospel of Jesus Christ saying that God loves you, while we are killing you in the name of the very same God. Jeremiah said that is not the way of God; Jesus said that is not how God is; and the writer of 1 Timothy said that is not what God wants. Where do we get the idea that now the Bible is different, and it no longer applies to us in the same way?

I must insert a statement of human compassion and, I hope, godly understanding. I believe that Jesus teaches that I should see every human being as a person who is loved by God. I have never learned how to watch war coverage on television news. In the comfort of my home I witness death, and I am repulsed and sickened by what I see. It hurts me very much when I see young American men or women being killed in war, no matter its name, because every human life is sacred. Every victim of war has a mother or father, a husband or wife, a sister or brother, or children. Their loss is unbelievably tragic, and my heart cries out for every one of them. But as I see mothers, fathers, and children of "our enemy" crying out to God because their own fathers, sons, spouses, and daughters are being killed—I find that pain to be equally unbearable, and my heart cries out to God in the same way. God's love for them is also profound, and their loss is equally tragic and painful.

I cannot condemn soldiers for doing what the nation teaches them to do, especially when the church is silent about the teachings of Jesus regarding how Christians should respond to war. I trust in a forgiving God, because I also need that forgiveness for myself. But I hold the nation accountable, not for going to war, because that is what nations do. Instead, I hold the nation to account for claiming *this war is God's war*, and that God approves of what we are doing to people whom God loves every bit as much as he loves us. I hold the church even more accountable for remaining silent or—even worse—for giving its support to the nation in fighting this war. The church has the Scriptures, the church has the Holy Spirit, and the church has the message. I plead today that the church might regain its voice and speak out for God. We should know better.

I want to close with four summary statements because Jeremiah, the psalmist, Jesus, and the writer of 1 Timothy all offer the same counsel:

1. Our salvation and our hope rest in God—not in any national military liberation carried out "in the name of God."

2. The message of the gospel is still salvation, peace, reconciliation, and healing as taught by Jesus, nurtured by the Scriptures, and

empowered by the Holy Spirit; and we are not free to change that message in order to be more politically correct.

3. As believers in God as revealed in Jesus, we cannot call upon God to destroy or kill others so that we can live in comfort and security—no matter how despicable that enemy is portrayed to us by our national leaders.

4. The call of God upon us is still the ageless message of Jesus: that God loves all people. We are still being sent into the world proclaiming and living this message of love, peace, healing, reconciliation, and salvation for all humanity.

I pray that God might fill us with God's love for all people everywhere. I pray that it might flow through us to others without our ever needing to stop and think about the person who is on the receiving end of that love. That is how God loves us, and for that I am very grateful. God also calls us to love others in the same way.

If God Loves Everyone, What Is Special About Us?[3]

One of the most dramatic events in recent years was the peaceful over-throw of the Marcos government by the followers of Corazon Aquino. Most of us watched from a distance, amazed to see the way in which a nonviolent resistance group toppled a military empire. It was an exciting turn of events. Not long after the Marcos family left the Philippines, the U.S. TV audience was given a tour of the lavish Malacañang Palace. One newsman, in commenting on that experience, casually remarked, "Marcos lived as though he thought he was God!"

That was a very interesting comment, but in truth it says much more about our American images of God than it does about the Marcos family lifestyle. Without being overly critical of an innocent remark by a news-man, I wonder if he really knew much about the biblical God. It is so easy for us to project onto God the pyramid values of power and wealth that we live with so comfortably, and then assume that this helps us see the nature of God. Is that really the way God is? Where do we go for our images of God? (From Luke 6:27–36.)

> But I say to you, love your enemies, do good to those who hate you, bless those who curse you, pray for those who treat you badly. If someone strikes you on the cheek, offer the other also, and if someone takes your coat, let them have your shirt, too. Treat people the way you want them to treat you. If you love those who love you, what credit is that to you? Even sinners love people who love them. If you do good to people who do good to you, what's the benefit of that? Even sinners do that. Love your enemies, and do good. Lend to people in need, expecting nothing in return; and your reward will be great. You will be children of the most high God, for God is kind to those who are ungrateful, and even to those who are wicked.

These are the words of Jesus. People who follow Jesus take these words very seriously. Those of us within Christian faith who reject vio-lence believe that these words are not simply good philosophic theory but are instructions from God that should be put into practice on a daily ba-sis. We who believe in the resurrection, who believe in conversion, who believe in being born again, believe these words say something rather important about this new life.

---

3. The biblical foundation for this sermon is Ephesians 6:10–20.

Again, from Jesus the familiar words of John: 3:16, "For God loved the world so much that He gave his only son, so that everyone who believes in him may not die, but have eternal life. For God did not send his son into the world to be its judge, but its savior."

From Jesus, the great commission of Matthew 28:18–20, "I have been given all authority in heaven and on earth. Go then to all people everywhere and make them my disciples, baptize them in the name of the Father, Son and Holy Spirit. Teach them to obey all the things I have taught you. And remember, I will always be there with you."

God's concern for the world is not a new idea introduced by Jesus or by Paul. From the very beginning of the people of God, way back with Abraham, the call of God included concern for all the peoples of the world. From Genesis 12:2–3, "I will make of you a great nation, and I will bless you, and make your name great, so that you will be a blessing, and by you all the families of the earth will be blessed.

At times, God had to push pretty hard to get Israel to see that call of mission to the world, because they very quickly got caught up in their own special status before God. In Amos, at a time when Israel's leadership was rejoicing in prosperity that they saw as proof that God loved them best, God said to them through the prophet (Amos 8:7): "Are not you Israelites like the Cushites to me? Yes I did bring Israel up out of Egypt, but did I not also bring the Philistines out of Caphtor and the Arameans out of Kir?"

God's people have always had this problem of trying to be the center of their own world, and then assuming that God sees the world exactly as they see it. We forget that God liberated Israel from slavery in Egypt because a nation of slaves in a foreign land could not do their God-given task of being a witness to the nations. Their exodus from Egypt was not for the sole purpose of making them feel better; rather, it was to free them again to be God's people in mission. But Israel soon forgot about mission. They preferred to get involved in self-protection and military battles. They forgot that to be in mission with God to the nations is impossible when in the name of God our nation arms its troops to do battle against those same nations in war. These basic scriptural truths still stand today.

We should acknowledge right away that arming for war is a defiance of God's call to be in mission to the nations. But this call gets lost so easily, which is why this is so critical for us. President Harry Truman, near the end of World War II said: "I call on all Christians to answer the call of the nation, for the goals of America are the goals of all true believers." President Ronald Reagan constantly mixed military defense language with Christian mission concepts. No wonder so many people are confused.

Make no mistake. We are heavily influenced by this kind of nationalistic religious piety, with its upper-middle class assumptions about faith being the sure road to economic prosperity. And because the words often sound right, we forget about the context and the meaning of how those words are being used. The result is that we are in danger of losing the very heart of the gospel in favor of fringe benefits and material blessings.

About nineteen hundred years ago, Paul was sitting in a prison cell in Rome, writing to the church at Ephesus. He wrote: "Put on the whole armor of God that you may be able to stand against the ways of the devil. For we are fighting against principalities and powers, against wickedness in high places" (Eph 6:11).

What is Paul referring to? Who are these principalities and powers of Ephesians 6? What do they look like today? They are still among us, but we are so comfortable with them that we no longer recognize them. We give them power today because we assume that what Paul was talking about was some spiritual, mystical force and not real people or real institutions. We need to remember, when Paul wrote this he was in prison, and some of these principalities and powers had put him there.

In 1987, the U.S. government budget called for $320 billion to keep American defenses intact, equipped with the latest in weaponry. I find $1 billion a hard amount to comprehend, much less 320 of them. So let's break it down a bit. One way of doing so is to note that this amount means spending nearly $877 million every day to defend ourselves from our enemies. That amount is more than ten times what the government is willing to spend for health and medical care. It is more than fifteen times what the government spends in a whole year for elementary through college education.

There are other ways to define this budget number. Let's begin in the year that Jesus was born (4 BCE), and every day we will spend $400,000. How many centuries will it take to spend $320 billion at $400,000 a day? On Dec. 31, 2012, we will still have $29,460,000 in loose change yet to spend. Are we really people of God if we quietly accept and sometimes even promote a government policy that invests that kind of money to kill people? By the way, the amount the United States spends for war every one hour and forty minutes is equal to what Mennonites give for all causes in local congregations and throughout the denomination in a year. That includes mission, education, Mennonite Central Committee (MCC), conference, and local congregations—everything. One hour and forty minutes!

When Paul wrote to the church at Ephesus, he said: "Put on the whole armor of God so that you may be able to stand against the evil ways of the devil."

How does the devil go about doing evil things in our day? One way is by trying to convince us that the ways of God are outdated and will no longer work. If we really want peace, the devil says, we must accept the more practical, tangible ways of death and destruction. Unfortunately, the devil continues saying that God's command to love your enemies has to be put on hold temporarily, because we have terrorists in the world—and if we don't kill them first, they will kill us.

That, my brothers and sisters, may make sense to the Pentagon, and it may sound like gospel to some radio and TV preachers, but it is not the voice of God. We are never instructed to kill our enemies before they get to us. We are called to love them, to share with them, and to be the presence of God to them for their salvation.

How should Christians respond to the overwhelming militarism of our time? How do we move beyond holding peace as a doctrine to be believed, until peacemaking once again becomes a way of life infused by the power of God's Holy Spirit? How can we move beyond seeing nations as friends or enemies, depending upon their political point of view, and start seeing them as people whom God loves?

What can Christians do if the United States (or any other nation) was invaded? How do you defend a country without having these vast military armies and enormous weapons systems? Richard Taylor, Ron Sider, and Gene Sharp are active Christian writers and leaders with concern for practical expressions of peace and justice. They say it can be done. They believe that Christians should be presenting positive alternatives to the "Rambo response" of our military world. The governments of this world spend billions to develop plans for the defense of a region. What might happen if we who believe that God provides a better way, would carefully develop a peace model so that it can be explained in believable terms, so that people might have an honest choice between guns and bombs, or the way of Jesus. Far too often Christians have been critical of what governments do without offering any counsel on what we believe God is doing. The Fundamentalist preachers of our day are quick to say that God supports increased military spending in the face of foreign threat. Do they speak for us? Or do we overlook what these preachers say about war and how to treat enemies because that is not a very important issue of ethics? Do we have something to say about enemies and how we treat them?

There is a very specific proposal that is receiving a lot of attention these days. This proposal, the original dream of Ron Sider, has been discussed, prayed over, modified, and discussed again. It is a concept that is built on the assumption that faithfulness to Jesus can be applied even in peacemaking. Called the Anabaptist Peace Guard, it assumes that peacemaking calls us beyond doctrinal ideas to actually move into places of conflict where we serve as agents of God's peace.

This Peace Guard would be comprised of maybe 500 people, both men and women, who have received special training in nonviolent responses to force. They would be mature Christians who believe in, and have experienced, the presence of God's Spirit. They would be committed to daily prayer, and would be supported by tens of thousands of other Christians in regular intercessory prayer *by name* every day. They would be a gathering of Anabaptist Christians from all over the world, thus resembling a Christian United Nations force, and not simply another American presence.

In military terms, these persons would be the equivalent of a Rapid Deployment Force, ready to move on a few days notice to any location in the world where major violence is occurring. They would position themselves between the warring factions in an attempt to deter or at least lower the level of violence. They would provide security for local citizens by recording and reporting violations committed by either side. They would attempt to establish communication between the two sides, encouraging each side to talk before shooting.

The authority of the Peace Guard would come from the godly power of self-sacrificial, nonviolent love; from the international good will of people committed to peace; and from the neutrality of the participants. This means that spiritual discipline, regular group worship, daily Bible study, and prayer are mandatory for all participants.

I would like to summarize several assumptions that lie behind this venture for peace:

1. Peacemaking calls us to work at ending conflict, not simply to keep separate from it.

2. The power of God's Spirit at work through God's faithful people is still a potent force on earth. This has been neglected by most

Christians, thus they turn to guns and bombs and tanks for a solution. But we believe the Spirit of God is also still a vital force. We believe that the prophet Isaiah was right when he called on Israel to trust in God and not in the chariots of Egypt. We believe that counsel still holds for the Christian church.

3. It is certainly possible that some members of the Peace Guard might be killed as they witness to God's way of reconciliation. But the military assumes that some soldiers will die in battle. Should we be any less willing to die for God's way of truth?

What is the biblical basis for peacemaking on an international scale? As I think about it, I am drawn to several situations in the Scriptures.

The first is Exodus 3, where a shepherd is out tending his sheep in the desert. This former civil servant in a dominant world superpower had lost his job because he chose to identify with the wrong social group. One day he had acted impulsively when confronted with a social injustice by killing a government official, and had to run for his life. He had since married and settled down in the security of nomadic life in the desert. But one day he saw a bush burning and was drawn to it. He heard the voice of God calling him; "I have heard the cries of my people in Egypt." Exodus 3:7. I want your help to set them free. The response of this shepherd, Moses, was less enthusiastic: In essence he said, "No, I want to stay here with my family where it is safe and comfortable." And He gave good reasons why that made the best sense in his mind. But God said, No! Go! So Moses went, and the history of several nations was drastically changed, because God called him to get involved in an international action that resulted in the nonviolent salvation of an oppressed people. The call of God is to bring aid to the oppressed and suffering people in other nations. For us, more explicitly, it can mean helping refugees who have been driven from their land and families because of war and famine.

A second text is in Isaiah 6, where a young man sits in worship in the temple. A good king had just died and the nation is in turmoil, trying to find its way. This young man, Isaiah, is discouraged because no one has any word of helpful counsel for the nation. But one of the Seraphim takes a burning coal from the fire and touched his lips. God spoke saying, "Go, and here is what you are to say" (Isaiah 6:9).

It is interesting to note that in the first six chapters of Isaiah, the content is all about domestic policy, with judgment and woes upon the people. But then God spoke again, and Isaiah's eyes are opened up to the nations around them, and he hears a message of hope for Israel and instructions on their foreign policy. These chapters talk about Babylon, Philistia, Moab, Damascus, Ethiopia, Egypt, and Tyre. The call of God is to mission, a mission that reaches beyond the individual and into the world around us. God's salvation and peace is for all people, not just us.

The third text comes from Luke 9. Peter, James, and John are having what today would be called a mountaintop experience. Peter is so completely thrilled by this experience that he decides the right response is to build a retreat center and revel in the glory of God's presence. Peter wants to stay there, on the mountaintop, but a voice came from the clouds saying: "This is my Son; Listen to him!" (Luke 9:35)." The next story tells us that Jesus went down in the city, confronting the pain and suffering of humanity as he engages in ministry to people (Luke 9:37–43).

It is so tempting to want to relive the mountaintop experiences of our faith. It feels so good to get together with the same people and retell stories of how nice it was back in the good old days, and then pray that God will bless everyone in the same way again. But these experiences are not intended simply for our own edification. They empower us to be a witness to the nations, and to those around us who are suffering. God's call to mission draws us into the suffering and hunger and pain of people everywhere. Not only do we see their suffering, but we begin to see what is causing it, and how we are contributing to their pain.

How do we work at being a witness for peace in the world? I believe there are some simple things that we can do. Probably the first thing is to become informed. There are many well-qualified relief workers and missionaries living in countries all over the world who can help us learn what is happening. We can read national news publications or watch the evening news. That gives us the broad perspective. But we should also read the *Peace Section* newsletter or MCC's *Washington Memo*. These publications provide excellent background information on world events through the eyes of Christian people who actually live in these locations. Other publications, like *Sojourners* or *Christian Science Monitor*, provide similar coverage. If God is God over all nations, then it is important for us to get a nonnationalistic view on current events.

One other straightforward thing Christians can do to be a witness for peace in the world is to follow the teachings of Jesus to love their enemies. Christians should love their enemies not out of some simplistic notion that says enemies are really wonderful, loving people. An enemy may be ruthless and truly evil. Christians do not love their enemies because they believe a smile will be returned with a smile, for indeed an enemy might not do that either. Christians love their enemies because God loves them, and God calls us to reflect that same compassion toward others. Our God, who is best known to us in Jesus, is a forgiving, loving, reconciling God. If Paul was speaking for us when he wrote, "It is no longer I who live, but Christ who lives in me," (Galatians 2:20) then it is safe to assume that the love of Christ for others will be seen in our lives.

Thus, in conflict at every stage of human experience, from the fist fight on the playground to the labor dispute in the board room; from the family shouting at each other to the nations that are shooting at each other; the Christian sees the world, its people and its wars, from the point of view of the cross.

We love, not because it always works in the political realm but because God has first loved us. We work at reconciliation, not because everyone in the world wants to be reconciled but because God has given us this ministry of reconciliation.

In very early church literature, there is a letter to Diognetus. (Jefford, "The Letter to Diognetus," pp.159–69.) In this letter, the writer makes a defense of Christians in the world.

> Christians cannot be distinguished from the rest of the human race by country or by language or by customs.
> They do not live in cities of their own.
> They do not use a peculiar form of speech.
> They do not follow an eccentric manner of life.
> Yet although they live in Greek and Barbarian cities alike, as each person's lot has been cast, and follow the customs of the country in clothing and food and other matters of daily living, at the same time they give proof of their remarkable and admittedly extraordinary constitution of their own commonwealth.
> They live in their own countries, but only as aliens.
> They have a share in everything as citizens, yet they endure everything as foreigners.
> Every foreign land is their homeland, and yet for them every homeland is a foreign land.
> They busy themselves on earth, but their citizenship is in heaven.
> They obey the established laws, but in their own lives they go far beyond what the laws require.
> They love all people, yet by all people they are persecuted.
> They are poor, yet others have more because of their presence.
> They are completely destitute and yet they enjoy complete abundance of life.

To put it simply: What the soul is in the body, that is what Christians are in the world.

To this, let us add what Jesus said (Matt 28:19–20): "Go to all people everywhere and make them my disciples. Teach them everything that I have taught you. And I promise, I will be with you always."

Finding Hope in the Cemetery

Most every American can remember where he or she was on September 11, 2001, when the plane of American Airlines flight 11 flew into the North Tower of the World Trade Center. I was teaching a Hebrew Prophets class that ended at 8:50 a.m. I found a television just in time to see the plane of United Airlines flight 175 fly into the South Tower. What followed was an eerie sense of not knowing what to do, and of being glued to a television set as though if we watched it often enough, we could make it stop happening. The next day I was asked to speak at a community gathering of grief, prayer and remembrance at the Oakwood Christian Retreat Center where I was then a member of the Board of Directors.

Oakwood is set in a very conservative Christian community about fifteen miles south of Goshen, the town where I live. This community's immediate and overwhelming response was for harsh military retaliation in the name of God against those who did these awful things to us godly people, even though as yet no one was sure exactly who these ungodly enemies were.

I had only one day to prepare for this community service. As I thought about what I might say, I asked myself, What should I do in a setting like this? Should I validate the national religious fervor that called for revenge in the name of God by declaring "us" innocent and "them" evil? What is the Word of God for a setting like this? I assumed that no one at Oakwood had friends or relatives who were killed in the tragedy. I had already seen and heard their immediate cries for strong military action, and, of course, I was familiar with the theological assumptions of the community.

I decided to attempt the impossible—to be both pastoral and prophetic at the same time. I pulled together experiences from the Scriptures where Israel had suffered unjustly, and noted how they had survived. I used an experience from Jesus and shared his counsel. These texts called us back to the core elements of our faith, called for healing, but also challenged the many calls for doing more violence in retaliation to those who had dared to do violence to us.

The response to this message was mostly critical, although there were one or two positive voices. The majority of this audience was not ready to move toward new life, because they were locked into "teaching those awful people they cannot do this to us!" There was a small minority who found the message immensely helpful, and who wanted to talk more about how to find healing, and what we might do so this would never happen again. Others, however, knew exactly what we should do. We should send in the military and kill them, for that is the only language these evildoers understand.

As I listened and engaged in conversation with members of the audience, I began to sense that how we respond to tragedy is often controlled by how we view the world, and what is included in our commitment to Jesus. If we expect our faith commitment to protect us and deliver us from evil because we know we are the righteous ones, then it is easy to call for retaliation against those who oppose us. But a few persons saw their faith commitment as being a way of living that is based on the teachings of Jesus. These individuals were aware that we often fall short in our faithfulness, yet they were prepared to look to the future without having to retaliate. They even dared ask the question (very cautiously), "Could it be that we did something which caused them to do this to us?" The majority group was intent on restoring the world to how it was before 9/11. The minority group was at least willing to think about how we could create a new world that just might be better than our pre-9/11 world had been.

Whether to be pastoral or prophetic is usually a tough call. Perhaps I could have phrased some things in a less confrontational way. But I was, after all, teaching a class called Hebrew Prophets when this event took place, and sometimes the prophetic tone of Jeremiah or Amos is not very audience-friendly. Jeremiah kept wishing that God would call someone else to proclaim the message. Amos never did get positive feedback for what he said. Nor did the Hebrew prophets get any personal joy out of declaring judgment on Israel. We must always be careful when we feel personal satisfaction in pronouncing judgment on others for their sins. But that does not excuse us from being a voice in the wilderness.

The following are the remarks I delivered that day. I leave it to you to measure its confrontational qualities in the same way that you, yourself, must decide which audience group to call your own.

* * *

Finding Hope in the Cemetery[4]

It had been a very painful year. All the traditional, comfortable symbols were gone, and it looked as though life would never be the same again. Some people were asking whether there was any hope that the people of God would survive. After all they had been through, maybe this was the end. Ezekiel found himself drawn back to the same quiet cemetery where he had often gone before. This was where his own wife had been buried just a few years before, where his personal hopes and dreams for the future had been painfully laid to rest. Not only was it personal for Ezekiel, but thousands of other people had buried their loved ones here in this strange land. There didn't seem to be much interest in either repentance (for what?) or renewal (of what?) in the life of Israel. Their identity, their way of life, their confidence in God had been shattered. What Babylon had done to them was not supposed to happen. After all, we are God's people and we deserve better from God. Was there any possibility that the nation could survive this tragedy?

Ezekiel's grief and despair is seen in his response to God's question, "Ezekiel, do you see any hope here?" [Son of Man, can these bones live? (Ezek 37:3)] His quiet response whispers the way many of us feel today: "Lord, no human being can find hope here, only you can see hope in this tragedy." [Lord, you alone know that. (Ezek 37: 3)]

I can imagine a modern Ezekiel sitting at Ground Zero in New York, or in Washington, or in a field in Pennsylvania wondering to himself, "How can anything good come from this?" I have wondered that same thing many times in these terrible days. I have watched people respond because how we react in the aftermath of tragedy says a lot about where we turn when we feel hopeless, and where we go to start rebuilding the future.

We have heard a lot of very strong language. Many people are replacing hope statements with believe concepts. We have always tended to do this, trying to reassure ourselves that the future is secure by reaffirming what we believe about God. If these statements are a true representation of what we believe, then it would make sense to me that we should trust in the God in whom we say we believe. But persons who make these statements usually turn to the government and to the military as the agencies that will make the future livable for us, often by promising to make the future unlivable for those who are responsible for this tragedy.

4. The biblical foundation for this meditation is Ezekiel 37:1–14.

Is there a word of hope that gives life to us in the Scriptures? There are many stories that run through my mind, where hope literally springs to life out of despair and tragedy that struck first Israel and then the new faith community of Jesus. Where do we go to have our faith strengthened?

There is a very helpful contrast painted for us by King David in Psalm 11. There is danger all around and his friends advise him to flee because the situation is hopeless. Yet David affirms his steadfast trust in God. He admits that people are shooting at him, and his friends ask, "When all hope is gone (when the foundations are destroyed) what can the righteous do?"(vs.3). Surely, David is fighting a lost cause. The moral and theological foundations were crumbling under the evil that people were doing to each other. What gives David the courage to stay? His response is indeed comforting: "The Lord is in his holy temple . . . the Lord examines the righteous . . . the Lord is righteous, he loves justice and the upright will see God's face" (Ps 11:7).

As with David, our hope is shaped by what we focus on. We have heard a great deal about the evil that is being done to us, and about the implication that there is no logical reason for it. But for David, focusing on the evil in the world leads to despair because there is so much of it. When we affirm again our belief that ultimately it is not evil that controls the world—but God—then we can see God still at work bringing redemption and healing.

What dominates our thinking these days? Certainly there are reports of food being shared and aid being given as people search for survivors. We hear stories about people making heroic sacrifices to save others, and to help others work through their grief. But overwhelmingly, the focus is on the unjustified evil done to us and how we who are righteous must punish those terrible people who have done these unspeakably horrible things to us.

What is the word of hope from David? Our hope rests in the assurance that God does not run away and hide. Rather, God can be counted on to be here in our time of grief and pain, and that ultimately, hope rests in God, and not in running away.

That raises an interesting point. What does hope do for us? Hope is a great motivator. I remember as a child working hard on the farm, saving my money hoping that I would soon have enough money to buy the bicycle that was on sale in one of the local stores in town. I worked hard because I knew what I wanted. But then in mid-June someone else bought the bicycle out of the store window and my hope of someday riding that bicycle up and down our road was gone. I was too young to think about how, maybe, there could be another bicycle at the store that would be just as good. I wanted *that* bicycle, and it was gone.

Our culture is committed to returning the world to the way it was before the 9/11 tragedy. But simply restoring the old ways is not the message of God. The hope that comes through God is that we will create a new world that will be more just and more loving, more compassionate and more understanding. It will be better than what we had because hope calls us to create new, not simply restore the old. If we believe that God is still on the throne, then Christians have no time to get sidetracked on retaliation and punishment because the purposes of God have not changed.

The 9/11 tragedy brought terrible pain and suffering into the lives of us all, and obviously some feel this pain much more intensely than do others. But when we affirm with David that God is still in the temple, then God's vision for a better world, where peace and justice and love are the dominant factors, continues to call us to do the things of God. Nothing has changed even though everything has changed.

We need to feel the experience of Jesus sitting alongside the road with his disciples. Things were not going well, and some followers were rejecting Jesus, choosing instead to search for simpler answers. Jesus turned to the twelve disciples and with sadness in his voice asked, "Maybe you want to leave, too?" As was usually the case, Peter spoke for the entire group: "Why would we do that? Where would we go? You have the words of eternal life" (John 6:66–68).

Perhaps in our own days of searching and questioning, that answer by Peter offers hope to us.

It just might be that tragedies like this force us to rethink our own faith and values. The world turns up the volume with their solutions on how to handle this crisis, and for many it is tempting to reach out for quick, violent solutions. We still need Peter to remind us that "You, Jesus, have the words of eternal life."

Now is the time for us to reaffirm our confidence that in Jesus we find truth; in Jesus we find the way; and in Jesus there is life. Thus, Jesus is still the foundation from which our hope springs fresh and new each day. Hope is not a shallow fantasy of how we might get what we want, nor is it a childhood daydream about presents under the tree. Hope is the motivating factor for action. Hope is the vision of what might be, of new life springing from death, of new buildings being built out of the rubble, and of new relationships (both interpersonal and international) being formed.

Jesus calls us to live in the day-to-day reality of this world, recognizing that sometimes terrible things happen to people who really don't deserve it. But throughout the Bible, the call rings clear. These tragic events do not derail God in the divine vision of creating a new community of God's people that reaches out to all people everywhere. The events of 9/11 are sobering data that tells us we have not done very well at reaching out. The real world wants us to destroy our enemies so that we can return to the past. Jesus calls us to live in the hope of a new future. This hope that comes from God, dreams not of destroying people but of creating new relationships. This hope is built not on avenging the injustices of the past but on the vision of God's new kingdom being realized in our midst. This hope comes alive again out of the affirmation that God is still on the throne, that Jesus still has the words of eternal life, and that ultimately, the nations of this earth are not the dominant shapers of history, for that belongs to God.

Our faith in God, our commitment to Jesus as Lord, and our membership with one another challenge us to live in this hope, for with Peter we still ask, "Lord, where else can we go?"

2

Theological Earthquake

Believe me, I am in my Father and my Father is in me.
If you cannot believe that, believe what you are seeing—
the works that I do.
The person who trusts me will not only do what I am doing,
but will do even greater things because I am giving you
the same work to do that I have been doing.
—Jesus
John 14:11–12

No one puts new wine into old wineskins.
If they do, the new wine will burst the skins.
The wine will be spoiled and the skins will be destroyed.
New wine must be put into fresh wineskins.
And no one who drinks the old wine will desire new wine,
for he says, "the old is good enough."
—Jesus
Luke 5:37

In living our faith we encounter God,
and in the encounter with God we find strength and joy for living.[1]
—John D. Roth

I do not understand the mystery of grace.
I only know that it meets us where we are
and does not leave us where it found us.
Lighthouses do not go running all over an island looking for boats to save;
they simply stand there shining.[2]
—Anne Lamott

---

1 Roth, *Beliefs: Mennonite Faith and Practice*, p. 58.

2. Lamott, *Travelling Mercies*, p. 143.

Theological Earthquake

"Even though I walk through the darkest valley I will fear no evil, for you are with me." Those words from Psalm 23:4 promise God's comfort for people when life is difficult. This Psalm was one of the first texts from the Bible that my parents expected me to learn by memory. It taught me to believe that this is how God would be for me.

I was the youngest of nine children in a traditional, religious home. We were taught to trust God to take care of us. The supporting evidence was persuasive. We were a very healthy family, and on those rare occasions when we did get sick Mom and Dad had lots of home remedies (mustard plasters, chicken soup, Vicks VapoRub, cod liver oil) that usually worked. Mom prayed for us when were sick, and when we recovered she always thanked God for being with us. God was identified as being, "a very present help in time of trouble!"

Growing up on the farm provided a level of security that sheltered us from almost every situation where we would have needed God's special help. One of my favorite cousins, Joel Blosser, was killed in an automobile accident over Christmas vacation during his junior year in high school. We could not explain this tragedy, but we were told God had a reason. This satisfied me because I knew that God was all powerful and all knowing, thus we accepted God's control even though we did not understand. The ways of God were to be obeyed, not questioned.

This attitude of acceptance stayed with me through college and into seminary. It was a comfortable belief that helped to make life meaningful because I was safe and relatively free from emotional stress. However, this luxury of an unchallenged belief system was quickly tested as I started my pastoral life at Freeport, Illinois. I had been at the Freeport church only a few weeks when a major tragedy struck in the congregation.

My safe, cautious theology did not provide the support I needed for my first funeral at Freeport. Eldon Kortemeier was a son of a family in the congregation, a young pastor serving another congregation in Illinois, who died in a tragic boating accident. His wife Caryl and three small children were forced into a future that was totally foreign from what they were expecting.

What is God's word of hope and comfort for a young family in times like this? Fortunately, Richard Yordy, (the former pastor) returned and took charge of the funeral, which allowed me to watch the process from inside. I tried to apply my family explanations of God's role in tragedy, but somehow they simply did not ring true. I felt inadequate and helpless. I wondered about this as I went through the motions of being a pastor. I assumed there had to be a good answer; I just did not know it yet.

The Freeport pastorate was a half-time position, and so I supplemented our family income by driving a school bus and doing some substitute teaching in the local high school. One Sunday morning in October a third grade boy on my bus route was killed when he got caught in the header of a corn picker. I attended the boy's funeral and heard a theological explanation that was unbelievable and offensive to me. "This accident" the pastor said in his funeral sermon, "was not an accident, it was God's response to the sins of the family for picking corn on Sunday morning. This was a sin against God, and sins against God do not go unpunished!"

This was my introduction to rigid, separatist Fundamentalism. I had never heard anything quite that crass, painful, or judgmental in any sermon, much less at a funeral. Why would any person want to believe in or worship an angry, vengeful, murderous God who would do that to an eight-year-old boy? I knew I did not have all the answers, but I also knew that I could not accept that concept of God. I had no idea how I would respond, but sitting in that church I could hardly breathe and felt a rising tide of nausea stirring within me. I knew I had to get out (both physically and spiritually). I felt deep within my soul that if this was Christianity, I wanted nothing to do with it. The theology of that funeral stayed with me for years as I wrestled with my own images of God.

Enter Erma, an elderly woman in the congregation who seldom made it to church because of her physical situation. Erma was a quiet, spiritual saint in many ways. She was at peace with herself and the stressful situation in which she lived. I enjoyed visiting with Erma because she had such a positive outlook on life. She shared her sense of God and listened patiently to my questions. One day she put her theology into a very simple statement: "Don, I learned long ago to trust God. I just don't ask questions. It is easier that way." But I had lots of questions, and I could not ignore them. I had to find answers that had spiritual integrity. But I did not expect that finding these answers would take me the rest of my life.

In most ways my traditional conservative evangelical theology served me well. I knew that God was in heaven watching over us. I knew that Christian faith invited people to believe in Jesus so that when they died, they would go to be with God in heaven for all eternity. I knew that God's kingdom was in heaven, and that we lived under the secular control of a different kingdom here on earth. I believed that people who had accepted Jesus as their savior would be actively involved in mission as peacemakers working for justice, feeding the hungry, and caring for the homeless. I considered myself to be something of a radical conservative evangelical with a traditional view of God.

In 1969 Carolyn and I moved to Akron, Pennsylvania, where I became pastor of the Akron Mennonite Church. Three years later John Howard Yoder's *The Politics of Jesus* was published. The title was intriguing because, for me, Jesus was a religious figure. Linking Jesus with the political world was a new concept. Dr. Yoder had been a stimulating teacher in my seminary experience, so I immediately bought the book and began to read. The book was exciting reading because it confirmed much of what I believed. Yet I did not understand the way Yoder talked about the kingdom of God as a present reality since my faith saw the kingdom of God as a future, spiritual, and heavenly experience that would be ours when we completed our life here on earth.

At about this same time, Rollin Rheinheimer stopped by the church office to tell me of the very exciting time he and Betty had just had at Koinonia Farm in Americus, Georgia. They had met Ladon Sheats who served as the resident teacher at Koinonia. Rollin was enthusiastic about how Ladon's message would be received at Akron Mennonite. As I listened, I thought Ladon sounded a bit radical, but that it wouldn't hurt anything to stir up the congregation just a bit. So we invited Ladon to lead a weekend seminar on "Following Jesus in Radical Faith."

On Saturday, Ladon led a Bible study in the Sermon on the Mount (integrity of faith, simple living, being truthful, loving enemies). With his quiet, straightforward treatment of the text, Ladon took what was left of my evangelical, fundamentalist faith and simply blew it away. Somehow I had gone through Goshen College and Associated Mennonite Biblical Seminaries (AMBS) without allowing anyone to challenge my childhood belief that the kingdom of God is up in heaven. Ladon saw the kingdom as a present reality where people live with an open commitment to Jesus as Lord. Ladon was a physical presence confirming what I was reading in John Howard Yoder's *Politics of Jesus*.

But seven years of study at Goshen College and AMBS had laid a good foundation on which Ladon built a new faith structure. Now, in the person of Ladon, God's Spirit reached out to me, and I had a conversion experience that can only be described as a theological earthquake. I could feel the pillars of my faith being shaken and reshaped. The best language

I can use is that I was born again, even though I had been a committed follower of Jesus all my life.

It was not that I had picked up a new idea. Rather, I had discovered a whole new paradigm into which my old faith simply would not fit. It was what Jesus was talking about when he said, "No one pours new wine into old wineskins, because if they do the skins will burst, the wine will run out and the wineskins will be ruined. New wine must have new wineskins if it is to be preserved" (Luke 5:36–39). Was I ready to let go of my old wineskins?

On Sunday morning Ladon pulled everything together for me with a multimedia presentation that contrasted the kingdom of God with the kingdoms of this world. As I watched and listened, I knew that something was happening within me, and that I could never go back to being who I had been before that weekend. I wasn't sure what it all meant, but I knew I had walked through a door into a new theological world that I had never known was there. *The Politics of Jesus* linked with the weekend with Ladon and was my "Damascus road experience." And like the apostle Paul, I would spend the next several years catching up with myself as I processed new ways of organizing my faith.

Over the course of the next weeks, I spent hours reading the New Testament. It was as if I was reading it for the first time. I saw things that I had never seen before. Preaching became an exciting adventure of sharing new discoveries with the congregation and testing the growing edges of my own soul. Members of the church began responding to sermons in new ways, and I had never been so excited about what it meant to be a follower of Jesus. What I had hoped might bring new life to the congregation had actually transformed my own faith. The prayer of St. Francis states it so clearly, "For it is in giving that we receive."

The congregation asked if I would follow up the Ladon Sheats weekend by leading a Bible study in the book of Acts. We started with ten members, and in two months we had fifty in the class, one fourth who were persons from outside the church. Several new small house church groups formed, and the congregation began looking at local mission opportunities in a new way.

Over the next year the dust from the earthquake began to settle, but life was never the same. Life went on much as it had before, of course, yet everything was quite different. I had discovered a peace with God, and a sense of comfort with myself that gave me more peace with others. I was on a path of faith that I could embrace with enthusiasm and integrity. Life did not suddenly become perfect and idyllic. Far from it. But I found a new confidence that gave me courage to move forward with new vision and excitement on a faith pilgrimage that was still filled with surprises, challenges, and a few testing bumps in the road.

I have been encouraged by the company of others who share this journey with me. I have learned that growing older in your faith does not automatically mean that life gets easier and all questions get answered. I have sometimes felt a little like Elijah as he wondered whether there were others who shared his faith vision. Over the years, scholars like Marcus Borg, John Dominic Crossan, and Brian McLaren each have, in their own way, been a challenge and an affirmation for my own faith. *The Heart of Christianity* by Marcus Borg gave me insights into and additional confirmation for much of what I believed. Thus it was with great excitement in 2008 that I attended a seminar on "Radical Discipleship in an Unjust World" with Marcus Borg and John Dominic Crossan. These two scholars led about two hundred of us in an exciting reshaping of the implications of faith for the church.

At this seminar, I heard creative, progressive theology that was solidly rooted in scripture and a commitment to following Jesus. This Catholic and Episcopal team of Crossan and Borg shared solid Anabaptist theology (although they simply referred to it as "biblical"). We examined radical discipleship issues of peace and justice, health care, poverty, environment, and economics. It was a theological feast of regal proportions.

Pastors and church leaders from different denominations were excited by what they were hearing. Many wondered aloud why they had not heard this gospel before, because in it they were finding integrity for their own lives and new reality of mission for the church. As we talked together in small groups over coffee, I was reminded that much of Christianity is far more comfortable supporting the status quo and staying away from the significant issues that Jesus dealt with almost every day of his ministry two thousand years ago.

John Oldham once told Paul Tillich, "Christianity has no meaning for me apart from the church, but I sometimes feel as though the church as it actually exists is the source of all my doubts and difficulties." (Oldham, *Life Is Commitment*, p. 79.)

Sadly, I sometimes experience church becoming increasingly irrelevant to a growing percentage of the population because, far too often, it does not side with the poor, the hungry, and the oppressed in our culture. The church has become chaplain for the state, approving its materialism, individualism, militarism, and nationalism; preferring instead to address only the safe, traditional spiritual issues of prayer, sin, and salvation that promise a future hope in a time and place quite separate from this life.

I remember when that was my theology, too. It was safe, comfortable, and usually well received. But those beliefs do not represent the gospel of Jesus that has given me new life and a new vision for faith. Earthquakes have a way of shaking things up. But they provide the opportunity to rebuild, to begin again, and to discover new life, even if that means I do not know what is going to happen tomorrow. I would have it no other way.

Let's Talk About It!

Historically, observance of Reformation Day has been a tradition in the Mennonite church. But, oddly enough, this tradition no longer receives much attention by most Mennonites. In 2006, the pastoral team at College Mennonite Church (CMC) asked me to preach on Reformation Sunday, doing something "appropriate for the day." CMC is a large congregation located on the Goshen College campus. It is theologically articulate, with a membership that includes more than fifty retired pastors and missionaries. A high percentage of the members are college graduates, and a significant number of persons hold PhDs. My first thought was to go back in history and retell the Martin Luther experience, but most of the congregation already knew that story. Then I wondered, what are the Martin Luther issues in our own day that could be posted on our church bulletin board as a way of starting a new set of intentional discussions? Could I become a modern Martin Luther and speak about contemporary concerns within Christian faith?

I felt the congregation would accept this approach, even though some members might be troubled by what this modern day Martin Luther would say. I did not want to offend anyone, because that is not the way to encourage conversation or change. Could this sermon present theological concepts that explore new understandings rather than doctrinal statements that demand acceptance? I identified five widely accepted beliefs, and then I suggested what I felt was a better way of thinking about each belief. I knew the congregation was not of one mind on these beliefs. Some persons would be troubled by the sermon content. But I also knew that there were others who were frustrated with the steady diet of traditional, safe theology we were hearing every Sunday from the pulpit. This would not be a traditional sermon that reinforced existing beliefs; but neither would it tell members of the congregation what they must believe.

The text of this sermon is provided in the following section. But it is important that I first provide a little more context for the creation and delivery of this sermon, the reaction it received, and some reflective assessments of the experience. For the previous four years I had been meeting with an adult Sunday school class that was struggling with the traditional faith answers they had learned as children. These class members had questions about what they believed (or didn't believe). Could they still be Christian and maintain their integrity? How should their faith intersect with their professional lives? As our discussion progressed, I wondered if we should invite the full congregation to join in the faith discussions that we were having during these Sunday school class sessions. When I asked this class for counsel, they gave an enthusiastic "go for it."

And so we did. The class suggested that we introduce the sermon by staging a three minute drama. While talking with a young woman, Martin Luther nailed his *Ninety-Five Theses* to a door. (The drama dialogue is included below.) We also prepared a PowerPoint presentation that projected each of the five points of the sermon on the church screens so that the congregation could read them as they heard them. Traditionally, I am not a fan of PowerPoint presentations in worship, but in this instance I felt that seeing the main points on the screen would assist in providing clarity of communication.

The response to the sermon was quick and emphatic, coming from all sections of the congregation. Some persons were upset and urged the church board to reassure the congregation that this sermon does not represent the beliefs held by our pastors or by this church. They told the pastors that if I was ever invited to preach again, they would leave the church. Other persons embraced the suggestions and requested that the church board provide settings where we could talk about these questions. The leadership agreed, and for nearly three years groups met to discuss Marcus Borg's *The Heart of Christianity* or to use "Living the Questions" as a discussion starter.[3]

Sermons are always set in a specific setting. It is important to recognize this fact. This sermon might not be appropriate for many congregations. However, College Mennonite Church is an unusual congregation, partly because of its location on a college campus.

This still raises important questions about the function of the sermon in worship. Is worship a legitimate place for presenting new theological ways of thinking? Are pastors expected to stay within the safe, traditional beliefs that we have always held, affirming what we already believe? Or is it appropriate to challenge traditional belief systems from the pulpit, urging members to think in fresh ways about traditional concepts that will nurture new life? Answers to these questions are not as simple as the questions themselves, for taking a "challenging" approach might mean that the pastor's tenure in the congregation will be threatened.

3. "Living the Questions" is an interactive video series in which progressive Christian scholars are interviewed on specific subjects of faith. These serve as springboards for group discussion. For more information visit the website, livingthequestions.com.

Are there ways that pastors can nurture and challenge the full range of beliefs held by congregational members, recognizing that not all members are at the same place theologically? Yes, of course there are. But how can the pastor address theological issues that some members face without alienating other members who do not sense the importance of these same issues for themselves? Where should the pastor go to work out the growing edges of his or her personal faith?

Some pastors meet regularly with other pastors for theological stimulation. But I know, after seventeen years in the pastorate, that these meetings are exceedingly rare. Should the pastor wrestle with faith issues in the study and then share his or her findings with the congregation? Or should the pastor lead the congregation in wrestling with the issues, trusting the Spirit to guide the membership in finding further insights that will deepen and strengthen their faith? Is it possible for a congregation to live together with a variety of faith answers? If so, how does the pastor nurture persons who are developing a more progressive personal faith, recognizing they are a minority within the congregation? Where can the church offer help for persons who have questions and concerns that deserve pastoral attention?

Again, answers to these questions are not as simple as they might appear. Suggesting new answers for traditional questions on how we approach Scripture may threaten the pastor's ministry in the congregation. I have wondered whether I would have preached this sermon had I been a thirty-five-year-old pastor with several children? What if I was dependent upon the church for my family's support? Did being a retired Bible professor-pastor who was financially free from dependence upon the church make it easier to say these things? I would like to think that is not the case, but I am persuaded that, in fact, this probably is true.

Perhaps the path to finding new answers lies in a creative restructuring of Christian education within the congregation. Most congregations attempt to be creative in Sunday school offerings, but usually this means trying to find creative methods in which to explore traditional materials. It is an unusual congregation that has a regular class that wrestles with new theological answers, or with new ways of applying biblical concepts to contemporary issues. Would it not be helpful if new approaches to theology and to Bible study were at least a regular option within the Christian education program?

As I prepared this sermon, I discovered that I was talking as much about my own faith journey today as I was about Martin Luther's centuries ago!

* * *

"Martin Luther and the Wittenburg Church Door"

(Martin Luther enters holding several pieces of paper and a hammer—he is met by a young woman as he enters.)

Woman: Father Martin, good morning.

Martin: Good morning Jayne. (He goes to the door.)

Woman: What are you doing with that hammer?

Martin: The more I read the Bible, the more I wonder whether we are teaching some things that don't really match with what Jesus taught. I think we ought to talk about them.

Woman: Like . . . what things?

Martin: Well, like . . . should any person have absolute authority over what another person believes? Or, is God really as judgmental as a lot of preachers say God is? Or even . . . the way we talk about God, and expect God to do whatever we ask Him to do? I don't know, but I think we ought to talk about things like this. Here, would you hold these for me?

(Martin hands her several pages and starts nailing one sheet on the door.)

(Woman takes pages, starts to look at them.)

Woman: This one—I never thought about that. And this one—I don't believe that either, but I never dared tell anyone. And this—Ohhh— are you sure you want to say this—some people are not going to like that!

Martin: Yeah, I know. When you talk about God, all you can do is make faith statements, and people don't like to have their faith challenged.

(Martin stands back and looks at the door.)

Martin: Will this make any difference? Nobody in Wittenburg cares about these things. Five years from now, will anyone even remember that we were here? I'll bet nobody will ever read this.

Woman: I'll remember we were here, and I'll read them.

(She goes to door, starts to read—then turns to a member of the congregation.)

Woman: Hey, John, you've got to come read this. (John comes up, starts to read—scene ends.)

* * *

Let's Talk about It!

What would *you* do? The church has been your whole life. But now, people are believing and doing things in the name of Jesus that just don't fit with what you see Jesus teaching in the New Testament. Your friends urge you to ignore your questions and stay with the traditional answers that everyone knows are true. Why disturb people by challenging what they believe? But Martin Luther felt he had to do something. His haunting questions led to profound changes in how we think about God, salvation, and faith.

Religious people usually think that what they believe is exactly what the Bible teaches. We know what the truth is, so our task is to defend this truth against all other false claims of truth. However, we grow in our faith—not by defending our version of truth—but by engaging in conversation with others about what we, and they, believe. British scholar C. H. Dodd once said: "How can truth prevail if we are not on speaking terms with those whose view of truth is different from our own?"[4] Luther's *Ninety-Five Theses* were not a defiant declaration of radical truth. He was simply saying, "Here are some things I wish we could talk about." On this Reformation Sunday, we still have a few things I wish we could talk about. I would like to suggest five things this morning to stimulate our thinking.

1. *God is a spiritual presence in whom we live and move and have our being.*

Biblical writers assume a flat earth with a three level universe where God is up there, we are here, and hell is down below. Virtually no one accepts that view of the universe today, yet we continue to talk about a God who is "up there," or "out there." This ancient belief says that from "up there," God runs the world, controls the weather, intervenes on our behalf, protects us from danger and blesses us with good things. At least sometimes, but not always.

This God, up in the heavens, watches everything we do. If we do bad things, God punishes us. If we do good things, we are blessed. This image of a distant, powerful God has a profound impact on how we think about life. God controls and judges the world. Since we are God's people, we now have the responsibility to judge and control the world in God's name.

I see a very different image in Jesus, one who says that God loves the whole world. Jesus tells us that God is best experienced as a living

---

4. I was given this by a pastor/friend as a framed quote. It is from Marianne Maye Thompson's book, *1–3 John (IVP New Testament Commentary Series)*, p 152.

presence of love right here in our midst. This all-encompassing God-presence is the source of all life. In this presence we find hope; we experience joy; we gather to worship. As we share together in this way, we discover God's truth emerging within us.

For me this is a tremendously freeing concept. God is not "up there" watching what we do like a speed camera at an intersection. Rather, God is here *experiencing* with us the joys and the pain of human life. This presence of God with us is something wonderful for us to celebrate. If we could talk about this God who lives among us and who shares every experience of life with us, it would give us a new sense of comfort and assurance. It would make us more sensitive to everyone and everything around us, and the world would be better for it. Is this something we can talk about?

2. The Bible must be read seriously (but not literally).

We look to the Bible as our guide for faith and life. But not everyone reads the Bible in exactly the same way. For many devout believers, the Bible is given to us almost directly by God. For other equally devout believers, these writings come out of the ancient faith community. The Bible reflects that community's experience with God, and this influenced their understanding of God. It is our task today to understand and interpret the message of the Bible. When we accept the role of the ancient faith community in the creation of the scriptures, our understanding of the message is greatly improved. If we understand what was happening in the church as these texts were being written, it is much more likely that we will correctly interpret what the text says.

Brian McLaren recently said: "It is the purpose of scripture to equip God's people for good works. Christians have thrived when we use the Bible to guide us in doing good for all humanity. We suffer when we use the Bible as a weapon to threaten or intimidate others, to prove ourselves right and others wrong, or as a defense of the status quo. God never intended it that way, and the world suffers when we do it."[5]

I see a growing tendency today to assume that the way Fundamentalists use the Bible must be the right way to read the Bible because they do it with such confidence and conviction. I wish that we could talk about these differing assumptions in how we read the Scriptures. Jesus has a very different message about war, poverty and wealth, salvation, and

5. McLaren, Brian. This quote is a paraphrase from personal notes taken during a conference at Goshen College, May, 2008.

hope for the future than what is sweeping across religious America right now. When we accept this fundamentalist American way of reading the Bible, we are on a road that historically has led to war and condemnation of others. We end up with a privatized, materialistic, domesticated faith that focuses on a future salvation in heaven reserved only for us. But Jesus calls us to go out into our world, not back to an ancient world. We need to say again that we take the Bible very seriously without reading it literally. Affirming this approach to Scripture would give us a more mature confidence in our faith. Is this something we can talk about?

3. *Jesus is the human experience of the God-presence, proclaiming the kingdom of God.*

The central message in the Jesus story is that in Jesus we experience the presence of God as one with us. Yet the way we tell the Jesus story today puts a primary emphasis on those elements that separate Jesus from our humanity. Here, Mark helps us. He tells us that Jesus came preaching the good news of the kingdom of God, and he makes this the central theme of his gospel (Mark 1:14–15). To paraphrase what Jesus once said, "You are the salt in the soup, and if you lose that, the soup isn't much good. You are the light of the world . . . if you don't let your light shine, you might as well turn off the switch." We share the belief that Christianity is a life that is lived—not a set of doctrines to be believed. This would give us a new, more faithful identity for Jesus that would change our lives and be a blessing for those around us. Is this something we can talk about?

4. *The church is a universal faith community engaged in mission to the world.*

Since this God-presence is experienced throughout the whole world, we, the people of God, dare never become so spiritually egotistical that we assume we are the only ones with access to this God-presence. One day the disciples came to Jesus and proudly told him that they had silenced a man who was casting out demons because he wasn't one of us. Jesus scolded them saying, in effect, "That is bad thinking, because those people who do what I am doing are one with us" (Luke 9:49–50).

Jesus calls us back to our original mission of being channels of grace, hope, love, and forgiveness so that all people will be blessed. We dare never exclude anyone simply because of nationality, economic status, social standing, gender, sexual identity, or theological interpretation. Our calling is to invite people to join with us in the movement of this

God-presence on earth bringing healing to the nations, food to the hungry, peace to the world, and hope to the children.

The body of Christ is a community of pilgrims on a daily journey of compassion and mercy because we believe this is the message of Jesus. This is the God-presence that we have experienced and are called to share with all people. This new vision would give us new purpose in living and would give new life to a lot of people around us. Is this something we can talk about?

5. *Christians are followers of Jesus, bringing healing, hope, peace, and salvation to all humanity.*

The popular Western concept says everything is about "what it will do for me." We are told that Jesus came to die so that we can be saved from our sins. So we preach a gospel that tells other people, "If you believe in Jesus like we do, someday in the future you will get a reward that only we have the authority to offer." In this faith system, Jesus came to die. Very little is said about the Jesus message that calls us to a new way of living right here, right now in this God-presence that is all around us.

Do we tell people if they believe in Jesus they will go to heaven where they will "rest in peace"? Or do we invite people to join with us in working for peace by loving our enemies, because in this God-presence we no longer see other people as enemies?

Do you see the dilemma? Is salvation something God promises off in the future? Or is salvation something God offers to all people right now? Can we see life as God sees it? I hear the business and science worlds saying, "We could feed the hungry, we could provide clean water and medical care for every child on earth if we just had the will to do that instead of spending our money to fight wars." I want Christianity to rally with them and say, "We'll provide the will. You provide the expertise and the resources and let's do it." We can feed the hungry; we can provide clean water; we can fight diseases that kill thousands of children every day. But American Christianity says we must fight wars to protect our borders, our own clean water, our medical care, and our freedoms. That just does not sound like the Great Commission that Jesus gave to the disciples. If we could gather together around this vision for healing and wholeness throughout the world, we might be much more effective in bringing peace to the world. Is this something we could talk about?

I have suggested this morning several theological concerns about God, about the Bible, about Jesus, about the kingdom of God, and about the Church. These are foundational for our discussion of Christian faith. The concepts that I have suggested are not given as dogmatic statements that you must accept—or even agree with. They simply offer contrasts to beliefs that we frequently take for granted. I wish the church would talk together about them, so that our common faith in Jesus Christ as Lord might be deepened, enriched, broadened, and given new life. Can we trust God and ourselves enough that we dare to talk about them?

God Still Speaks—Are We Listening?

What should a congregation do when their pastor leaves and they need to find new leadership? The standard procedure is to engage in a search to find another pastor who could be persuaded to leave his or her church to fill the vacancy in our church. One Goshen congregation was involved in this process. When some members of the leadership team saw the number of congregations who were looking for a pastor, they decided to encourage members within their own congregation to consider the call to be a pastor. Their dream was to do more than meet their own pastoral needs: they wanted to call persons who would go to seminary, and then be available for other churches, as well. The leadership team asked me to present the need for pastors, and encourage persons to consider responding to that call.

In this sermon, I wanted to present the image of the pastor as being a person of faith who cares about people, who cares about peace, and who knows how to listen. I wanted to contrast the popular image of a pious saint who is out of touch with how life is. I decided to share very personal stories from my own life in order to humanize the pastoral calling.

Usually, pastors do not re-preach sermons. We may recycle some of the ideas, but most sermons are a "once and done" experience. However, some members of the Church Relations Office at Goshen College heard the sermon I delivered on the subject and urged me to consider sharing it in other churches. They believed that the call for pastors needed to be heard in many local congregations.

One very unexpected result came from this sermon. My home congregation (College Mennonite) asked me to share my personal story of depression in more detail as part of a four week series on depression. Other churches and other persons have asked me to talk with them about depression. This was not my intention when telling the story. Sometimes good things happen in sermons that were not intentional. Perhaps that is one sign of a good sermon.

I do not know exactly how often I have preached this sermon. But many congregations have requested that I preach it and then lead a discussion on being a pastor during the church's Sunday school hour.

* * *

God Still Speaks—Are We Listening?[6]

When I read the Bible I am amazed at what I learn about how God works in human experience. Often on the first reading, I am bewildered at some of the things Jesus said, and by some of the unorthodox things that he did. As I try to figure out what is going on, I am reminded that in Jesus' own day there were religious people who had the same difficulty that I have in trying to understand Jesus. But when that thought hits me, I don't like it very well, because in our day it is not considered a compliment to be identified as a Pharisee. But yet, sometimes, I bring some Pharisaic ways of thinking when I reflect on what God is doing in my own life. This might also be true for you.

One of my responsibilities as President of Oakwood Academy has been to hire staff members. When I look at the people whom Jesus called to be his disciples, and those whom he told to go out and tell others, I don't think I would have hired some of them. Would you really accept a former demon-possessed man as a youth counselor at your child's summer camp? I am not sure that I would have sent this demon-possessed man out into his own community as an evangelist for the good news. But when we experience Jesus as Lord, and when we recognize that the kingdom of God is a present reality in which we all live, even though very often it is a minority vision in the world, even among Christians, then the reality of being called to a new way of living becomes critically important. This almost instantly leads to a second step. If we are going to live in the midst of the grace of God, committed to following Jesus, then we need to call leaders who will help us discover, experience, and then share this grace of God with others.

I am going to work with three basic assumptions this morning:

1. The primary purpose of the people of God (church is our simple word for it) is mission—sharing the grace of God, bringing salvation, healing, and hope to the world.

2. If we are going to be faithful in this mission of salvation, healing, and reconciliation, then we need leaders who understand that vision. We need leaders who keep inviting us (encouraging and sometimes even kicking us) out of our comfort zone of simply reveling in the joy of God's grace shown to us.

---

6. The biblical foundation for this sermon is Isaiah 6:1–8 and Mark 5:1–20.

3. We need help in moving into this creative ministry of loving, caring, feeding, healing, and bringing hope to a world that just doesn't recognize what God is doing.

Now that is so easy to say. I think all of us, if it were our worship style to do so, would say "Amen," because we all agree. So what do we do about it? Let me share some observations from the text, make some suggestions about what this might mean for us, and then issue a call for new leaders who keep pushing for new life in our churches.

Over my twenty-plus years of teaching New Testament, I have developed a new appreciation for the Pharisees. I give Kathleen Kern (*We Are the Pharisees*) a lot of credit for this appreciation because she has urged me to think about them a bit differently. The Pharisees were a minority religious group (that's familiar with us); they were intent on doing careful study of the Scriptures (I hope that feels right with us); and they were committed to living holy lives (we share that one, too). In many ways their concerns are our concerns. I happen to think that is good. So what happened? We can see it in the contrast of several stories in the life of Jesus. We heard one story from Mark 5 this morning, where Jesus tells the healed man to tell everyone about his experience. There are several parallel stories in Mark where Jesus heals a person and then tells that person, "Don't tell anybody."(See Mark 1:25, 43; 3:12; 4:11; 9:9.) Now, why would Jesus do that?

One reason is the difference in community vision. If the person had spread the word about Jesus, the local community would have pulled out their traditional assumptions about God and would have tried to anoint Jesus as messianic Savior on the model of King David. But that was not the model Jesus was using for his own ministry.

This, then, is my first challenge: So often when congregations call pastors or discern gifts for leaders, we look for good preaching, teaching, and administrative skills. These are the public institutional tasks that we want the pastor to do. I would like us to look for something different. Trust me, we can teach you how to preach, how to teach, how to study the Bible, even how to do administration. Instead of these basic skills, let's look for vision of what God is doing. Let's look for experience in knowing what the grace of God feels like. This demon-possessed man didn't know much about theology, but he had experienced the mercy and healing of God's grace. *That* is exactly what Jesus told this man to share with his friends—tell people that God is a God of mercy and healing.

Now, let's put this right alongside the call of the disciples: Jesus called a rather interesting group of people to be his disciples. And what was the first thing he did with them? He taught them. Luke 6:20 says he looked at his disciples, and he began to teach them what the kingdom of God is all about. When we call leaders, let's be careful that we don't get sidetracked on the easy stuff and in the process miss the crucial sense of God's vision for a people who are caught up in the power of Jesus and the presence of the kingdom. Thus, the important question for each of us this morning—what is our vision? Do we have dreams about what God could be doing in our individual lives, and in our life together as a congregation? That goes far beyond just running an organization or planning worship services each week.

How then, do we call leaders with vision? Let's begin with how Jesus called his disciples. What do you know about them? The diversity of this group is truly amazing. We know from some brief snippets of New Testament storytelling that they did not always like each other very much. Sometimes they argued among themselves, and even after three years of being with Jesus, they still did not fully understand what Jesus was all about.[7]

I'd like to suggest something from this. We don't call leaders to be perfect models of saintliness. We call them to be human channels of God's grace among us. There are many Christian people who expect pastors to be perfect saints, and these folks make life miserable for pastors and for everyone else in the congregation (themselves included). When we demand that pastors be saints, we assume that all the rest of us who aren't pastors must be sinners. And we treat each other as sinners because we treat people the way we perceive them to be.

Let me tell you a story. I grew up in a very healthy family. I have been very fortunate in my life to have had basically good health. I am very grateful for that. But this meant that when I became a pastor I did not like to make hospital visits. I wasn't very understanding of persons who were struggling with issues of health and sickness. I just sort of expected these people to get their act together and get well. But then at one point in my life, for about a year and a half, I got sick and struggled with severe depression that almost made me nonfunctional. Ask Carolyn, she knows what it was like in our home. It was tough, it was painful, and it was totally, completely exhausting. It took all my energy to get through

7. See Mark. 8:27–34.

the morning, and I still had the afternoon, plus evening meetings to attend. I had had classes in seminary that talked about depression, but I never understood it until I walked through my own valley of the shadow of death. Unless you have been there, you don't know how scary that valley can be. I got help from a congregation that was merciful when they didn't understand and from a good psychiatrist who helped me understand; and I survived it. I learned a lot about life, and about myself. I think I became a much more compassionate, merciful person because of that experience. I could share with people in the pain of their suffering because I had learned about the grace and mercy of God. I had learned that grace is not just a good theological concept; it is an experience of liberation, of healing, and of hope.

When we call persons to lead us, I hope we look for persons who know what the grace of God feels like because they have experienced it in their own lives. I hope we can look for persons who have been forgiven—and who know it. I hope we find persons who have been forgiven for things they would really prefer not telling you about, because the sin was so personal, so painful, and so embarrassing. Persons like that can help the rest of us develop the courage to come to God and to our faith community and ask for forgiveness. Persons who have been there know more than just the Bible verses telling us to forgive. They know the pain and the fear that comes when what you have done becomes public. Saints don't always do so well at forgiving. They expect you to be good—just like they are. I pray for pastors that they might be quick to forgive because they know God has forgiven them.

Why is this so important? When biblical concepts become a living reality in our lives, we become changed persons. When we become changed persons, we can offer new life, forgiveness, and hope to others around us. So I wonder. Are we seen as a forgiving, merciful people, or as an achieving, spiritually judgmental people? When we expect perfection from our pastors, then we are telling people that spirituality is linked with ethical perfection. And we are usually uncomfortable around people who think they are perfect.

I have a friend in Goshen whom I see rather regularly. He grew up in a good home. At one time he declared his faith in Jesus, but now he doesn't have much interest in church. As we visit together, I keep encouraging him to come back to church. One day, he put his coffee cup down, looked at me and said, "Don, I know you want me to come to church, but I'm just not good enough. If I came to church, people would look at me and wonder, What's he doing here?" *Ouch!* That one hurt. That tells me the community sees achievement—not grace; they see judgment—not forgiveness. That tells me that Romans 5:8, "while we were still sinners, Christ died for us," has not yet soaked into the core of our spiritual being.

So I ask another question this morning. What if we told you that we don't expect you to be perfect, and we will forgive you when you are not. We want you to help us be more honest and loving with God, with ourselves, and with each other. Could you say, "Yeah, I'd like to do that!"? Maybe God is calling you. Could you hear that call of God to help the rest of us become sources of hope, of healing and salvation in a world that is really hurting, confused, and destructive?

One more thing this morning. How do we call persons to be leaders? Our Western culture encourages us to be very private and internal with our spiritual experiences. Yet our understanding of church urges us to be more open, sharing, and communal in nature. But when it comes to inviting persons to consider being a pastor, we have relied almost exclusively on the internal, personalized, secret call of God upon that person. Now for some, that is a very legitimate starting place. But I personally know of students who have felt this internal nudging of God, but because no one in their church ever added the human confirmation to that inner Godly voice, they began to question their experience. If nobody else senses these gifts in me, maybe this isn't really God calling. Maybe it's just me living in a fantasy world. Look again at the disciples. They didn't come to Jesus saying, "I've got this internal urge that I should follow you." No! Jesus went around saying, "you, and you, come on, follow me and I will make you leaders (fishers of men)."

We say we believe that God is present in our midst. What might God do if we had the courage to quietly say, "John, you have integrity and compassion, have you ever thought about being a pastor?" Or "Mary, I see the way you listen to other people and seem to understand what they are feeling. I see how people trust you. You'd be a good pastor."

I'd like for us to be more intentional in suggesting that persons consider the call to be a pastor. This applies equally well to those adults who are successful in their current occupations. The disciples were all successful in their chosen vocations. Paul was a well-respected teacher and religious leader in his day. Maybe the excitement, the challenge, the privilege of sharing life with others that you now enjoy is good preparation for you to consider being a leader in the faith community.

I want to make one disclaimer. I do not believe that being a pastor is a higher or more spiritual calling than being a teacher, or a counselor, or a business person, or a member of the medical profession, or a social worker, or a farmer. God is at work in all these professions. But what I do want you to know is that being a pastor is also rewarding, fulfilling, and very exciting (most of the time). I would like to nudge you to think more intentionally about calling, nurturing, and sending persons to be pastors.

Do you know what it feels like to be forgiven? Do you find it invigorating to listen to and walk with people who are trying to make sense of their lives? Do you think that there ought to be a better way to live in this world than what you see on TV? Do you believe that Jesus makes sense when he tells us to share and love and forgive? Can you accept yourself as a human being, and risk letting other people walk with you? Do you get excited when you see other people mature and grow in their excitement for living with God, with others, and with themselves?

Maybe you ought to think about being a pastor. Or maybe you should be offering a word of encouragement to someone else here in the congregation this morning about being in ministry. God is still calling. The question is whether we are still listening.

If That's a Blessing, I'll Pass!

Congregations often plan worship around a series of sermons on a given topic or biblical text. A local congregation asked me to introduce a worship series on the Sermon on the Mount. My assignment was to help the congregation understand the Beatitudes. The Beatitudes can be problematic because they seem to be very nice sounding platitudinous statements that are out of touch with reality. They seem to be teaching that we should be passive and piously happy in the midst of painful experiences. That sounds like asking people to deny how they are experiencing life. How should we understand what these statements mean?

I decided to approach this sermon by sharing true stories about real people (changing names to protect the innocent). Each person gave me permission to tell their story on that condition.

* * *

If That's a Blessing, I'll Pass![8]

David and Olive live in Portadown, Northern Ireland. David owns a small sporting goods store, and Olive is a member of the Parades Commission. This group has the task of approving and then supervising the parades that have very deep religious-political meaning in Northern Ireland. David and Olive are active members of a new emerging Mennonite Community in Portadown. Carolyn and I met them in June when we visited Portadown with friends. David and Olive believe the gospel speaks to issues of justice, love, reconciliation, and healing. Along with other members of the Greenfield Community Fellowship, they are trying to bring healing to the tensions between Catholics and Protestants. In Northern Ireland, that is not an easy task. In late July, David's store was firebombed, just a week after he had received a major shipment of inventory for the new autumn changeover. The fire damaged the store and ruined the entire inventory and computers with all the records of orders that had been received. It was economically devastating and emotionally terrifying. The Beatitudes say, "Blessed are you when you are persecuted for righteousness' sake, for yours is the kingdom of heaven." How can this discouraging experience of economic destruction be a blessing for David and Olive? Why should they see themselves as being blessed?

8. The biblical foundation for this sermon is Matthew 5:1-12.

Janet is a leader in the church. Because of her own experience with the love of God, she has devoted her life to working with persons who have been deprived of love and acceptance by church people. She speaks up publicly for these hurting people. She has written some articles in the church press that challenge us in how we treat people whom we see as not being "like us." The result is that some Christian people discredit her faith. They say that she does not believe the Bible, and they actually challenge her right to speak in Mennonite churches or at denominational assemblies. The Beatitudes tell Janet, "Blessed are you when people revile you and say all kinds of evil things against you for my sake. Rejoice and be glad." I know Janet and I know how badly it hurts when people try to dismiss her for what she is doing. I just can't bring myself to tell her that she should be glad when people tell lies about her. How is that a blessing?

George has lived on the edge of poverty and bankruptcy his whole life. He has very little hope of ever owning his own home, or driving a new car. He struggles, and life is hard for his family. Luke's version of the Beatitudes tells George, "Blessed are people like you who are poor for you will receive the kingdom of heaven" (Luke 6:20). George doesn't care much about heaven, but he does worry about having enough money to pay the rent and have food for his family. Now with school starting, buying shoes and school supplies for his children presents an economic crisis. Help me understand how George is supposed to be glad because he is poor.

This is the image that is commonly held in the Beatitudes. Jesus is saying sweet things to people about having an upbeat attitude in the midst of their suffering. This is not new. If you go back and compare the Matthew and Luke accounts, you will note they are slightly different. Luke says, "Blessed are the poor," while Matthew says, "Blessed are the poor in spirit." Luke says, "Blessed are you who are hungry," while Matthew says, "Blessed are those who hunger and thirst for righteousness." Do the Beatitudes really teach the right internal attitudes that you should have, so that in the midst of your poverty, your hunger, your abuse, and your oppression, you discover that these terrible realities are only temporary external conditions? Do they really tell us that someday in the presence of God, you will receive a special blessing to make up for what you went through here on earth?

I want to suggest this morning that Christians sadly miss the true point of what Jesus is saying. They turn Christian faith into an internal, spiritual, private experience that tells us to hope for the future, rather than to expect the love of God to make a difference here in this life. The gospel does not tell people to "hang in there; you'll get better treatment after you die." The gospel call to mission is to bring change to people's lives today. The call is to do something about the suffering, the lies, and the abuse, not simply to encourage those who are suffering to develop an attitude of denial about what is going on around them.

Where does this come from? It is found in the beliefs that one has about what Jesus meant when he talked about the reign of God. Jesus proclaimed a new way of living that is present, something that is already here, even though it is still emerging and developing. It is a new reality, a new way of living, of thinking, of reacting to life, of deciding what things are important. Jesus did not primarily teach doctrines and ideas (although you have to have doctrines and ideas in order to carry on a conversation about what the reign of God means). And Jesus is not primarily inviting people to have an internal religious experience that makes them feel better when they are suffering (even though you cannot fully respond to Jesus without it being personal). It is a decision that impacts who you are and what you do, so it is emotional, it is personal, and it is life changing. Second Corinthians 5:17 says, "When a person is in Christ, there is a whole new world, everything has become new."

That is point number one: Jesus is talking about a new order where God rules, where there is a new reality, not just an internal attitude. Point number two: The stuff that Jesus says you will be blessed for doing are not things you simply decide to do. You don't get up in the morning and say to yourself, "I am going to hunger and thirst for righteousness today," or "I think I'll mourn for a while," or "I'm going to be meek for a change." Jesus is not talking about actions for which you will receive positive rewards. He is talking about experiences in which people are already living.

Don't read the Beatitudes as, "Blessed are those of you who work hard at mastering the art of being poor in spirit, or who struggle to be meek, or who are good at mourning, or those who can get other people to spread all kinds of evil lies about you, because if you suffer these things here, you will enjoy the good things of heaven all the more." That is like beating your head against the wall because it feels good when you stop.

When Jesus says, "Blessed are you . . ." he is saying, "You don't realize how fortunate you are," or "good for you." Now, why is that you are so fortunate?

Jesus is saying that there are people in the world who are poor and hungry, and they are fortunate. But they are not fortunate because there is some special virtue in being poor and hungry. That is old system thinking. The reason they are fortunate is because the reign of God is here, and in the reign of God, people give food to the hungry so they don't have to keep on being hungry. In the reign of God, people help poor people, because that is just what happens in the reign of God. Let us never forget that when empires are the ruling power, they stomp on the poor, they take advantage of you, and they push you aside and try to ignore you.

Do you remember Atlanta in 1996, the year of the Olympics? The powers that be bussed all the homeless people out to surrounding towns so that these people would not be a blight on Atlanta's two weeks on the world stage. But people living under the reign of God don't do that. Poor people will be blessed because God's people see poverty differently. God's people see their own wealth differently. They share it with those who are poor. They buy food for those who are hungry. And *that truly is good news*.

You see, the words of Jesus are not directed at helping oppressed people convince themselves that they shouldn't really mind being oppressed. Jesus tells people who have already decided to follow him what their faith is going to mean for oppressed people who live all around them. It is a mission statement directed at the church, not a psychological statement aimed at oppressed people.

For those people in the world who are hungry, the good news is that there are people here who live by the values of God seen in Jesus, and they will share their food with you so that you don't have to go another day fighting hunger—*and that is good news*.

You folks who are peacemakers, you really are lucky because in the reign of God there are people who will see what you are doing and will rightly identify you as a child of God. They don't write letters to the local editor calling you a traitor or an enemy-lover who should be deported. These reign-of-God people recognize the godly nature in what you are doing, and they will support you in working for peace—*and that is good news*.

There are people in the world who live simply, claiming no status or power for themselves. In the world around them, other people take advantage of them. But the good news is that the new reign of God is here, and these reign-of-God people will treat you with respect and dignity. They affirm what you are doing with your generosity and your simple living, and they honor you for it. *And that is good news*.

There are people in the world who show mercy to others, and they are fortunate, because there may come a day when they will need mercy to be shown to them. Now I can imagine there will be some people who will say to them, "That's tough, you should have saved something to take care of yourself." But people living by the reign of God will remember that you showed mercy, and they will show mercy to you.

The Beatitudes are not internal, spiritual attitudes aimed at people who are suffering or who are trying to do good all by themselves, yet end up being abused for their good intentions. The Beatitudes are aimed at people in the faith community who are already clear in their commitment to follow Jesus. The Beatitudes help us understand how people who follow Jesus will live. And when we do that, the poor, the hungry, the meek, the peacemakers really are fortunate. Why? Because they discover that they are living next door to people who know the reign of God is a present reality. People who know this truth lead lives of thankful gratitude for all that God has done, and they share that gratitude with others who are less fortunate.

So we are called to look at ourselves. How does the reign of God show in the way we treat people who are abused, lied about, persecuted, work for peace, choose to forsake power, wrestle with what it means to be righteous, or have hearts that focus on the will of God? The Beatitudes call us to be in mission, walking alongside these people, sharing with them, caring about them, helping them, joining with them in their work for peace, and defending them against the lies created by the empires that are in power.

Let me end where I started this morning. Recently we received an email from David, the shopkeeper in Northern Ireland whose store was firebombed. It reads:

> Thank you so much for your note. It is so encouraging to know that we are not alone. I have never known more than I do right now what it means to have the support and love and compassion of the faith community. The folks at Greenfield have been so wonderful, helping us process our feelings of fear and anger, encouraging us to continue on with our lives. This has been very difficult for Olive and me, but your prayers, your words of encouragement give us hope. The persons who came from Goshen to help us rebuild did more than rebuild the store, they helped us rebuild our lives. Today we open for business again. My suppliers and customers have stayed with me, and life will go on. Three months ago, we were discouraged and afraid. Today, we

have hope and we are excited. We now believe that this event can open new doors for reconciliation and healing here in Portadown. Please continue to pray for us.

That is the Beatitudes at work in human experience by the grace of God through the faith community. It is my fervent prayer that it might be that way for us as well. *For that truly would be good news.*

3

What Really Matters?

Do not judge and you will not be judged.
Do not condemn, and you will not be condemned.
Forgive, and you will be forgiven.
Give and it will be given to you.
A good measure, pressed down, shaken together, running over.
The measure you give will be the measure you get back.

—Jesus
Luke 6:37–38

In the Christian scriptures,
the most virtuous form of love is not agape, but koinonia,
the mutual, reciprocal, committed and celebrative love of intimate relationship,
authentic community and responsive fellowship.
To live in koinonia is to rely on a web of relationships of loving, caring community.[1]

—David Augsburger

No preacher stands in front of a congregation hoping that everyone
will go home exactly as they were before the sermon.
Every minister is dedicated to bringing the life-changing love of God
into the lives of those who gather for worship.[2]

—June Yoder

1. Augsburger, *Dissident Discipleship*, p. 69.
2. Yoder, "Preaching as an Agent of Change," *Vision*, Vol. 2, p. 60.

What Really Matters?

If you had asked them, Sandra and Miriam would have told you they lived in the worst of all possible worlds. In our average-sized three bedroom home, our two youngest daughters had to share a bedroom. They had bunk beds and their own personal desks. It was a nice room. I never thought about how the two sisters "suffered" by having to share that particular space. That is, until one evening. I was downstairs when I heard louder and louder shouting coming from their room. That was not terribly unusual because our family had a way of being openly verbal with life. When Carolyn suggested I go see what was going on before someone got hurt, I went up, tapped on the door and walked in on a heated shouting match.

I asked them to calm down and tell me what was going on. That didn't help much, because it started another argument about who got to go first! So I sat down on the lower bunk bed and talked with them about what it feels like when you are fighting. Do you enjoy it? They each shook their heads "no" without looking up. So I began with the standard parental lecture, "I don't know how this got started, but why don't we just forgive each other and start to play nice together. It's a lot more fun for all of us when you get along. Do you think you could do that?" Both girls sighed, "Okay." And I said, "Thank you, that's much better."

I headed for the door, feeling rather proud of myself for having averted World War III. Just as I closed the door, I heard Sandra mutter under her breath to little sister Miriam, "You did too, and you know it!" Apparently, not all was forgiven. Forgiveness in my childhood was "forgive and forget." While this approach momentarily might have stopped the actual fight, we seldom forgave, and we never forgot. Like father—like daughter!

I remember being told in church, "As far as the East is from the West, so far has God removed our transgressions from us." I had no idea how far that East-West thing was, so it made no sense to me; especially because when I transgressed, I was usually reminded how this is the third time I had done it, and when is it going to stop?

I also remember the two or three times when, as a child, I was part of the worship service when a member of the church was excommunicated because of some particularly offensive action. I don't recall that our congregation ever disciplined anyone for *believing* the wrong thing, but members could get quite agitated when a person *did* the wrong thing.

I guess that made sense in a way, because most of our sermons in our church focused not on what people believed, but on what people did. It also seemed as though some sins were more offensive than others, and these sins warranted congregational action. Other sins could be quietly ignored because they were less important. At least that is how it seemed to me. But I could never figure out how people knew which sins deserved which response.

One of my first experiences with church discipline was directed at my older brother Carl. Carl had violated church ethics by joining the army in 1945. One Sunday morning, several months later, it was announced that Carl Blosser's name had been removed from the church roles and that he was no longer considered a member of the church because of this grievous sin in his life. The church leaders had not actually talked with Carl about this, and they also neglected to warn Mom and Dad of what was coming that Sunday morning. It hit Mom particularly hard. She was a Sunday school teacher with a very sensitive, caring conscience. This told her that she had failed as a mother and as a Christian teacher in her own family. It was not one of Mom's better days in church.

In seminary I was taught that *discipline* and *discipling* come from the same word. The goal of church discipline is always to strengthen or correct an individual with the intention that the person's faith would become stronger and their witness in the world would not be tarnished by destructive behaviors. We were told that discipline should always be done in love, with the goal being the repentance and restoration of the transgressing member.

At home, discipline (spanking or having privileges taken away) was administered so that I would learn not to do those bad things again. In church, discipline was always applied because a rule had been broken, thus there was a sense of objectivity, a violation of something that was written down. Somehow there was the belief that punishment would pro-duce redemption and change. Therefore, those of us who are righteous must take the responsibility of punishing sinners. This led to the obvious conclusion that we punish behaviors that we ourselves are not guilty of, and that we determine sinfulness by criteria that exempts us and focuses on others.

As a young pastor, this troubled me. Most of the disciplining that I had seen was not very redemptive. It appeared to me that church disci-pline focused more on protecting the good name of the church than in redeeming the person. More and more often, it seemed to me, the church perceived itself as the gathering of saints who guarded against the intrusion of those who do not match our level of perfection. Rather than offering redemption, forgiveness, and nurturing, it was much easier to simply condemn and exclude. It was only after we disciplined you, and you exhibited appropriately changed behavior, that we could talk with you about forgiveness. I wondered if this was the best approach.

My first experience as a pastor with church discipline was a touchy one. One member of the congregation had done something in public that was inappropriate. It was truly unacceptable behavior. Most might even say it was sinful. I was told I had to do something about it. The person was embarrassed, and ashamed of what had happened. He had come to me as pastor and had apologized (confessed) to me for his actions. The church board insisted he make a statement to the congregation and offer the same apology to the church. This was a long time ago. It was just the way we did things back then.

The week before this "confession" was to be made, I met with the man's Sunday school teacher and suggested that the class have a noon carry-in dinner at church that day as a way of saying "we forgive you, we care about you, and we want to be your friends." The teacher agreed. The man made his confession statement to the congregation during the worship service, and then we had a truly celebrative time that Sunday noon as we ate together. Class members hugged each other and a few cried. All of us indicated very clearly "let's move on with our lives."

On Monday morning two older church leaders were waiting for me at the church office. I did not know what they wanted to talk about, but their demeanor told me I was not going to like it. They explained that I was young and probably did not know "how we do things around here." The clincher was, "It used to be when people sinned we exercised discipline in church, but now it looks like we throw a party. We don't know what they taught you in seminary, but that's not how we do it here." Without waiting for an explanation they left, which is probably a good thing because I had no idea what to say.

I closed the door behind them and felt duly chastised, but only briefly. I remembered the prodigal son and how glad the father was when his son came home and acknowledged his unsavory actions. That thought made me feel a little better. Then I remembered the Pharisees who got so angry at Jesus when he did not punish people for "sins" they knew were clearly punishable. That made me feel even better yet, although I still did not know what I would do about "how we do things here" if another situation came up.

Is it necessary to embarrass people and make them pay before we can forgive them? What is it that we really want to have happen with either church discipline or church forgiveness? It was clear to me that both groups (the Sunday school class and the two senior leaders) wanted the same thing: that the destructive behavior should stop. The two church leaders assumed that the experience of punishment would effectively stop the behavior, and once that happened, we forgive, accept, and reinstate the member.

The Sunday school class had a different premise. If we walk alongside each other as friends, we can assist the person so that the behavior will take care of itself. There is no need to kick someone when they are already hurting. As I look back, I think I gained the tiniest twinge of new insight along with the accompanying regret for what I had done. A few years later I was the pastor in a different congregation, and it was there I discovered that this tiny twinge of insight was not dramatic enough.

Mary was a local elementary school teacher. She was creative in her teaching methods, and she possessed a quiet way of listening while you talked that made you feel important. That means a lot to a fourth grader. One day our daughter, who was in Mary's class, told us that her teacher was in the hospital. A few days later I learned that she had been admitted to an area psychiatric center. Mary and her husband were not active in any of the town churches, and since Carolyn and I knew her as a teacher for two of our daughters, we visited her at the hospital. Mary was depressed, withdrawn, and not very responsive, and we stayed for only a few minutes. As we left, we asked if we might come back again. She nodded without looking up. Over the next two months, Carolyn and I visited Mary each week, and we could see marked improvement in the quality of interaction week by week.

When Mary returned home, she asked whether she and her husband might visit our church. In our small town she already knew many of the children and their parents. She and her husband were soon regular participants in worship and in other events in the life of the congregation. About six months later she came to my office and wondered if she could be a teaching assistant in the fourth grade Sunday school class. I was surprised: "Teaching assistant? You are the best elementary teacher in the school system; you want to be an assistant?" "Yes," she replied. "I just want to be of help where I can."

A year later, Mary and her husband asked about becoming members of the congregation. They had been church members in another town just after they were married, but had not been active for quite a few years. Our congregation felt like home to them and they wanted to make their membership official. Several other couples had expressed similar interest, and so we formed a group where each shared their own faith pilgrimage. We talked about questions of faith, we explained congregational life, and we learned to know each other better. I was looking forward to an exciting celebration for the congregation.

However, a few people were not happy. They wondered how much I knew about Mary. I said, "I know her as an excellent teacher with a warm, vibrant faith."

"Do you also know that she is divorced and remarried?"

"Yes, I know that. But that is not an issue in her situation."

"It might not be an issue for you, but it is for the church. Before we can receive her as a member we must have a biblical study of this issue, because divorce is a clear violation of Scripture!"

I disagreed, but the church leaders were insistent, arguing that such a study would be good for the congregation and would be helpful in preserving church unity.

The next Sunday morning I went to church with a letter of resignation that I intended to read in protest of this decision to have a study. The chair of the congregation caught me between Sunday school and worship. He knew I was angry about the decision, and he was afraid I would do something in anger and haste. He urged me to reconsider my decision to resign because the study would help the congregation be more accepting, and the process would be good for everyone. I finally agreed that I would tear up the resignation letter. The church board then organized a biblical study of divorce and remarriage for the congregation.

Attendance for the divorce study was very strong, participation was enthusiastic, and all went well. Or so I thought. At the end of four weeks, the congregation joyfully agreed that because God had graciously forgiven us, we would extend that same love and forgiveness to Mary and her husband. We would warmly welcome them into full fellowship in the church. But by the time we made that decision, there was no one there to love, or forgive, or accept. Once again, Mary's past was used against her, and she felt the pain of being rejected. She was gone and she never came back.

The pain that I felt because of what we had done to her has never gone away. It was wrong for me to have succumbed to church pressure from a minority faction. I had sacrificed a person in order to protect the "sacred unity" of the church based on an inappropriate interpretation of a biblical text. I had, in that experience, become a Pharisee and had withheld the love of Jesus from a person who was finding the liberating joy of new life.

I vowed within myself that I would never, ever do that again. I remembered the times that Jesus clashed with the Pharisees who preferred to judge others rather than offer forgiveness in the name of God. I remembered the anger Jesus had with their stubborn, self-righteous attitudes. Jesus offered grace, forgiveness, and acceptance to persons whom the Pharisees saw as sinners. I became convinced that offering healing and hope is far more important in the great sweep of God's dealing with humanity than any technical reading of Scripture that condemns a person to live in their past rather than be freed from it.

I remained in contact with Mary over the next few years until we left that particular community and I enrolled in graduate school. She forgave me for what I had done, and we found healing in our personal relationship. She and her husband became members in another church, but she lived for a long time with the pain caused by what I had allowed to happen.

This experience stayed with me for years as I wrestled with my commitment to be more accepting of persons who struggle with relationship issues, or who have lived through personal experiences that others identify as being destructive. I grew in my belief, and I came to understand, that following Jesus means getting close enough to persons in order to understand them. The alternative is to keep a distance, and in so doing run the danger of judging them from a distance. This new process also helped me understand that sometimes Christians will be critical of a pastor if he or she does not hold fast to "the clear teaching of Scripture" on a very specific point. I have learned to expect that criticism, but I have also learned not to accept it. If I were to accept it and allow it to control my commitment to share God's love with others, then that would mean a rejection of the love God has shown to me.

This experience, in addition to three years in graduate school where I wrestled with the biblical text, influenced how I read Scripture. Do we really represent the spirit of Jesus when we use Scripture to condemn or exclude others? Conversely, are we not representing the spirit of Jesus when we apply the hope and grace we find in the Scriptures? Must a traditional interpretation of Scripture be defended even if today's setting is quite different from the original experience of Jesus? Should defending Scripture or church doctrine ever take priority over the acceptance of a person who is honestly seeking healing?

In my "Jesus and the Gospels" class at Goshen College, I always included a discussion of "Forgiveness," in order to look at how it works and why it is important. Jewish philosopher Hannah Arendt has been helpful in shaping my thinking. Among other very good things, she suggests that forgiveness releases persons from their past and also frees us to be who we want to be. She argues persuasively that not forgiving reduces our options, thus allowing choices like revenge or "getting even" to rise to the top. When this happens we never get even, we simply prolong the battle. Forgiving allows us to get off the escalator of violent temptations. If we do not forgive, we allow other persons to control our lives by giving the event power to continue. When we forgive, we remove the control that event has over us. We then can recover for ourselves the power to set our own agenda.

I have spent my adult life as a pastor interpreting Scripture in the church or as a professor teaching the Bible in the classroom. For me, Christian faith is about grace and mercy that helps others become whole (and holy) persons. I continue to believe that we would be a better faith community if we would read the Scriptures with the same spirit and understanding that Jesus had as he interpreted and applied the Scriptures in his own day. Some persons may not feel this is the best way to interpret Scripture, but I am convinced it is the best way to capture the Spirit of God, shown to us in Jesus Christ, who is Lord in our lives.

Good Enough for God's Grace

How do Christians connect salvation that is purely by God's grace, "for by grace you have been saved through faith, this is not your own doing, it is the gift of God, not of works lest any man should boast" (Eph 2:9), with a strong ethical call to do the will of God, "What does it profit if a man says he has faith but has no works? Can his faith save him? . . . You see a man is justified by works and not by faith alone" (Jas 2: 14, 24 NRSV).[3]

For me, graduate school was a very exciting time of making new connections. Our whole family moved to Scotland where I enrolled in a PhD program at the University of St Andrews. My doctoral studies (Jesus and the Year of Jubilee: Luke 4:16–30) forced me to wrestle with the faith–works tension in a new way.

In Leviticus, chapters 24–25, I found the recurring theme: "I am the Lord your God who brought you out of Egypt," followed by instructions on how the Israelites should live together. I saw that the recurring prophetic call for ethical living in the Old Testament was rooted in what God had already done for Israel. This same theme fit perfectly with the New Testament call to action based on one's belief that, in Jesus, God was fully present with us. Thus, I began to see that ethical behavior does not save us, but it is a living witness to the depth and quality of our faith.

Several years later, I was teaching a Sunday school class in my home congregation. I asked what I thought were two rather innocent questions. "Why are you a person of faith? Why do you believe in Jesus?" The quick response by several people was "because I want to go to heaven." That answer stirred an intense discussion on the purpose of "saving faith." These questions kept dominating the class for several weeks. Some persons insisted that all we have to do is believe, because salvation is by grace, not by ethical behavior. They were concerned that too many Christians (Mennonites in particular) believe that their salvation is in doing good works (Matt 5:16).

Others felt equally strongly that simply believing the right religious answers is not what identifies a person as being a Christian. They felt that our faith is best reflected in our lives, rather than in theological doctrines. For them, faith has little validity if how we live is not in harmony with

---

3. A brief comment regarding the biblical text that appears in the sermons found in this book: The reader should know that these sermons were preached over a 30 year period. During that time I used the RSV, the NIV, and the NRSV versions of the Bible. Currently I use the NRSV.

the teachings of Jesus. Still others tried to bring faith and ethical behavior together, insisting that we need both. But no one could identify how that balance should be maintained, or which had priority. Underneath all this discussion was lurking the unspoken assumption that "grace is what sinners need"—a quiet implication that *we* in the class do not need it because we know (or do) the right things.

This was not the first time I had heard these themes. They seemed always to be just below the surface for many Christians. Yet, often, these Christians are not comfortable in their own faith. Is there a way to help persons feel secure in their faith, yet retain their radical commitment to peace? What is the right motivation for loving others, for feeding the hungry, clothing the naked, or visiting the sick (Matthew, chapter 25)?

I grew up in a religious setting where fear or guilt was often used to motivate good behavior, or at least to keep us away from bad behavior. We were challenged to be sure that we were good enough for God's grace to be given to us. In graduate school I discovered a new way of seeing how the Scriptures integrated believing and doing into a holistic life. I wanted to share this concept with the congregation in a way that both the right-belief people and the right-works people would feel affirmed, yet be encouraged to think in some new ways about their own faith.

And so I set to work on a sermon. It was, in retrospect, an ambitious task. That is, this sermon raised some additional questions that pastors often face: Do we sometimes try to do too much in a single sermon? After I gave this sermon, a number of persons asked for a copy of it, saying, "I liked what I heard, but it was just too much for me. I want to read it so that I can think about it."

I suppose that is good criticism. Pastors often get so involved in what they want to say that they feel they have to say everything. One of the benefits of being a pastor is that, in most cases, after seven days there will be another Sunday with another sermon. Perhaps a series of two or three sermons allows the development of a theme in smaller steps in order that the congregation does not feel exhausted or breathless in simply trying to keep up.

An alternate side benefit of this particular sermon was that I received a good number of requests to have a cup of tea with members of the congregation to talk about some things I had said. People frequently wanted to talk about feelings of guilt, or the importance of "being saved to go to heaven." The concept of seeing what we do as a response to God's grace, rather than a way to earn God's grace was most helpful.

These notions of grace highlight some important pastoral decisions that are worth considering before we move on to this particular sermon. Generally speaking, how might follow-up conversations to a given sermon happen? The answer, it seems to me, depends on whether a pastor preaches with an attitude that invites conversation or with words and style that dares listeners to raise questions or disagree. Should sermons be a one-way conversation where I speak and you listen?

It has been my experience that the education level of most congregations has increased dramatically. But information is one thing and expertise is another. For example, at College Mennonite Church, where the following sermon was preached, no matter what subject the pastor chooses for a sermon he or she knows that there are at least five or six persons in the congregation who are specialists in that area, and that these persons will know far more about it than he or she does. Is this intimidating for a pastor? Absolutely. But, in my experience, this knowledge helps a pastor express the best possible sermon, both in terms of content and delivery.

Although a pastor may not face a congregation of experts on a weekly basis, would it not be helpful to use a sermon about grace as a way to initiate an ongoing discussion in a congregation, rather than using it as a tool to pronounce edicts that must be accepted without question?

* * *

Good Enough for God's Grace[4]

What would you do? How would you feel? You have always been a religious person. You have tried hard to obey the Scriptures. Then one day you hear about a young rabbi from Nazareth who is telling people the following: "I know this is what you have been taught. I understand that this is how you read the Scriptures. But I am telling you, you have turned God's will inside out. You use it to meet your own needs, to justify your own actions, and to convince yourselves that you are the only ones who have the truth."

Could this really be true? God had given them the teachings and they honestly did believe they were right in what they were doing. But over the generations, their godly traditions had gradually changed just

---

4. The biblical foundation for this sermon is 1 Corinthians 3:10–17.

ever so slightly. Their sacrifices, for example, originally intended to celebrate God's presence and grace, had become symbols of their own status before God and the exclusion of others from God.

Listen to the prophet Micah: "My people, what have I done to you? I brought you out of the land of Egypt and redeemed you from the house of bondage." But the people ask, "With what shall we come before the lord, and bow ourselves before God on high? Shall we come with burnt offerings, or with calves a year old? Will the Lord be pleased with thousands of rams, with tens of thousands of rivers of oil? Shall I give my first born for my sins?"

The prophet answers them: "He has shown you, O people, what is good and what the Lord requires of you—to do justice, to love mercy, and to walk humbly with your God."[5]

About forty years after Jesus, Paul writes to the church at Corinth: "According to the grace of God I laid a foundation and expect others to build on it. Jesus Christ is our foundation and you dare not lay any other foundation."[6]

Why did Paul need to warn that congregation about laying another foundation? We know from his letters that the church at Corinth was facing a rather long list of problems. They were rallying around personalities, so that following Jesus had actually become a divisive element within the church. People in this congregation were basically saying:

"We intellectual Apollos Christians have the right theology . . ."

"We experiential Peter people really feel the grace of God . . ."

"We social activist Paul types are the ones who are really doing God's will . . ."

Paul had the courage to tell them, "Folks, your house just doesn't fit the foundation." But the congregation did not like that. They reacted so strongly that Paul had to make a special trip back to Corinth to patch up the relationship. Then, like now, most people don't take very kindly to having their faith challenged.

About fifteen hundred years later, Menno Simons quoted this same verse: "For no other foundation can be laid than that which is laid, which is Christ Jesus."[7] If Jesus called the people at Nazareth back to the original will of God, and if Paul called the church at Corinth back to the

5. See Micah 6:8.

6. See 1 Corinthians 3:10.

7. Wenger, *Complete Writings of Menno Simons*. This verse was the motto for Menno Simons' life and occurs frequently in his writings.

original will of God, what was Menno Simons trying to say? Menno saw Christians in his day using the name of God to justify war, and Menno said that was just not the Jesus way. He saw the more radical Anabaptists at Munster setting up a harsh theocratic political system where God ran the city government, and again Menno said that was not the foundation that Jesus laid.

The foundation laid by Jesus is God's grace, God's peace, and God's gift of salvation. When we build on that foundation, we bring healing and hope, and we invite others to be people of peace, to be forgiving, to show grace. We commit ourselves to be people of God—holy, righteous, and merciful toward others.

But what is happening with the foundations in our own day? Christians tend to distort their faith in a way that often justifies themselves and condemns others. We don't really intend to be mean about it, it just happens. In his ministry, Jesus told sinners that God loves them, and he told the religious leaders that they should get their act together and live holy lives. The religious leaders did not like that.

Today, we still don't like it, so we have turned it around. We tell ourselves how much God loves us and then we tell others (the sinners) that they need to straighten up and repent so that God can love them like God loves us.

Several years ago I audited a class at a graduate seminary in Southern California. The professor asked the class to define the term *grace*. One student responded, "Grace is what God gives us when we obey him." I felt a shiver go through me, because that is very scary. And it's also bad theology. You see, we aren't here because we are the good people of God. We are here because we know from experience that we are hurting, that we are struggling, and that we need help. We believe as we gather to worship, to pray, and to share, that we can find healing. We believe that together we can make sense of life when it really doesn't make much sense.

This is particularly difficult right now, because we are surrounded by good people who are telling us that we should find meaning in a very different way. Their approach is to force their beliefs and their will upon other people, often by military might. We have drifted back into a mentality that says, "We are God's people and that makes us right." And since we are right, that gives us the authority to demand that other people think like we think, and do what we want them to do.

But discovering resurrection for ourselves calls us to become intentional people of healing and reconciliation for others. Because eternal life has burst in upon us in the person of Jesus Christ, we no longer have to live under the power of death and destruction, even when it is present all around us. Jesus moved eternal life from being a promise that we anticipate getting some day, off in the future, to it being a present reality where we have the Spirit of Jesus all around us *right now.*

But unfortunately, people usually think of the resurrection as something that happened to Jesus two thousand years ago. That was a marvelous event, and it is one of the central elements of our faith. But we usually don't think about discovering resurrection in our own lives. John reports that Jesus said, "This is the will of my father, that all who believe in the son will have eternal life." [8] Not "will get it," but "will have it. When we recognize this, then we can begin to see that the things Jesus said about peace and being peacemakers start to make more sense. Christians are called to be people who have discovered that the resurrection of Jesus leads them to a whole new way of thinking about this world.

Certainly we pray for peace. We pray for the leaders of our nation. But the gospel calls for a more comprehensive image of peace. What troubles me is that so many of us only know how to make peace when we are not at war. When our nation is at war, we aren't sure what to do because being a peacemaker is seen as a reaction to national policy. Many Christians talk about salvation as gospel and then add peacemaking as a special footnote that only a few of us have discovered. It is seen as something for those who have mastered the basic stuff and are now ready to move toward a more elite expression of faith. Thus peacemaking has become an external, optional thing that you can choose if you want to be a super-special Christian, but is not necessary for your salvation.

What does this mean for us? Sometimes we need help thinking about how to love people who aren't our enemies, but who are just annoying neighbors. I learned back in high school geometry that two things which are equal to a third thing are equal to each other. That seems to be good theology as well. Two persons who claim to be reconciled with God should find themselves being reconciled to each other. When we say the gospel is only about reconciliation with God, we lose a major portion of what Jesus told us God is all about.

About a year ago, I had had a really tough week. A number of things had not gone very well. I felt that I had been mistreated. I was angry, and frankly, I wanted to get even with a few people. I think most of you know

8. See John 6:40.

that feeling. I woke up on Sunday morning and seriously debated staying home. I knew that people would be cheery and ask me how I was doing. I knew I would not be comfortable telling them. But I went, because that is what I do on Sunday morning. I go to church. Carolyn and I went in, sat down, and I looked at the worship folder. The opening meditation was from Psalm 24:3–4: "Who shall ascend the hill of the Lord and who shall stand in His holy place? He who has clean hands and a pure heart, who does not lift up his soul to what is false, nor swear deceitfully." I leaned over to Carolyn and whispered, "I don't feel like I belong here this morning." She read the meditation and whispered back, "I think you need to be here this morning."

I think now I understand better when people tell me that sometimes they don't feel good enough to come to church. How do I explain that God loves us and cares deeply about us, and that we care about each other? How do I explain to others that you don't have to be perfect because none of us are either, even though we try awfully hard to act like it sometimes?

You see, when the gospel becomes something that we have, and if you become good like we are, then you can have it too, we've got our shovels out. We are digging a new foundation that just does not match the one laid for us in Christ Jesus our Lord.

I pray this morning that we will resist the temptation to lay new foundations that protect us while excluding others. I pray that we might remember that we are all persons saved by grace so that we might offer a faithful, Christlike response to persons, for example, who are in the military, who while worshipping with us have experienced that grace of God in a new way, and who are trying to sort out what that means for their lives. I pray that we might fight the temptation to lay ethical requirements that other people have to meet before they are good enough to worship God with us. Can we discover again that all of us are growing, that all of us have areas where we need forgiveness and grace, and all of us need help from each other in learning how to do better in experiencing, and then expressing, that grace.

Jesus had a conversation with the Pharisees in which he made a very simple, yet important statement: "Everyone whom my Father gives me will come to me. I will never turn anyone away who comes to me. For this is the will of my Father, that everyone who believes in the Son will have eternal life, and I will raise him up at the last day." [9] The Pharisees did not like that, because Jesus included people whom they felt were not worthy. I wonder at times whether we might be guilty of putting stumbling blocks in the way of people whom the Father is calling, and who are trying to discover how to respond to that gracious God who says, "I will never turn anyone away who comes to me?"

There is a song that I learned as a boy in Sunday school. I think some of you will remember it too. "Oh, be careful little hands what you do. Oh, be careful little hands what you do. For the Father up above is looking down in love. Oh, be careful little hands what you do." There are other verses for little feet, little eyes, and little mouth. It pretty well covers the whole body. It has a nice melody; but as an adult, I look back and see quite a mixed message. God up in heaven is looking down in love—you'd better be careful what you do!

My mother was a good mom, and we always felt loved as kids. But when I misbehaved, one of her favorite lines was, "You'd better not be doing that when Jesus comes." Or, "You'd better not let God catch you doing that." Very early in life I learned that there are eternal implications for little human things I did as a child.

Philip Yancey in his book *What's So Amazing About Grace* writes: "Grace means there is nothing I can do to make God love me more. The message of the crucifixion is that there is nothing I can do to make God love me less." [10] That is where we must start when we talk about following Jesus. In the New Testament, Jesus frequently offered healing and forgiveness to persons who had done nothing to deserve it. That caused all kinds of grief for the Pharisees because they thought these people had done things that proved they did not deserve God's grace. It made them even more angry when Jesus scolded them for thinking that way.

We are tempted to tell people: "We believe in forgiveness. We'll give you a chance to prove yourself. Once you show us that you have stopped sinning, we will be glad to forgive you and accept you." When we do this, following Jesus becomes something you have to do in order to be forgiven. But the Jesus model is that we forgive others because through God's grace, we ourselves have already been forgiven.

This approach to following Jesus calls us to be more willing to nurture others who are still learning. It also means that as we use this same

9. See John 6:37, 40.

10. Yancey, *What's So Amazing About Grace*, p. 70.

process we will learn from them. It calls us to share our time, our faith, and our resources with those who are in need without demanding specific behavioral changes before we dare to trust them. It calls us once again to be a community of God's caring redemption. This community includes not only those of us who gather here, but also our neighbors who are not here in worship but who are lonely, are hurting, and are afraid.

I have this dream that the day will come when others experience us not as people who think we have all the answers but as a community that listens to their questions. I pray that our neighbors would see us as people who are compassionate and self-giving, not simply people who work hard and who are very successful at it. I wish the world would see us as people who joyfully and willingly offer help without the unspoken look that says, "You know you really should not let yourself get into this kind of mess."

We should learn to focus on the love that God has shown for us, rather than on our ability to do good things. If we do that, then others will see the good that we do and praise God for it, rather than live in fear of our judgment of them because they don't do it. I pray that we might find the grace and the courage that we don't turn them away. I pray that we will reach out and invite them into the mercy and grace and love of God whom we serve and worship and love, so that these persons might grow and learn that not only does God love them but God's people also care about them.

I pray that we might return to the foundation that is laid in Jesus, who showed hurting, frightened people that there is hope, there is peace, there is safety, and there is salvation with the people of God in this place. There is no other foundation, only the one already laid in Jesus Christ, and for that I give thanks. Let's not yield to the temptation to lay new foundations that divide and judge and exclude those for whom Christ died. I pray that we can trust the Holy Spirit to give us wisdom, to give us strength, and to give us courage that we might build on Jesus Christ, the author and finisher of our faith. When we do this, we are not tempted to improve on what Jesus has already done. I pray that we can feel secure and comfortable enough within ourselves that we can be welcoming and accepting of people who feel, "I'd like to come to church, but I'm just not good enough."

I pray this morning that the grace of God will be felt by us, and then through us to those who share life with us. Listen to this paraphrase from the words of Paul and John: "I have been crucified with Christ, and

I no longer live for myself, but for Christ who lives in me. The life I live right now, I live by faith in Jesus who loves me and gave himself for me. I cannot ignore the grace of God, for if I could be saved by what I do, then Christ died for nothing. But the love of God urges me on, and when one is in Christ, they have a whole new way of looking at the world. My dear friends, if God loves us that much, surely we can love one another." [11]

11. See Galatians 2:20–21, 1 John 4:11.

Slave of Duty, Servant of Love

Every year, the Goshen College faculty opens the school year with a faculty retreat. The goal is to build faculty cohesion, review college goals, and signal the start of the new academic year. One year, the faculty presented *The Pirates of Penzance* for the incoming students and the wider college community. Several of us who had lead roles used the month of August to learn lines and music. A weekend was devoted to staging and final rehearsals. Then the students arrived, and along with members of the community, were treated to three performances.

On Sunday morning the faculty met for worship. I was asked to prepare the sermon for this particular service. It seemed appropriate to connect this worship service with the Gilbert and Sullivan operetta. This sermon draws from the life experience of Onesimus, the runaway slave described in the book of Philemon, and places those experiences alongside Frederick, the hero of *The Pirates of Penzance*. The sermon follows.

* * *

Slave of Duty, Servant of Love[12]

For many of us, this weekend has been given to learning how to tell a story. Storytelling is important. But have you noticed how frequently people use very simple concepts to tell very complicated stories? Nowhere is this truer than in Christian faith. Stories of how God works in one's life often have something of an unreal quality that makes you wonder if life can really be that nice.

I saw this phenomenon the other evening in a *Pirates* rehearsal. What would *The Pirates of Penzance* sound like as a personal testimony in the hands of the popular religious media? How would they tell the story of Frederick? I discovered that after you strip away all the Gilbert and Sullivan mythology, there is in *The Pirates of Penzance* a very simple religious story. With apologies to all concerned, here is that story.

Frederick, for many years, lived a life of sin as a pirate. Then he began to come under conviction about the direction of his life. On his twenty-first birthday, he was dramatically converted and vowed henceforth to leave the ways of sin for a new life. Soon after his conversion he met Mabel, a beautiful young girl from a fine, respectable family who

12. The biblical foundation for this sermon is Philemon 4–25.

encouraged him even more along the paths of righteousness and truth. Even though his former partners in sin tried very hard to entice him back to his old sinful ways, Frederick stood firm in his resolve to always do his duty. In the end, he is instrumental in the conversion of these old pirate friends to a new life of born-again responsible living. Even the leader, who had sworn to "live and die a pirate king," came to see the error of his ways. Frederick and Mabel lived happily ever after, praising God for his miraculous grace and mercy.

But as most of you already know, and the rest of you will soon find out, that doesn't quite tell the whole story. In fact, it basically ruins it. But far too often religious stories, particularly biblical ones, get told this way. The impression is given that, with God, all things are possible because everything just falls neatly into place.

Let me tell you another story. Once upon a time there was a slave who ran away from his master. Sometime later, in a far away country, he heard an itinerant preacher, talking about God; and he was converted. The preacher sent the slave back to his master who immediately forgave his new Christian brother. Thus God is to be praised for his miraculous grace and mercy.

Now, if you were to ask this slave, named Onesimus, if that was really how it happened, he would probably give a qualified, "Well, yes, but . . . you didn't say anything about how it felt having to go back to my master Philemon, not knowing if you would be forgiven . . . or killed. You didn't saying anything about the heated arguments that I had with Paul, the itinerant preacher over why he thought I had to go back to Philemon at all. Let me tell you what it was really like.

"I was in charge of purchasing and paying bills for Philemon. A group of us slaves had created a system. When we bought something, we simply overpaid, got a kickback, and then kept the difference. It worked very well until one member of the group was careless and got caught. Philemon became suspicious and told me he wanted an immediate audit of the books. I knew our system would be exposed; I would get caught and probably be killed. So I ran away. I ended up in Rome. That seemed like a good place to lose yourself. It was in Rome, quite by accident, that I met Paul. I heard him talking about justice, about forgiveness, and a God who loves. He was very persuasive. I went back a couple of times, talked with Paul about what he was saying, and I became a believer. I stayed with Paul because he needed help. He didn't ask about my past and I didn't see any reason to tell him. Those were the best days of my life. I had discovered new purpose. I was making new friends. It was good to be alive.

"One day, Paul got a letter. It made him very excited. 'Onesimus,' he told me, 'We are getting company. Epaphras, from Laodicea is coming. I know you don't him, but he is a good friend of mine. You will love him.'

"That letter signaled the end for me. The coming of Epaphras made everything different. You see, I did know Epaphras. And worse yet, Epaphras knew me. He was a close friend and business associate of Philemon. You see, it was one of Epaphras's slaves who got caught in our old group back at Laodicea.

"I didn't know what to do, so I decided to run away again. Paul heard me leaving and demanded to know what was going on, so I had to tell him. Have you ever told the best friend you ever had that you are a liar and a cheat, a thief, and a runaway slave? Then Paul quietly reminded me that what I had done made him guilty of harboring a runaway slave, and thus had put a death penalty on his head, too. I wanted to die right there.

"Paul and I spent the rest of the night arguing about what we should do. He argued that the only chance either of us had was to write a letter to Philemon and ask Epaphras to serve as our personal ambassador. I argued that if I just left, Epaphras would never have to know anything about me and everything would be okay for Paul. But as I said, Paul was very persuasive. He could be ferocious in an argument.

"Epaphras came two days later, and was he ever furious when he saw me. We had to physically restrain him to keep him from calling the Roman guards on the spot. It took Paul a week to convince him to talk to Philemon for us. That was the worst week of my life. I couldn't eat, I couldn't sleep. All I could think about was running away.

"Paul worked for days on that letter to Philemon. Finally, Epaphras and I set out for Laodicea. I still didn't want to go. Do you enjoy being forced to face up to mistakes that you have made? Do you look forward to going home when you know that your own death is a very distinct possibility? Paul kept insisting that it would be alright, that I should trust God—but believe me, sometimes trusting God can be awfully hard to do."

At this point we lose the story of Onesimus. We don't know what Philemon did, but the evidence is pretty strong that Onesimus was forgiven and received by Philemon as a brother in Christ. But there is more. About forty years later, Ignatius (a bishop at Antioch) is on trial in Rome. We know now that he was executed in Rome. Ignatius wrote a letter to the believers at Ephesus. In this letter he refers to the bishop at Ephesus, a man named Onesimus. In his letter Ignatius makes the identical play on words that Paul had used forty years earlier about Onesimus being useless, yet being very useful. Many scholars believe that Onesimus the runaway slave and Onesimus the bishop of Ephesus are one and the same person.

If that is true, and I believe the evidence is very persuasive, that helps answer another question. How did this intensely personal letter between Paul and Philemon get included among the books of the Bible? Undoubtedly Paul wrote lots of personal letters that are not in the New Testament. We know about a few of them. What is special about this one?

We also know that it was during the time when Onesimus was the bishop of Ephesus that the letters of Paul were brought together into a single collection. It may well be that Onesimus had kept this particular letter, and that he added it to the Pauline collection. Thus Philemon is not a timid statement about slavery and Christian justice, but a powerful, bold personal witness to the power of God's saving grace in the life of one of the most important bishops in the church.

In this letter, Onesimus, the bishop of Ephesus, tells the world that once he had been a thief and a runaway slave. He tells the world that he owed his life to the gospel of Jesus Christ and the forgiveness of a Christian brother named Philemon. It is a statement of personal testimony by one person that God, working through other people, can make a profound difference in your life.

With this understanding of Onesimus and the purpose of that letter to Philemon, I'd like to make several brief observations for our own setting at the beginning of a new school year.

1. The story of Onesimus is a challenge to each of us to be open with each other about how we have experienced the grace of God. I have observed that we have a wide variety of religious experiences among both the student body and the faculty. What bothers me is that most frequently among the students, only one type of religious experience is being shared. Would not growth be encouraged as students learn from us a variety of experiences? Might they discover that their experience is not the only valid one, and that they do not have to be threatened by those who experience faith differently. As they see us living comfortably with a multiplicity of religious experiences, they will learn to be comfortable with diversity in their own faith. Thus

the door is opened for new insight and another step is taken toward a more mature faith.

2. I also see an interesting contrast in how Paul and Philemon look at Onesimus. Paul sees hope, promise, and new life—the future. Philemon probably saw a thief and a runaway slave—the past. Yet in fact, it was the very same person. Perhaps just as Paul asked Philemon to think differently about Onesimus, he would ask us to reflect on how we see other people. For example, do we see students as immature adults whom we tolerate until they learn enough from us to grow up or graduate, whichever comes first? I suggest that this is an example of Philemon's point of view. Paul is urging us to see something else—the creative potential for growth and new life in every person. He wants us to seize the opportunity to walk with them, believing that as we share our lives with them, their lives will become more open and more mature.

3. A third thing I only want to mention. In the experience of Onesimus we get a very personal glimpse of the awesome potential of forgiveness. Forgiveness is one of the delightfully freeing gifts that God has entrusted to us. It can be given—or withheld. The next time you are called upon to forgive someone and something inside you rebels, think about Onesimus the slave and Onesimus the bishop. Remember that it was the forgiveness of Philemon that helped make that transition possible, enabling a slave to become a bishop. That is the transformation power of forgiveness.

Philemon is a personal letter, but there is much here to speak to our own hearts as Paul writes:

"I always thank my God as I remember you in my prayers, for I have heard about your faith in the Lord Jesus and your love for all the saints. I pray that you may be active in sharing your faith, so that you will have a full understanding of every good thing we have in Christ. Your love has given me great joy and encouragement, because you have refreshed the hearts of the saints.

"I suppose that I could use my authority in Christ and demand that you do what is right, but I'm not going to do that. No, I am simply appealing to your love. I make my appeal on behalf of Onesimus. Now I know that you have found him to be pretty useless in the past, but he is going to be useful now, to both of us. I am sending him back to you. Will you receive him as my son, as part of me? I would dearly have loved to have kept him here with me, for he could have done what you would have done—helped me while I am here in prison. But I would not want to do anything without asking you first, for if you have a favor to give, let it be spontaneous and not forced upon you by the circumstances.

"It occurs to me that there has been a purpose in your losing him. You lost a slave, but you are gaining a Christian brother. Then do welcome him just as you would welcome me. If you feel that he has wronged or cheated you, put it down to my account. I'll see that it gets paid. Do grant me this request. Such an act of love will make my heart rejoice. I send you this letter knowing that you will do what I ask, believing in fact that you will do even more.

"May the grace of our Lord Jesus Christ be with your spirit always. Amen." [13]

---

13. This is a careful paraphrase of the Philemon letter.

How Does One Feel Forgiven?

She was an active mother and a regular participant in church life. Thus, I was quite surprised as she told me about her fears about not being good enough to deserve God's love. She had grown up in a rather traditional religious family with a lot of good behavior expectations put upon her by her parents. She had been a student of mine several years before, and she now wanted me to know that my class in Jesus and the Gospels created stress for her. We had talked about the love of God and the process of forgiveness. She heard me say that God is a loving and forgiving God, and that we should reflect that same love and forgiveness for others. But last year, her husband of four years and father of their one-year-old daughter left her for another woman. She could not stop thinking hateful thoughts about him, even to the point of wishing he were dead, much less consider forgiveness. He continued to dominate her life even in his absence. How do you make the shift from theological concept to pragmatic faith experience?

He was a student who had done some things for which he was quite ashamed. He was not yet willing to talk about what these things were, but he did say he had apologized and was trying to make things right. His problem? He could not forgive himself because what he had done was so out of character for how he perceived himself to be. How could he have done it? Other students treated him as though he was a very good person. But what if they ever found out what he had done! He could not forgive himself, so why should he believe that God would forgive him?

As a pastor and professor, I heard other stories like these almost every year. From young and old alike, persons wanted joy and freedom in their lives, only to be tormented by fears about not being good enough to be loved and being too bad to be forgiven, all at the same time. So I prepared this sermon on forgiveness. In the week following, several persons came to my office and wanted to talk. They began the conversation by saying, "How did you find out about me? Did somebody tell you about what I did?" Maybe the need for forgiveness and healing is a universal human trait!

* * *

How Does One Feel Forgiven?[14]

Have you ever tried to convince a child of something when they already know exactly what the truth is? When our children were small, I remember there were times when they were afraid in the dark. I would try to convince them that there really are no ghosts in the closet or monsters behind the door or under the bed. Do you remember how that felt when you were a small child? If you have been a parent of small children, you will no doubt remember that all of your good, careful logic never seemed to work. As a parent, you simply took the time to sit on the bed and hold the child until they stopped shivering and fell asleep in your arms. Do you remember how comfortable it felt to be held when you were a child; and how good it still feels to be held when you are afraid, or when you feel lonely, or if you have had a bad day?

Let's think together this morning about forgiveness and the simple joy of being held when life is hard. The concept of forgiveness is a profound theological belief that is awfully important in Christian faith. But, unfortunately, a lot of us who have very good theology about forgiveness still have a hard time actually feeling that we have been forgiven.

We see this in a slightly different way in the story from Luke this morning. Here are four friends who go to considerable effort to bring their friend to Jesus. When Jesus forgave the man, the Pharisees and the teachers were quite upset, saying, "You aren't allowed to do that—only God can forgive sins." This is good, standard Jewish theology. All forgiveness comes from God. Jesus senses their tension and recognizes that anybody can say the words, "Your sins are forgiven." That is really easy to do. We can say lots of things. So he turns to the man and says, "Why don't you get up and walk?"

Do you catch what Jesus has just done? The Pharisees believed that only God can forgive. But the Pharisees also believed that only God can heal! But do you sense the difference between forgiveness and healing? How do I know that you are forgiven? I have to trust you when you say that, because there is no external evidence unless your life is changed. But if you are a paralytic and are healed, and you get up and walk, the evidence is instantly obvious.

Now the Pharisees have a major problem. They don't like it that Jesus claimed the power to forgive. When he goes one step further and heals the man, they really get irate. In the mind of the Pharisees, Jesus is not

14. The biblical foundation for this sermon is Luke 5:17–26.

allowed to heal or forgive, because that is usurping power that belongs only to God. But how do you argue that point when the man is standing right there in front of you holding his sleeping bag?

How do we capture that assurance and public expression of forgiveness in our lives? The ministry of Jesus is filled with stories of people who were forgiven. But back then, just like today, we still have people standing around who aren't exactly thrilled when other people are forgiven.

Do you remember Zacchaeus, the tax collector in Luke 19? Jesus ate dinner with him (that made the Pharisees angry to start with), then Jesus forgave him (they didn't like that, either). Then when Zacchaeus started knocking on doors, telling people, "I've come to apologize, and give you back some money from a couple of years ago," the Pharisees just didn't know what to do.

I remember hearing that story when I was a young boy. You know what got the most attention? It wasn't the fact that Zacchaeus had been forgiven. Instead, the focus was: if you are going to be forgiven, you have to go around making things right. And so I went home and made a list of all the bad things that I had done, so that if I ever had to ask God to forgive me, I would know what I had to do. But then I had a bigger problem: where could I hide the list so that mom would never find out about all those bad things that I had done. We are caught in a legalistic religious world that says, "Sure we'll forgive you. But we want to make sure that from now on you will only do the right things. And by the way, if you aren't sure what the right thing is, we have ways of telling you."

Here is another story from Jesus, this time the prodigal son (Luke 15). The wayward son who ran away with part of the family inheritance comes back home and his dad throws a huge party because he is so glad to see him again. But the older brother comes in from the field and is quite angry, insisting this whole thing is so unfair. "I've worked for you, I never said *no*. I have always been here for you, I didn't waste your money, and what thanks do I get?"

And, you know, he's right. Forgiveness is not fair. It is an expression of grace, and God's grace is based on generosity, not legal bookkeeping.

Most of us gained acceptance as children by being good. So we have some natural carryover that says acceptance with God also depends on good behavior. But forgiveness forces us to look at those areas where we have not been good. As a child, for me these things brought a fear of punishment. So now, coming to God asking for forgiveness creates the same emotional overlap. How can I know that I am accepted by God when I confess my sins, when all through my life I received acceptance when I was good, not when I was bad. Being bad led to punishment. I was grounded, I lost the freedom to play basketball with my brother, or worst of all, I had to clean my room. Now with Mom, I could say certain things and convince her that I was really sorry, and I would get a slight reduction of the sentence. But in church, I am told that there is nothing I can do to earn God's favor. So I am really in trouble.

Here is where the rest of us come in. If we are going to experience forgiveness, we need persons who will model God's approach to forgiveness for us. When God's people show us the acceptance that God promises, then we will do better able at sensing within ourselves that God really has forgiven us. Did you ever think about that? You may be the agent of God helping another person experience what it means to be forgiven.

A second concern about forgiveness comes out of a long history of American preaching, wherein I have my own personal story of forgiveness. This history often used language intended to create feelings of guilt, so that I would know that I had to ask God to forgive me. Then when I did ask for forgiveness, these preachers proceeded to tell me how I should feel now that I was forgiven. But the problem was that I did not always feel the way preachers told me I should feel. That led me to question whether I really was forgiven, because I didn't feel right. And this started a vicious cycle within me. I knew I didn't have the feelings I was supposed to have, so in public I tried to act like I thought people who had those feelings would act. Then I would hear a sermon on hypocrisy, and I was really dead in the water.

First John 3 helps me with my feelings: "If our own heart makes us feel guilty, God is infinitely greater than our hearts and God knows everything."[15] Now, what does that mean? Let me rephrase that in a different way: "If we have certain feelings, those feelings do not make us bad, for God is not limited by how we feel. In fact, God is fully able to understand the turmoil that is going on inside us." My salvation, my relationship with God, and my own forgiveness are not controlled by the fickleness of my day to day feelings, and for that I am very thankful.

You see, there is hope. If God knows everything, then God certainly knows how I feel. If that is true, God will also know that sometimes my feelings get all confused by things other than theological or biblical truth. What we have done is to take a verse that is intended to bring comfort,

15. See 1 John 3:20–21.

"God understands how you feel and why you feel that way, so relax," and have turned it into a club that creates even more fear: "Be careful, for God knows everything, even how you feel." This has an unspoken implication: "God will take those feelings that you have and will punish you for having them." That is so unlike the God who Jesus says loves us.

Now, what do we do with this? Sometimes people find themselves in a situation where they think, "I don't feel forgiven because if I really were forgiven I would feel a certain way. I don't feel that way, so I must still be condemned for my sin, and that means I must be even worse than I thought I was." And that cycle rather quickly leads to despair and depression. Any of you who have been there know it is much harder to climb out of depression than it is to slide into it. But that cycle is not a biblical cycle. However, my telling you that won't keep you from using it on yourself.

That brings us back to where we started this morning. What do we do when we just don't feel the way other people tell us we should feel because we have been forgiven? I'd like to suggest a few things and then ask for your response.

First, forgiveness of sin and confession of sin belong very closely together. Confession of sin does not mean beating up on yourself because you are so evil. Confession of sin means accepting responsibility for one's behavior, rather than denying it or trying to blame someone else for it. When we do that, we open up that part of our lives for growth and change so that dealing with the problem becomes a possibility. But confession of sin carries tremendous emotional tension for many of us because of past experiences, most of which were negative. We tend to handle sin in the context of the legal court system. If I confess my sins (plead guilty), someone in authority (the judge) will tell me what the punishment will be, and I will have to suffer accordingly.

Now that may be the American judicial system, but it is not the biblical Jesus model.

"Brothers and sisters, when someone among you commits a sin, you who are spiritual should gently restore him." (Gal 6:1). Confession of sin calls for support, counsel, and help. Punishment is easy. Support and love is much harder.

But you see, when we take the Jesus route, I can accept who I am and what I have done, even when it is painful. When others walk with me in my search for healing, together we all find new life and hope, and the whole community is blessed.

Second, the Lord's Prayer has a phrase that helps us in this area. Jesus prayed that God would "forgive us our sins as we forgive those who sin against us" (Luke 11:4). It is possible to forgive and still not be a forgiving person. In Luke 7:47, Jesus tells Simon the Pharisee, "a person who has been forgiven only a little shows only a little love for others." I may not like what you have done to me. But when I have an honest awareness of the things I have done, I will be much slower to condemn you because I also know I have benefitted from God's forgiveness. But if I depend heavily upon my good behavior as my method to achieve my status with God, I will easily assume that you will get your relationship with God in the same way. That means I will approach you with a spirit of expectation. You should be good like I am good, and if you do that, God will love you like God loves me.

But instead, we are challenged to approach others with a willing spirit of forgiveness. We are to be ready to accept them even before they have a long list of good deeds to show they deserve my forgiveness. Here I need to remember Romans 5:8, which says: "While we were still sinners, Christ died for us." That's gospel.

Unfortunately, I have to fight the inner urge that says, "Okay, I'm willing to forgive. But first I want you to hurt as badly as you hurt me." But then I hear this quiet voice of God inside me: "Okay, Don, but do you remember what happened to me one day on a cross outside Jerusalem? What if I made that same deal with you?" Then I have to say . . . "Oops, wait a minute. Let me rethink that."

Third is a challenge to each of us: If we are right in what we are saying from the Scriptures, that each of us plays an important role in helping others feel the reality of their forgiveness, then perhaps we need to ask God to help us become more forgiving persons in a more forgiving community. There is a verse in 1 John 4 that says: "How can you love God whom you have not seen if you don't love your brother or sister whom you see every day?"[16] May I rephrase that? "How can a person feel forgiven by God whom they cannot see, when they do not feel forgiven by God's people whom they see every day?"

Are we prepared to become God's agents of forgiveness? When we claim the forgiveness God has shown to us, will we also extend that same forgiveness to others? If we do, it is just possible that we might all become new persons in Christ, with new hope, new life, and a new experience of healing and wholeness among us . . . Right here . . . Right now.

16. See 1 John 4:20

4

Same Book, Different Message

The law of the Lord is perfect, reviving the soul.
The testimony of the Lord is sure, making wise the simple.
The precepts of the Lord are right, rejoicing the heart.
The commandments of the Lord are pure, enlightening the eyes.
The fear of the Lord is clean, enduring forever.
The ordinances of the Lord are true, and righteous altogether
More to be desired are they than gold, even much fine gold.
—David
Psalm 19:7–10

The word became flesh and lived among us,
and we have seen his glory.
From his fullness we have all received grace upon grace.
The law indeed was given through Moses,
Grace and truth came through Jesus Christ.
—John
John 1:14, 16–17

I do not know if everything happened exactly this way,
but I do know this story is true.
—American Indian chief

We should read the Bible as an inspired library that preserves,
presents, and inspires an ongoing vigorous conversation with and about God,
a living and vital civil argument in which we are all invited,
and through which God is revealed.[1]
—Brian McLaren

---

1. McLaren, *A New Kind of Christianity*, p. 83.

Same Book, Different Message

I was only eight years old. It was 1945 and World War II had just ended. My oldest brother, Howard, came home after several years of Civilian Public Service work with the government, and he immediately volunteered for service with Mennonite Central Committee (MCC—the relief and service agency of the Mennonite Church). MCC assigned him to work with UNRRA (United Nations Relief and Rehabilitation Agency) in Italy where he helped staff and then operated an orphanage in southern Italy for children whose parents had been killed in the war. I had never been more than 150 miles from home, so I could not imagine what it would be like to go to Italy.

This turn of events was also hard for Mom, but for very different reasons. I knew it was far away, but because I did not know exactly how far, my main concern was that Howard might get lost. Mom knew that Italy had been a war zone, and she was afraid Howard might get killed. Howard tried to reassure Mom with his theological logic: "God took care of me for three years when I was in Iowa, I think I'll be in good hands in Italy." That made good sense to me. Iowa and Italy sounded like they were not very far apart.

We had a globe in the living room and on it Mom had marked where we lived and also where Howard was working. When we heard Walter Cronkite reporting from Europe on the evening news, I would try to find that town on the globe (usually with no success because small towns in Italy don't make it on a world globe).

When Howard came home several years later with exciting stories about Europe, the mountains of Switzerland, strange new languages, exotic foods, and different ways of doing things, I was spellbound. I wanted to go to this faraway place called Europe. But I knew it could only be a dream. No one in our family, other than Howard, had ever been that far away before, and I saw no reason to think that it would get any better in my lifetime.

Thirty years later, in July of 1975, Carolyn and I were in Eureka, Illinois, for the Mennonite General Assembly (with delegates from Mennonite churches all over the United States and Canada). Goshen College President J. Lawrence Burkholder was making the Board of Education report to the conference delegates. He shared the concern that there was no one "in the system" to replace the New Testament teachers in our church colleges who would soon be retiring. He presented this as a serious concern for the church. Where were we going to find New Testament teachers for our colleges? As I heard this, and even though I was sitting off in the side bleachers among perhaps a thousand delegates, I felt as though J. Lawrence was talking directly to me. It was a very personal, overwhelming feeling. I don't remember anything else that he said, only that the church needed New Testament teachers.

On that particular day, Carolyn and I were not sitting together. Immediately after the meeting was over, she came directly to me and the first thing she said was, "Did you hear what Lawrence Burkholder said? He was talking about you!" In our fifteen years of marriage, I had learned that Carolyn is a very perceptive listener, and when she said something, I should listen carefully. She had heard exactly what I had felt. It was an intensely powerful and confirming moment for me.

As Carolyn and I drove home to Akron, Pennsylvania, three days later, we talked about what this might mean. We had five young children. We had no extra money, and graduate school would be expensive. Things were going well in our church and neither of us had any interest in moving. We had built a new house, and we were finally building some financial equity and security for our future. Our children were doing well in school, and we asked ourselves if we really wanted to disrupt their lives. Ultimately, we agreed to "table the discussion" for a few months in order to let any spur-of-the-moment surges of inspiration settle down. But almost every time we sat down at the table to eat, we were aware of what was on the table that we weren't talking about.

As we had done several times before, we shared our questions with Paul and Doris Longacre. Doris was chair of the Akron congregation, thus I was accountable to her. But more important, we trusted her. Doris and Paul were good personal friends. Doris affirmed the teaching I was doing in the congregation, and suggested that we share this discussion openly with the congregation to hear their counsel.

In early February 1976, we shared this sense of call with the congregation. For three months the congregation talked together in family gatherings, in small groups, and in various committees. The question was simple: "Should Don go to graduate school in New Testament or should he continue here as pastor?" In the meantime, Carolyn and I began to talk about where we might go for my studies. My immediate thought was Princeton University because we had friends with biblical and theological degrees from Princeton. But there was a side of me that wanted to study outside the United States in order to have a wider world orientation for my faith. I thought about Basel, Switzerland, because I had read books by Marcus Barth of the faculty there. But that would have meant studying in German, and we wondered how it would be for Carolyn and the children to live in a culture where they did not know the language.

Robert Bowman, pastor of the Ephrata Church of the Brethren, was a good friend and colleague, and so I shared this concern with him. He said, "Your children might have an easier time adjusting to the German language than you would, so don't use them as an excuse for giving up on Basel. But," he went on, "I would recommend St Andrews in Scotland because everything would be in English, so both you and your children would have an easier time. I studied there for a year and it was a good experience. I would be glad to write a letter of recommendation."

That was helpful counsel. I wrote a brief letter to five pastors and teachers whom I respected in the field of biblical studies asking, "I am considering going to graduate school in New Testament. The University of St Andrews has been recommended, and I wonder what counsel you might have?" Each person responded positively, telling me that the British system of PhD work would be primarily a research degree, and if I had the self-discipline, it would be fine.

So Robert wrote his letter of reference, and I applied for graduate school at the University of St Andrews. As I sent the letter, I remembered my oldest brother, Howard, and how I had always dreamed of going to Europe. Now that I was actually thinking about doing it, I wondered whether this was truly God's leading or simply my own reckless desire for adventure!

In June 1976, I received official notice that I had been accepted to study with the graduate faculty of the University of St Andrews. That same week, Doris Longacre met with me and reported that the counsel of the congregation was that I should go to graduate school. Indeed, I had the congregation's blessing. The following Sunday I shared with the congregation that we would be leaving for St Andrews, Scotland, around the first of September. This gave us ten weeks to complete our ministry at Akron, say goodbye to the members of the congregation, sell our house, find suitable living arrangements in Scotland, and figure out where the money would come from.

This last item was a matter of significant concern. We literally had no money. One Akron businessman hired Carolyn as a secretary so that we could buy airline tickets for our family to fly to Glasgow. We held a garage sale so we would not have to put so many things in storage. That was an emotional day. We sold dishes that had been given to us as wedding gifts, chairs that had made our house a comfortable home, books and kitchen appliances that we had lived with for years. An especially poignant moment was seeing eight-year-old Sandra fight tears as she watched another little girl buy her bicycle and then ride off down the street.

One Sunday after church, Peter J. Dyck asked, "Don, have you picked a research subject, yet?" I hadn't given this any thought. Peter referred me to *Jesus and the Nonviolent Revolution* by André Trocmé. Trocmé had a deep commitment to peace, with a Jesus ethic that was based upon the Jewish Year of Jubilee. I remembered having read a chapter in *The Politics of Jesus* by Dr. John H. Yoder. In that work, Yoder had introduced this Jubilee theme to me. So I went back, reread the chapter in *The Politics of Jesus*, and I was hooked. I had found my research topic.

The day to leave Akron came far too quickly. We had breakfast at The Akron Restaurant with our small group from church. We did a final walk-through of our as-yet-unsold house, locked the doors, and climbed into Les and Lydia Weber's Chevy Suburban for the trip to New York and our flight to Glasgow. I felt like I was sleepwalking. Did it really make sense to walk away from the security of a very good job, the luxury of a delightfully comfortable home, and some of the best friends we had ever had? I slid down in the back seat of the Suburban, shut my eyes tight and swallowed hard, fighting back tears. We were leaving everything I had ever wanted to do in order to plunge into a whole new world. Is this what it feels like to follow your dream? What if . . .? I was afraid to finish the sentence.

We arrived in Scotland with a commitment to stay for at least one year of a three year program. Our children had to be enrolled and then fit into the appropriate classes within the Scottish school system. Scotland schools operate on a two year class cycle and we arrived at the start of the second year. Carolyn and I watched the difficult adjustment process our children faced—all because I had decided to uproot the family so I could study in a foreign culture. I had severe doubts about the wisdom of my decision when I saw what was happening to our children. Lois (always at the top of her class) had to drop back a year in order to start with first-year French and first-year science. Miriam's first grade teacher, a man in a black robe with a yardstick, was dramatically different from her grand-motherly kindergarten teacher in Akron. It was traumatic for all of us.

Church was another adventure. On our first Sunday, we chose a church within walking distance of our home. The pastor used a box of

Gordon's Allsorts, a popular Scottish candy with a licorice center, as an object lesson for the children's story. The lesson was that children are of all colors on the outside, but inside we are all black, and Jesus wants to make us white! I could not believe what I was hearing! As we were walking home, my son John asked, "Dad, do we have to go back there next Sunday? I don't believe what that pastor told us in the children's story." I was really proud of John.

That first month we got to know a few people in town, and we were invited to visit the local Church of Scotland. (I share our first Sunday experience in that church in the first chapter of this book.) A few weeks later the local pastor was hospitalized, and the church board asked Deane Kemper (an American Presbyterian pastor on sabbatical) and me if we would lead worship and do the preaching until the pastor was able to return. This invitation gave us almost unlimited acceptance in the community. Church attendance increased dramatically as the townsfolk of Anstruther came out to hear the new pastors with their Yankee accents. Shopkeepers wanted to visit, people stopped us on the street to talk, and we soon became known as "Starsky and Hutch" of TV fame!

Eight months into that first year, we knew we were going to stay. We loved Scotland. Our children had made lots of friends, and I had joined the Crail Golfing Club. I was learning to know the local community, my studies were truly exciting, and in a totally unexpected way our finances had fallen into place. Our house in Akron had been sold. We also discovered that we were eligible for government child support and rent rebate because I had very minimal income. Carolyn set up a sewing business, working halftime out of our home. She replaced zippers, adjusted hems and waistbands, and even made dresses for a complete wedding party. Women would bring something to be fixed, then stay and visit for the hour or so that it took to make the minor repairs. Carolyn became well loved by the local women because of her listening skills. We joined the community Operatic Society and the Philharmonic Chorus. I auditioned for and was accepted into the Pittenweem Madrigal Society, a twelve-member choral group of substantial local reputation. We moved into a larger house across town and settled in for the full three years. Life was good!

Two years and nine months after arriving in St Andrews, I delivered what I hoped would be a final copy of my doctoral dissertation to the St Andrews University faculty. This work, titled "Jesus and the Jubilee: Luke 4:16–30, the Year of Jubilee in the Gospel of Luke" was accepted by the faculty and sent to an external examiner who, six weeks later, approved it with only minor editorial corrections. I had heard horror stories about the ultimate, unquestionable God-like power of the external examiner. Having my dissertation accepted in this way was a tremendous relief for both Carolyn and me, and a tribute to the excellent help of Dr. Matthew Black, my supervisor.

Now that the dissertation was finished, it was time to look for a job. I took a long weekend to attend an International Fellowship of Reconciliation meeting on the island of Iona off the west coast of Scotland. It was a wonderful mixture of vacation, celebration, and inspiration. While I was gone, Goshen College President J. Lawrence Burkholder called our home to invite me to Goshen College to fill a one-year opening resulting from a faculty sabbatical.

We returned to Goshen in July 1979, and I accepted the exact position (albeit a temporary one) that I had dreamed of three years before when I first applied to St Andrews University. This temporary position grew into a tenure track teaching position that lasted for twenty-two years.

I had always enjoyed being a pastor, and I felt strong fulfillment in that responsibility. People often ask me whether being a pastor was more rewarding than being a college professor. I humorously respond that, in the pastorate, if you have a difficult parishioner, you are stuck with them for life. But as a college professor, you know that in four years the problem student will graduate and go on to be a problem for somebody else! I believed that being both a pastor and a teacher were important responsibilities, because each one deals with critical faith formation and character development.

Several things were driven home most clearly for me in those three years of intensive study at St Andrews. These discoveries shaped my life as a follower of Jesus, and were the foundation of my teachings as a professor of New Testament at Goshen College.

First, I discovered a relationship between salvation and ethics that has guided my faith ever since. Leviticus 25 is the foundation for the Year of Jubilee. Five times in this chapter, the text says, "I am the Lord your God who brought you out of Egypt . . ." and each time, this phrase is followed by ethical instructions about land use, about slavery, about economics, and about social justice. This Jubilee theme provides the core for shaping biblical ethics.

Indeed, it is the basis for a central focus that remains constant throughout the Scriptures. Salvation is based on the undeserved activity of God (grace). How we live (ethics) is rooted in how we respond to that grace. We love others *because* God has first loved us (1 John 4:19). We do not live moral, upright lives hoping that we will earn God's love by doing it. God's love for us is based on the nature of God, not in our own ability to do good. This is essential to our understanding of faith. As a pastor, I had met many people who felt they had to tell the truth, or tithe, or not commit adultery so that they could go to heaven. This is built on the assumption that entry into the presence of God is dependent upon our ability to do what is right. That is not what I was finding in the Scriptures during my time at St Andrews.

Furthermore, we do not do things for God so that God is obligated sometime in the future to reward us with entry into heaven. We love our enemies not because they are lovable but because, while we were enemies, Christ died for us (Rom 5:10). We tell the truth because, in Jesus, God has been honest with us. We share with others because God has already shared abundantly with us. This means, for me, that we don't believe the right things or do the right things so that we are assured of going to heaven when we die. We do what we do because of what God has already done for us in Jesus Christ, whom we claim as Lord. This perspective changes how we understand faith, how we live our lives, and how we trust God for our future. It was a liberating and refreshing discovery for me.

Second, and closely related to this first discovery, is a more holistic approach to the Bible. As I traced the Jubilee theme through the Scriptures, I began to see that the great themes of the Scriptures, and indeed the salvation story itself, are much more important than any individual story that is used to tell the larger salvation story. And the salvation story is much more important than the technical accuracy of any particular detail within any individual story.

It is far more exciting, and far more important, to look at the great biblical themes of salvation, of following Jesus, of peacemaking, of the presence of the kingdom of God, than to argue over the historical accuracy of whether every detail really happened exactly the way a biblical story tells it. This removes the modern, often intense, debate over inerrancy, because inerrancy focuses on the wrong issue as we read the Bible. Arguing over how we got the Bible sidetracks us from the far more critical question of how we are going to live out the biblical message. During my study at St Andrews, the Bible started to tingle with new life as I saw God's vision for daily living appearing repeatedly in the full sweep of biblical history. I began to see salvation as a fully human experience of a life lived *right now*, modeled on the teachings of Jesus. Salvation became an incarnational experience in the present, rather than an anticipated hope for the future. Suddenly, the lordship of Jesus took on a vibrant new meaning that gave my faith new and very exciting integrity.

A third understanding reinforced what I had learned years before as I sat in classes at Associated Mennonite Biblical Seminary (AMBS) with Dr. Howard Charles. When I was a child, I had been taught that God gave us the Bible, people then read the Bible, and that led them to form groups so they could worship God and tell other people about Jesus. But, as I learned while studying under Dr. Charles, an honest encounter with biblical history shows this is not a correct reading of history. Rather, a faith community, formed by the followers of Jesus, provided the people and the setting for writing the Scriptures. We had "church" long before we had the New Testament. The Scriptures emerged out of actual historical settings. Quite often the Scriptures were addressing specific theological or congregational concerns in specific geographic settings at a given time in history. This historical context frequently impacted how the writers shaped the content of the message and the language used as the message was written down. It is important that we read the Bible within the setting in which it was written. When we see Jesus living and teaching in a culture that was dominated by the Roman Empire (via brutal taxation, oppressive troop presence, and emperors who claimed divine status for themselves), we better understand the context in which Jesus spoke. When we see this, the radical contrasts of life in the Roman Empire with life in the kingdom of God jump out at us with dramatic clarity. Thus, we can learn something from Jesus about how we should live as people of God in our own nation that is also committed to an empire mentality. That puts an urgency, intensity, and practical application into the life and teachings of Jesus that cannot be avoided.

The fourth reflection is less traditional and thus more troublesome for many people. As I wrestled with Paul's theological background, as well as the social and political context in which he lived, I began to see how these forces impacted Paul as he was shaping his own theology. I saw elements of Paul's Pharisaic theological background showing up in his new thinking as a follower of Jesus.

I began to wonder. Even if we assume that Paul's counsel is genuine, and that it is solid, godly, spiritual counsel for his day, does this mean that his first-century counsel on women, or slavery, or relationship to the state, and so on are God's determinative counsel for all of history? We know things about human sexuality that Paul had no way of knowing. We do not share his view of slavery, as seen with Onesimus in Philemon. His counsel on women pushed the acceptance barriers of his day in a very positive way, but is it appropriate to retain that application as God's eternal intention for our own day? It became increasingly difficult for me to accept a literal, inerrant reading of Scripture. I wondered, must we assume that God's presence and creativity stopped with Paul's death in 64 CE, or the apostle John's death nearer 100 CE? Does Paul set the parameters of faith for all time, or does he point us in a direction that leads to freedom, equality, acceptance, and grace that is in harmony with, yet goes far beyond, that which Paul was suggesting for his own day?

If we recognize Paul's background as a brilliant Pharisaic scholar, and see how his life was changed as he met Jesus on the Damascus road, then we will see much more clearly how our own lives can also be changed. When we see what Paul encountered as an itinerant missionary and church planter, we are much less likely to misuse his counsel by automatically applying the words to our own church setting without recognizing that the culture and history of Paul's world are different from our own. I came home from graduate school with a new appreciation for the Bible, and a driving vision of teaching others how to study the Bible and find this new understanding for themselves. Does the Bible serve as the brakes for the church to keep it from ever changing? Or is the Bible the launching pad that allows us a journey and trajectory toward those even greater things that Jesus promised we would do (John 16:12–13)?

I am profoundly aware that, for many people, their dreams are not achieved in this way. I was blessed by a congregation who caught the vision and believed in me enough to keep me on partial salary for two of the three years while in graduate school. Our family was blessed by other people who stayed in contact with us, and even visited us while we were in Scotland. I was given the privilege of coming to Goshen College and having the opportunity to invest my life in studying and sharing the Scriptures with others.

I claim no special privilege or status before God except the responsibility to be faithful with the opportunities that have come to me. For that, I am eternally grateful.

You Have Heard—But I Say

In 1996, the Bible-Religion-Philosophy department at Goshen College sponsored a conference "Teaching the Bible in the Classroom and in the Congregation." We invited several pastors to share experiences on using the Bible in the pulpit. Several faculty members talked about how the Bible was being taught at the college level.

I was scheduled for the opening lecture on reading the Bible. I developed this lecture as a personal statement of faith regarding reading and teaching the Bible. The setting was academic and I drew from sermons that I had preached, and from things that I had said in classroom lectures. Thus, in this lecture, the reader might well recognize ideas and illustrations that appear in other places.

* * *

You Have Heard—But I Say[2]

I'd like you to use your imagination for a moment. We are in a small town tucked in among the rolling hills of Palestine. It is Friday evening and we are in the village synagogue. Excitement is running high because a young visiting rabbi is going to be the speaker. This young rabbi has quite a reputation for the way he handles the Scriptures. What makes it even more exciting is that this rabbi is a local boy. Everyone knows him. His mother still lives in a small house just down the street.

As this young rabbi speaks, you can feel the excitement and the empowering presence of God in what he is saying. He is talking about something that you have been praying for all your life: the day when God will once again be present with us and we will hear the voice of God in our worship. You feel a tingling warmth starting to creep through your body as a hope that has been dashed so many times in the past begins to burn once more. You can feel it. This is a new day, and the hope for the promises of God for Israel once again begins to stir within you. You hear the soft murmurs of prayers and the whispered words of approval all around you as the congregation begins to respond to what the teacher is saying.

"Today, this Scripture is coming true in your hearing . . ." he says. As he speaks, you can literally feel your heart pounding with an excitement

2. The biblical foundation for this lecture is Luke 4:16–30.

that you haven't felt for years. But then the teacher stops. "No, you don't understand. All throughout your history, you have been expecting God to do it for you. God is calling you, right now, to do the things of God. Don't wait for God to do it for you. You are to be God's agents bringing good news, healing the blind, giving hope to the oppressed. *You* do it!"

Suddenly a deathly silence sweeps across the congregation. "What is this?" you ask yourself. "We all know what the promises of Scripture are. The Scriptures say we will be liberated from this terrible Roman oppression, we will get our land back, our sick will be healed, and we will be blessed like we were back in the days of King David. That is what God has promised. That is God's truth, and we have always known that!"

Now you don't know what to think. This young rabbi is telling you that what you have always believed is not right. He has the audacity to say that your interpretation of the sacred texts is wrong. Then when he uses the words of famous prophets like Elijah and Elisha, right out of your own history to prove that you are wrong, well that is just too much. You are not sure what you think, but instinctively, you join in the pushing and shoving that is happening all around you. As a single voice you reply to this rabbi, "No one interprets the Scriptures like that in our synagogue!"

The Bible tells us that this audience forced Jesus out of the synagogue and tried to kill him. What would you have done if you had been there that evening in Nazareth? Would you have joined in the pushing and shoving?

Jump ahead a year or two. This young rabbi is gaining quite a following. There are more and more rumors about people being healed—lame people, blind people. You are an important teacher in the religious community, so the next time he is in town you go to hear him. But you listen with critical objectivity. As you listen, you think, "This really isn't so bad, except I just wish he would stop saying, *I know this is what you have been taught, but I am telling you!* . . . *Or, I understand this is what you believe, but I am telling you that is not what God is saying.*"

You find yourself getting a little angry. You would like to argue with him, but he speaks with quiet integrity, and he certainly does know the Scriptures. What would you do? The Bible tells us that the religious leaders got together and decided they had to do something about Jesus. Eventually, they killed him. But we also know this teacher voted against taking such radical action.

Now, let's jump ahead a good many generations. You are in a university town in central Germany. There is a young priest who pastors a local congregation and does some university teaching on the side. He is a powerful preacher, but he just goes too far sometimes. He has had the nerve to say that our theological thinking is wrong. And it is not just a lot of wild charges. He has a very specific list of ninety-five things that Christians are doing that he says are not faithful to the Bible. Now that would not be so bad, but he has Bible verses that he quotes to prove it.

You have seen his list, everybody has. It is posted on the cathedral door right in the middle of town. That list challenges some of the very basic, central principles of your faith, things you have always believed, without question. Now you are being told that what you believe is not right. He says that these beliefs are not based on Scripture, and he is calling you to change.

This young priest is, of course, Martin Luther. History tells us that Martin Luther lost his job and almost lost his life because he dared to challenge the religious thinking of his day. What would you have done? Whose side would you have been on?

Many people today are concerned about the life of the church. There is a feeling that something has gone wrong. These people are convinced that had they been there at Nazareth they would gladly have defended Jesus from the crowd. When Martin Luther nailed his ninety-five theses on the door of the church in Wittenburg, these same people say that they would have been first in line to support him, thanking God that finally someone is taking the Bible seriously around here. Or would they?

We live in a very different world that is, curiously, almost identical in many ways. We hear the call for renewal and a transformation of faith. We agree that something must be done, but our solutions usually argue that we simply need to work harder at what we are already doing. We need to pray more often, worship more sincerely, read our Bibles more faithfully, and talk about Jesus more openly. And we must do these things with the assumption that we are doing the right things, and that we just need to do them better and more often. I wonder, is this how Ezekiel felt when he sat down in a cemetery in Babylon, asking, "How can we breathe fresh life into these old, dead bones?" (Ezek 37).

Have we decided that God is no longer doing a new thing in our midst? Is our calling, as religious leaders, to protect the answers we already have, because we know they are the right answers? How do the Scriptures give us new life? Maybe we really are back in the synagogue at Nazareth, or standing at the church door in Wittenburg, wondering why anyone would believe that God has something new to say. We don't need new answers. We simply need to package our right answers more persuasively.

When I was in graduate school, Matthew Black, my supervisor and friend, once told a group of us that there is a second unforgivable sin that is not mentioned in the Bible. It is very simple: "Thou shalt not make Bible study boring."

If we are going to allow the Bible to come alive for students in the classroom, or for members in the congregation, we need to discover again what it is that the Scriptures are trying to say. Dr. Leander Keck, professor of biblical theology at Yale wrote recently, "The future does not belong to those who fight the shortcomings of the past."[3] If we believe that God is active and alive, that the Scriptures are dynamic and life-giving, then every generation is called upon to search the Scriptures so that we do not simply repeat the answers learned by previous generations.

Dr. Keck quotes Deuteronomy 2:3 where, in effect, God says to Moses, "You have been going in circles around these mountains long enough. It is time to head north. Get these people ready to move."

If we are going to hear the voice of God calling us to move, there are several things that are important.

First, we must stop worrying about the Bible and be more concerned about what the Bible says. We have a long history of worrying about how we got the Bible. We have often felt the need to protect the Bible from criticism. We tell people that the Bible is inspired by God, but we are secretly afraid that someone might discover that, in fact, it isn't. Then what would we do? Keck suggests that no faith community can remain strong if it uses all its energy defending its own Scriptures. To stop worrying about the Bible does not mean to ignore it, or deny it, or stop reading it. I am urging that we let the Scriptures speak with their own authority, and that we commit ourselves to listen intently to hear what they say. It was Mark Twain (hardly a paragon of biblical insight) who once said, "It's not what I don't understand in the Bible that bothers me, it's what I do understand."

Second, we need to stop using the Bible to serve our own needs, and start living with the Bible in a long-term commitment. By *using* the Bible, I mean searching the Scriptures to win an argument, prove a point, or provide support for the sermon we have already prepared for Sunday

---

3. Keck, "The Premodern Bible," pp. 130–141.

morning. When we use the Scriptures to defend our arguments, we are actually diminishing the authority of the Bible.

Dr. Keck reminds us that living with the Bible is not like living with a crotchety old grandfather who only wants to talk about the good old days. Rather, it is like living in a multigenerational extended family, where you keep learning new things simply because you are there. To live with the Bible does not blind us to its limits or its involvement in historic events, some of which we might now see as primitive and oppressive, anymore than living with your spouse blinds you to their humanity. Quite the contrary. Living with the Bible enables us to see these things, to understand them as historic reality in that day without having to believe that we must duplicate these ancient realities in our own time.

The Scriptures call us to create new communities of faith. We are not called to reconstruct the old world, or the ancient tribal family patterns of Abraham, or even the first-century world of Jesus. To live with the Bible is to come to know and experience what is important, life-giving, and emancipating. We should never allow its obvious narrowness in certain ancient cultural practices to trip us up.

This is the risk we must take. We must open our Bibles and allow God to speak to us through the written Word. We should be reading the Bible with all our heart, *and all our mind*, with all our soul, *and all our strength*, bringing a commitment of faith which dares to let the Spirit of God change us and call us to new life. People quickly get bored with Bible study when we keep running around the same tree, giving the same answers without ever noticing that people are asking different questions.

The Bible is a book about God's activity in history. To separate God from that history is destructive to history, and to separate history from God denies an essential aspect of God's nature. The Bible must be studied in its historic context so that it can be correctly applied to our own context. Faithfulness does not mean trying to recreate first-century society. We are trying to be God's people in our own culture so that other people can come to know the saving love and grace of God in their own lives. To do this, it is very helpful to recover the feelings, emotions, and anxiety of biblical characters.

It is easy to get excited for Mary. How wonderful it must have been to have an angel appear to you and tell you that God has chosen you to be the mother of the Messiah. But how did Mary feel when she told Joseph and he blurted out, "You're *what*? If you are pregnant, I'm out of here. You are on your own young lady. How could you do this to me?"

That is not exciting, that is devastating. And don't tell me that she sang the *Magnificat* on the way home because she knew that an angel would appear to Joseph in a couple of nights, and he would come crawling back begging for forgiveness!

What was Mary's source of hope? She turned to a member of the faith community who she knew would be understanding because of this member's own experience with an unusual pregnancy. What is the biblical message of hope when your life falls apart six months before your wedding day—or when your marriage falls apart six years after your wedding? That is the stuff the Bible is made of. It tells of real people wrestling with real issues in life and discovering how to experience God's grace in the midst of it all.

Let me suggest a couple of things that I believe the Scriptures teach us about how we can give expression to the grace of God in our own world.

The first is seen in the prophet Hosea as he wrestles with an exceedingly painful marriage with Gomer. Out of that experience he comes to some new understandings about the love of God. What he learned literally came to life in Jesus. The apostle John writes, "Beloved, let us love one another, for love is of God, and anyone who loves is born of God and knows God."[4] Jesus put it this way: "Love your enemies, do good to those who hate you, bless those who persecute you."

One of the exciting new edges for faith in our day is the call to rediscover the depth of God's love. I don't mean God's love for us, because we have always known that, but rather God's love for people in communities we don't find very lovable, and even God's love for our enemies. We claim to be the people of God. When we make that claim, it demands a conscious decision to center our lives in Jesus. This centering is often in direct contrast with the pressures of our world that try to tell us that some people are not very lovable, or not even worth loving. What makes this worldview so tragic is that much of it comes from a segment of the Christian community that claims to have a special relationship with God and the Bible.

There is a tendency in our religious culture to tell others, "Get your act together, change the way you live, become like us, believe like we do, and then we will love you." But would it not be more faithful to the Scriptures for us to love and accept persons not on the basis of how nearly they

---

4. See 1 John 4:7.

match our spiritual maturity, but rather on how open we are to share the love, grace, and mercy of a forgiving God?

Our nation has many outstanding religious voices. But as a country, we still have many who thunder with the voice of Mars (god of war) and not of Jesus (prince of peace). I pray that we might be accepting of those who are at different places in their faith. But I also pray that we will continue to teach and share that God is a God of love—even for our enemies.

A second theme comes out of the hills of Judah. As Amos went to Bethel, he was overwhelmed by the greed, oppression, and luxury of that community. Jesus emphasized this theme in his own ministry. "Don't lay up for yourselves treasure on earth, where moths or rust can ruin it, or thieves break in and steal it, for your values and your character are all wrapped up together."[5]). One of the biblical concepts for our day is for us to live simply and responsibly with the resources of the earth. There are major pressures calling on us to accumulate for ourselves, spend on ourselves, and save for ourselves in the future. Where do we find our security? Is it in the stockpiling of mutual funds, trusting in the market to safeguard our investments? Or is it in God, through the people of God who commit themselves to share so that no one is in need? How do we teach the biblical message of trust in God so that we share with those in need as God has blessed us?

Finally a word from Ezekiel as he sits in discouragement looking out over an old burial ground near Babylon, wondering if there is any hope for new life and whether these people really can start over again. God responds to his question with a vision of new life, of bones and muscles and tendons coming back together again, and of dead bodies springing back to life. Jesus took this prophetic theme and expanded on it, calling for a radically new way of looking at life, a way so radical that the only way to describe it is to talk about being *born again*. In his own words, "No one can enter the kingdom of God unless they are born again"(John 3:5).

Unfortunately, this term has become a religious cliché that has lost much of its biblical meaning. We have domesticated it to fit into our modern, comfortable, and cultural values. We have watered down this radical word from Jesus so that it simply means rearranging our theological ideas to provide a corner for God on Sunday morning. In much of Protestant Christianity *born again* speaks only to how you think about God. It says nothing about how you treat enemies, how you spend money, how you

---

5. This paraphrase comes from Matthew 6:21, which says: "Where your treasure is, there is where your heart is also."

use God's creation, how you see other persons, or how you use your own body. Being born again has become an emotional, theological cliché that no longer sounds the trumpet call for a dramatically new way of living under the guidance and power of God's Holy Spirit.

The Bible teaches us that when we join with the people of God, we take upon ourselves the confession "Jesus is Lord." Being born-again people means that instead of fighting wars, we follow the way of Jesus in being active peacemakers—even with our enemies. Instead of pushing and shoving to get into positions of wealth and power, we serve so that others may live. Instead of accepting society's images of male and female sexuality, we see every person as a child of God. We pledge to live pure, open, honest, and holy lives, treating others with dignity and respect, so that all of us are free to be fully human. Instead of surrounding ourselves with cultural symbols of wealth, of prestige and security, we covenant to live simply, with our security being in God and God's people. We rejoice in sharing with those who have need, just as God has shared with us in our time of need.

Where is our hope? Is it in God and the possibilities that the Scriptures teach us about being made new—of being set free from yesterday's sins because God is a forgiving God? So often in Christian faith we focus on the sins of yesterday and the hope for tomorrow without extending to others the joy and excitement of the life that is ours in Christ Jesus *right now*!

The Bible calls us to live as people of God, so that through us others might experience the grace, love, and mercy of God in their own lives. As we study the Scriptures we hear the call of God to be a new people, shaped and inspired by God's Spirit as we serve the God of history who is always ahead of us, saying, "Come, follow me." It is my prayer that we might have the courage to study the Scriptures so that we might better learn how to follow him who is the way, the truth, and the life.

That You Might Know the Truth[6]

Where do you go to find the truth these days? We live in a society where truth is defined by the hard sciences: through observation, research, and data. The news provides on-the-scene reporting of floods, wars, and famines, complete with pictures so that you can see what is going on. If you remember Walter Cronkite, he always used to sign off the evening news with "And that's the way it is." When he told us that, we believed him. We knew that really was the way it is.

Where does God fit into Tom Brokaw's world of reporting the news? I am told that Brokaw is a religious man, but when he reported the collapse of the Berlin Wall he did not use the same language that the Bible used to report the collapse of the walls of Jericho. Jericho was seen as a miraculous act of God. The Berlin Wall was the result of politics and the persistent dream for freedom on the part of a divided people.

Has NBC news replaced the Bible in determining how we see life? Can educated people continue to rely on a book that is almost two thousand years old to give counsel in a sophisticated, technological age?

The Bible is essentially a religious book. Its central story is the relationship between God and humanity. It describes that relationship in terms of specific events in history. Thus, the Bible not only reports history, it theologizes about history, meaning it interprets history on the assumption that God had something to do with what was happening. By the way, it is interesting to note that the rallying point for the people of East Germany was the church. People met in church basements to pray, to plan, to lay strategy, to build community, to find freedom in an oppressive system through the leadership of a few Free Church pastors. Just maybe, the more we learn, the more the Berlin Wall looks like Jericho after all. Maybe God is still involved in liberating people. Maybe NBC news just doesn't know that!

You see, it is so easy to read the Bible as a spiritual book filled with instructions on how to escape to another world where God is. Paul got hit with that very same issue at Ephesus. It also shows up in 1 John. There was a group of people in the early church who believed that salvation was in knowing the right doctrinal facts. These facts would guarantee that you would be received into the presence of God. These people had turned faith inside out. For them faith did not mean being Christ-like in their lives here on earth, it meant finding the fastest way to escape back

6. The biblical foundation for this sermon is Luke 1:1–4.

into heaven where God is. Paul confronted this group, saying, "Why do you want to do that, because God has given to us in Christ every spiritual blessing that you are trying to find in the heavenly places"(Eph 1:3). That information should change dramatically the way you look at life, the way you interpret history, and the way you make history. That is what the Bible brings, not simply a recording of history, but an interpretation of God's activity in history.

Some of the events in the Bible can be documented from the records of secular history, but some cannot. The reason why they can't is not because they did not happen; it is because secular historians didn't think the event was very important. Egyptian historians showed little interest in the social conditions among the Hebrew slaves in Egypt. It was only when these slaves erupted in a major social revolt and Pharaoh, with several battalions of the Egyptian army, was lost in a freak accident at the Red Sea that the Egyptian press picked up the story.

For example, how much did you see on the evening news about Bosnia? Probably not much. What did you see in the news about the slow buildup of social and racial tensions in Los Angeles last year or even last week? Unless something momentous occurred, you probably saw very little. People who live in poverty don't get the headlines today any more than they did twenty-seven hundred years ago in Egypt. Not until there is a radical disruption of life as usual, or when war erupts, and the people in power are directly affected by it, does the press pick up the story. But the Bible has a lot to say about people living in oppressive, dehumanizing situations.

The book of Jonah speaks directly to racial prejudice. Nonetheless, people with racist religious backgrounds miss everything God is trying to say about race, nationalism, and social justice because we still get devoured by that whale.

That is what makes the Bible so exciting and also so confusing. The Bible is not primarily a philosophy book about the nature of God. It assumes that God exists, and then reports on how the activity of God impacts history. It reflects with us about how people got the message, or why they didn't understand.

When you put the story in its social, economic, and historical context, you suddenly discover that the Jewish year of Jubilee as described in Leviticus 25 has something profound to say to us about labor management relations, about ecology and the environment, about wealth and poverty. But we miss it because we want to focus on God and the blessings of heaven. Because we spiritualize the message, we do not realize that the Bible shows us how the people interacted with God in this world, feeling God calling them to be godly people in an increasingly ungodly world. It is a lot more comfortable to dream about heavenly mansions than it is to wrestle with problems of homelessness here in our own corner of the world. Yet that is a central concern of the biblical message. God has become known to us in Christ trying to reconcile the world to God's way of living, and this ministry of reconciliation has been entrusted to us (2 Cor 5:19).

Once again, the contrasting observation: History normally is told by the winners, the powerful, and the wealthy. Official Egypt of twenty-seven hundred years ago had a very different way of recording the story of how a major portion of their labor force disappeared and how a freak of nature led to the loss of several battalions of their military. By contrast, the Bible approaches the story from the perspective of the people of God.

Let us consider the exodus story in terms of a clash between two stubborn, determined, and powerful people—Pharaoh and Moses. Official Egypt told the story of Pharaoh. The Bible tells the story of Moses. Why? Because the Bible was written by descendants of the slaves. It tells the story of God's liberation of people calling them to be in mission—not in slavery. But secular history tells the story of people in power doing all they can to stay in power and control the world. There is a difference.

It is no surprise that the "Jerusalem press" did not cover the story of a baby that was born in Bethlehem. Maybe the visit of the Magi to Herod made the social pages. Babies were born every day in small towns throughout Palestine. No Babylon news agency paid any attention to the story of a wealthy family emigrating from Ur because they wanted to find a new way of living with less social and political pressure. People moved all the time. No one was concerned about reporting on the actions of a Jewish teacher surrounded by a dozen rather simple disciples who was challenging the religious traditions of his day. It wasn't until Rome started feeling threatened that they paid any attention to Jesus.

Perhaps you might remember the old telephone party lines that we used to have in the country. For those who don't, it was a system of shared lines. You could tell by the ring exactly who on your line was getting a call. You could also be pretty sure that two or three other people were listening to everything you said on the phone. That is what all of us kids did on those party lines—we listened in. There is a conversation in the Bible that I wish I could have listened in on. Two people are walking down the road from Jerusalem to Emmaus after the crucifixion. Jesus falls in step with them and gives them a course in Old Testament Christology. Now that would have been an interesting seminar. The Bible has such a polite way of telling stories. As you might remember, Jesus said to these two persons, "Oh, how foolish you are and how slow of heart to believe."[7] Allow me to translate: "Oh dear, you dumb guys, aren't you ever going to get it?"

I suggest that we have trouble with the Scriptures because of our own stubbornness and ignorance about what the Scriptures teach. Let me suggest a couple of things.

Jesus moved from a focus on the book to a commitment to the person. Back on the road to Emmaus, the biblical text tells us, "Beginning with Moses, he explained to them in all the Scriptures the things concerning himself."[8] The purpose of the Bible is to confront us with the living God known to us in Jesus. We learn that by seeing how the people around Jesus saw the presence of God in him. Jesus affirmed their enthusiasm for the study of the Scriptures but despaired over their inability to make connections within the biblical message.

The apostle Paul is a good example of this. Paul was thoroughly trained in biblical knowledge, but it wasn't until he was confronted by Jesus on the Damascus road that he really got the message. And then he spent three years in the desert to rethink everything he had learned in rabbinic school, because he now believed that Jesus was the Messiah. Are we willing to rethink what we know? How many of us think we know what is in the Bible, so our calling is to tell others what we already know? Do we dare to expect the Holy Spirit to help us discover new things as we study the Scriptures?

To this I add, our salvation is in Jesus, not in the scriptures. I say that very deliberately because I am convinced that the never-ending debate about inerrancy and biblical inspiration is not our issue. When we let that become our issue, we lose sight of the central message of the Bible, which is a call to follow Jesus in doing the will of God. Arguing over how God was involved in how we got the message gets in the way of doing what the message says.

The Bible is intended to be a guide for those who confess that Jesus is Lord. It invites other people to join the God movement. It is not a club

7. See Luke 24:25.
8. See Luke 24:27.

that excludes people who don't think exactly in the same way. Jesus put it this way: "You search the scriptures because you think that in them you have eternal life. They bear witness to me, yet you refuse to respond to me so that you can have eternal life" (John 5:39–40).

Study of the Bible should change our lives, because in the Bible we confront the person of Jesus. It is in Jesus that we learn about the will of God. That study should result in our joining with others to feed the hungry, to offer support and love to those who feel rejected, to visit the elderly and the lonely, to share with the poor, and to make known to everyone that God is a God of forgiving love. The Bible wants us to allow the love of God to be felt in the lives of other people. You can study the Bible to win arguments, or you can study the Bible to be a better reflection of God's love in your own life.

As the Spirit leads us in study and discussion of the Scriptures, we begin to get insight into how God would have us live. When that happens, we start to recognize the foolishness of some of the things the world tries to do. When we see how God sees things, we start to think differently, and as we think differently, we start to live differently. It is as we live differently that the world begins to see the Spirit of God shining through us, because we are living by a different vision, guided by a different understanding of God.

My second observation: I continue to be amazed by people in church. On their jobs, they recognize the need for competence, knowledge, and the importance of continuing education. But many of these same, exacting professionals have a level of biblical faith knowledge that has stagnated at about the eighth grade level. Is it any wonder that when an eighth grade biblical knowledge clashes with college level scientific theory, or college level economics, that the Bible doesn't come out looking so good. I would challenge all of us not to simply review your knowledge of the Bible but to make a commitment to learn something new about life from the Bible.

In John 16:13, Jesus talks with the disciples. He says, in effect, "I have lots of things to say, but you can't handle them right now. But when the Spirit of Truth comes, he will guide you into new truth." Or, to quote 1 Corinthians 2:12: "We have received the spirit which is of God, that we might know the things that are feely given us by God."

Learning new things from the Bible does not automatically mean a rejection of what you already believe. The decision to drive a car does not mean your great grandparents were wrong for driving a horse and buggy. But simply repeating the answers of one hundred years ago without rethinking the questions is a way of saying that God can be dated and boxed in history. It assumes that God does not have anything new to say to us today. If you believe in a God who is alive, dynamic, personal, and powerful, then you owe it to yourself, to God, and to the world to keep up with what we are called to do as children of God. It will be more exciting than you ever imagined.

I Promise!

Be Careful What You Read!

I thought it was a strange question: "Do you still believe the Bible?" I was professor of New Testament at Goshen College. I had a PhD in New Testament from the University of St Andrews in Scotland. Why wouldn't I believe the Bible? But it seemed that some people needed to be reassured that graduate school had not ruined my faith. I did not like the question, nor did I care for the assumptions behind it. Why would three years of intense graduate-level study of one biblical theme (Jesus and the Year of Jubilee—Luke 4:16–30) destroy my love for the Scriptures? It had been intense, but never destructive. I had learned a great deal and this increased my appreciation of Scripture. For three years, I had been digging into the biblical text, as well as examining the history and culture of the various biblical periods. Every morning I had checked into the small, unheated university room that I shared with three other PhD students eager to see what new insight or connection was waiting for me that day.

Now, I was beginning a new career as Professor of Bible at Goshen College. The college was willing to pay me to do what I absolutely loved doing—study the Bible and teach students how to study the Bible. I could not understand why people were asking these questions.

One day I shared this confusion with an older pastor and good friend. "Ah," he said. "You don't understand. They are not asking whether you believe the Bible. They want to be sure that you believe the Bible *the way they believe the Bible*." When I was a student at AMBS, Dr. Howard Charles shared a comment from a former student: "I didn't take this class to learn anything new, I just want better proof for what I already believe." Dr. Charles kept wanting us to learn new things. He was a superb teacher and a major contributor to my love of the Bible.

I had been at Goshen less than a year when College Mennonite Church asked me to be part of a short sermon series on the Bible. They asked, "How does careful, critical Bible study increase faith and give credibility to the message?"

I wanted to encourage young people to read their Bibles, not simply to review what they already knew but to expect to learn something new. I wanted to help them walk alongside the biblical figures and experience how they had discovered God and what it meant in their lives. I wanted students to see the Bible as a living story of how real people interacted with their concept of God, and from that, to learn better how we might also interact and respond to God. Paul once wrote, "When I became a man, I put away childish things."[9] How can we encourage adults to read the Bible as adult thinkers, seeing the problems that are there but also seeing behind the specific problems to the message that the Scriptures have for us?

* * *

Be Careful What You Read![10]

Imagine with me for a moment. Your son is a sophomore in college and is home for the weekend. One evening you find him curled up with a book he brought home. He tells you it is required reading for a class. You are interested in what colleges have their students reading these days, so you ask about it. Your son tells you it is sort of a religious history and ethics book. It tells the story of a tribe who were trapped in slavery, how they revolted against the government and escaped through the desert to start a new life. This tribe had some religious leaders who were pretty hypocritical. Private property is frowned upon by the central group in the story, and this group wants to form a new economic community. But the government kept arresting their leaders, who kept finding very exciting creative ways to escape. The hero of the story is arrested and then executed by the state for political treason. It's a good story. But you wonder, *Whoa!* What are college students reading these days?

Let's change the image just a bit. Your daughter is home from college. She tells you about a class she has to take where they are required to read the Bible as a story about real people who are trying to make a new life for themselves. She is intrigued by this story of people who have a vision about how life could be. "You know," she says, "this story makes sense. I wonder what life would be like if we could pick up their vision and do something with it? If we could stop going to war all the time, get off this crazy economic escalator and be generous with what we have, start feeding the hungry, and learn to treat people like people; we could do a lot of good in the world."

How do you respond to that? You recognize, of course, that both students are reading the same book. We assume that the Bible is a very safe book. We expect it to help people settle down, to make them more

9. See 1 Corinthians 13:11.

10. The biblical foundation for this sermon is from Leviticus 25 and 2 Timothy 3:10–17.

socially responsible, clean up their lives, and turn them into law-abiding, good middle-class American citizens. We think that way because in our culture most of us read the Bible that way.

Turning the world upside down—or downside up?

Years ago a young German theologian, Karl Barth, wrote that when he reads the Bible, his spiritual assumptions get shattered because he finds that he is not always headed in the same direction that God is going. More recently, Don Kraybill, of Elizabethtown College, said, "The Upside Down Kingdom which is so central to the message of Jesus is upside down only to people who don't recognize that they are already standing on their heads. These people complain that we are turning their world upside down. But what they don't realize is that they are the ones who are really upside down. We are simply trying to get the world back to the way God intended it to be."[11]

That sounds a lot like what happened to Paul and Silas at Thessalonika as the crowd said, "These people who are turning the world upside down have come here also" (Acts 17:6). How long has it been since anyone has accused us of turning the world upside down?

We would all like the world to be a better place, with peace, food, and decent housing for everyone. But we use our own situation as the model for how God would have us live. We believe quite innocently that what we are doing is obviously biblical and godly. We don't think much about Jesus and what he might say about how we should approach stewardship, ecology, and poverty. We witnessed Mother Teresa working among the dying in Calcutta, and we say, "What a wonderful model of Christian saintliness." But we give our money to TV evangelists and parachurch organizations who promise success and prosperity to those who "name it and claim it for Jesus." We don't stop to recognize that there is really something wrong with this behavior.

Motivation for giving!

There is a story about Jesus and his disciples in the gospels. Allow me to modernize the tale. One day, Jesus and his disciples were in the temple when they saw the press getting out their notebooks, setting up their TV

11. Kraybill, *Upside Down Kingdom*.

cameras, and milling around while the temple Pharisees were straightening their beards and checking their robes. This was the day to kick off the annual "Support Your Local Temple" fund drive with wealthy people bringing their major contributions so they could be seen on TV talking with the High Priest. The disciples were really impressed. But Jesus said, "Hey, you guys, look over there—see that? Over there—that is generosity." They turn just in time to see the tattered robe of an elderly woman disappear behind a pillar out of range from the TV cameras (check Mark 12). Jesus tells the disciples, forget these guys on TV with their checkbooks, and instead check out that woman and her anonymous generosity.

The Bible is full of stories like that. It tells us about people who have been caught up in God's grace and their lives have changed. They didn't plan it. God's grace just sort of does that to you. While working on the Leviticus text about the Jewish Year of Jubilee, I first thought it seemed to be rather boring. But as I kept reading, something started to jump out at me. It starts in Leviticus 24:22: "I am the Lord your God"; in 25:17, "I am the Lord your God"; in 25:38, "I am the Lord your God who brought you out of Egypt"; and in verse 42, "They are my servants whom I brought out of the land of Egypt."

I grew up in a family where "I am the Lord your God" did not always sound like good news. More often than not it implied, "You are in trouble and judgment is coming." But that is not the biblical message. In Leviticus, every time Israel is told how they should organize their new life, it is prefaced with the phrase, "I am the Lord your God who brought you out of Egypt." The message is clear. Israel was to base their new life as a community upon their gratitude to God for liberating them from slavery in Egypt.

This is true for Christian faith as well. Jesus does not call us to do things so that we can be saved, become healthy, or even get rich here on earth before going to heaven when we die. Jesus calls us to share with others because God has already shared so abundantly with us. We are called to reach out in compassion because God was reaching out to us while we were yet sinners. Throughout the Scriptures, it is always God who takes the risk. It is God who takes the initiative. It is God who blesses and forgives us, and then urges us to pass that on to others by blessing them, forgiving them, and caring for them.

I do not get much joy out of being critical. It makes me very sad to see what many Christians are doing to God these days. Our religious culture tells people, "If you give to us and our organization, God will bless you abundantly. If you support us financially, God will meet your every need." This is called "seed faith," and it has a certain appeal. It fits comfortably with American capitalism (work hard, invest wisely, get rich). But God calls us to be thankful for what we have received, and then share it generously with those who are less fortunate.

Who sets the standards?

After tracing the Jewish Year of Jubilee through the Scriptures, I have developed this belief that God calls Christians to live simply and responsibly. Carolyn and I feel pretty good about how we are doing, because I compare myself with Michael Jordan, Bill Gates, and Donald Trump. When we do that, it is really easy to think we are being frugal, tight even. But when I turn on the evening news and the newscaster shows me a war-torn place where refugees carry everything they own on a little two wheeled trailer, suddenly life looks very different. They don't deserve what is being done to them, but that is their reality. Now I happen to like Michael Jordan. Bill and Melinda Gates have been a blessing for millions of people with their Gates Foundation. But I wonder if God's truth about stewardship is seen most vividly through these refugees fleeing for their lives or if it is seen through the luxurious living patterns of sports heroes, movie stars, and mega-business executives.

Back to Leviticus. There is one more point to be made. The focus is on what God has done for Israel. And because of that, they were challenged to think about their own future as they were preparing to live in their new land after escaping from Egypt. How about us? How does what we do impact the lives of our children? In Leviticus, God provides hope for the next generation. You could only be a slave for six years and then you were set free. Debts were cancelled in the seventh year; and once every fifty years, the land, which was the primary source of living for most Israelites, was recycled back to the original owners. In such a society, you always had hope that God would provide for you. But it is important to note that this hope came from God, through the believing community, by being faithful to God's intentions for humanity. Those who had been blessed were supposed to share, even give up some things, so that others might live. There was no emphasis on personal divine rights or privilege connected with what people owned.

Paul picks up this same theme in Ephesians 4 wherein he outlines some very practical steps for Christian ethics. With each step he adds a note saying why we should do these things. In Ephesians 4:28 he writes, "Thieves must give up stealing, rather let them do honest work so that they might have something to share with those who are in need." That is an important Christian principle. Even when we are working, we should be aware of those around us who are in need.

A lesson in creative generosity

Let me share a story that happened recently at Goshen College. In our opening chapel, President Shirley Showalter presented three Goshen College lanyards. These had been an exceedingly popular item among the youth at Mennonite General Assembly in July. She proposed that we auction them off to raise money for earthquake relief in Turkey. Faculty would bid on one, the staff on the second, and the students would bid on the third lanyard. The winner had a month to raise the money needed to cover their bid. I dropped out when the faculty bidding reached $250. Our lanyard eventually went for just over $300, and I was impressed with the generosity of a specific faculty member. I knew the students would never match that amount.

Then the students started bidding, and almost immediately it got exciting. Their lanyard quickly passed $300, to $500, to $1,000, to $2,000, to $2,750, to $3,000. By now everybody was on the edge of their seats. It finally went for $5,000 to a second-year student who I doubt had ever seen $5,000. A couple of students (Bible Religion majors even!) had put their heads together and said, "We don't have it, but we can raise it!" For four weeks they did creative campus programming. They made home-made ice cream. They sold tickets for faculty-student athletic competitions. They talked the touring choir into giving a charity concert. They even organized a student fast where the dining hall donated the price of each uneaten meal. Their final total was over $14,000. In the process, they encouraged the faculty (actually they shamed us into it) to get together and increase our individual $300 bid to become a collective $5,000 contribution. The final total for earthquake relief was over $24,000.

That should be a model for us. We do our theology in a sharing mode. We talk about community, but we still do most of our economic thinking in a very individualistic mode. It is as though it violates our human dignity and privacy to talk together about money or the resources we have for our own use. We have effectively moved that topic out of the faith discussion circle. We allow the culture to dictate how we think about money, about our standards for living, and what good stewardship means.

Who owns what?

The biblical model is built on the theme that the cattle on a thousand hills belong to God. Yes, we hold legal title to that which we own. But can we begin to recover the image that God is the creator and ultimately everything that we have belongs to God? Can we together find ways to affirm and support each other as we struggle with issues of responsible stewardship?

Are there ways that we can meet together and learn how to share so that we have more to give to those who don't have anything to share? Are there ways for us to rejoice together and celebrate the blessings over which God has granted us responsibility? Can these things remind us how fortunate we are, and encourage us to buck the prevailing culture that keeps telling us how much better life would be if we just had more of what we already have?

Let's go back to where we started. Stewardship (thankful living) begins with God, not with us. It is not just keeping track of how much we have given (that's a legal tax issue), but rather becoming more aware of how much God has given us. We need to rethink who our role models are, and who our discerning community is going to be. When we give because we have been blessed with abundance, the feeling is ever so much better than the feeling of obligation because there are just so many needy people out there who will starve if we don't give. So shame on us for not giving more! Who is it that determines the direction and the vision for our lives? Does it bring obligation and anger, or does it provide joy and thanksgiving?

God gives to us out of the joy of God's creative love for all people. When we share with others, we are telling God how grateful we are for God's love and generosity shown to us. Can we also give and share with that same joy?

You see, the biblical message is not dry history about the past; it is a living message that impacts how we live, how our world functions, and how we can create a better, more just world that better reflects the nature of God whom we say we believe in. May God give us the courage to be who we say we are.

5

Finding God without Even Looking

Are you tired?
Worn out? Burned out on religion?
Come to me and you will recover your life.
Walk with me, watch how I do it.
Learn from the unforced rhythms of grace.
I won't lay anything heavy or ill-fitting on you.
Keep company with me and you will learn to live freely and lightly.[1]
—Jesus
Matthew 11:28–30

Our first task in approaching another people,
another culture, another religion, is to take off our shoes,
for the place we are approaching is holy.
Else we may find ourselves treading on someone's dreams.
More serious still, we may forget that God was there before we got
there.
—Anonymous

Jesus did not bring a corrected ritual, or a new theory about God.
He brought a new peoplehood and a new way of living together.
Such a group, if it lives faithfully, is the most powerful tool of social
change.[2]
—John Howard Yoder

---

1. Peterson, *The Message.*
2. Yoder, *The Original Revolution*, p. 31.

Finding God without Even Looking

Continuing education seminars usually promise change for its attendees: a new approach to old problems, a better quality of life, or perhaps better methods for conducting a ministry. I attend such seminars because they also offer me an opportunity to visit with pastors from other denominations. One seminar particularly stands out in my memory. Dr. Gerald May of the Shalem Institute in Washington, DC, talked about the psychological pressures of the pastorate. He told us, in effect: "Twenty percent of what you do is best described as carrying out the garbage. Those are jobs that have to be done to keep the organization working. Nobody sees them unless you don't do them, because if they aren't done they create a real stink. You don't have to like these jobs. Most of us don't. But they still have to be done."

Most college professors put committee meetings into that category of carrying out the garbage. We are teachers, not administrators. Committee meetings are a necessary evil that should be avoided whenever possible. At Goshen College I was a member of the Judicial Board (well known as "J-Board"), which was then chaired by Dean of Students, Dr. Norman Kauffmann. J-Board worked with students who were in violation of the "Campus Standards of Our Life Together."

On J-Board we listened, gave honest confrontation, and insisted on personal accountability. When students were in conflict with each other, we would bring them together and help them mediate and come to their own decision. Students participated actively in the resolution of problems and the restoration of relationships.

J-Board met nearly every week for ninety minutes. It quickly became clear to me that I was near the bottom of the learning curve on how to handle conflict. My family system had taught me to deal with conflict by avoiding it. Our family rule was: "We ignore, or deny, conflict hoping that in a week everyone will have forgotten what happened and life will return to normal." This seldom worked, but it was how we operated.

As a J-Board member, I discovered how often conflict could be resolved when it was treated not as a problem that called for punishment, but as an opportunity that offered growth in self and social understanding. I began to wonder whether we could teach conflict mediation skills as an academic discipline that could be open to all students. This course would take a proactive approach that would benefit more students than just those who appeared before J-Board. It also fit quite well with the church's belief in peace and reconciliation.

After ten years of teaching, and seven years as a J-Board member, I was eligible for a sabbatical. This sabbatical was an opportunity for me to try to transform my ideas for a conflict mediation course into something tangible. I titled this new course, "Introduction to Conflict Mediation," and I hoped that it could become a regular part of the curriculum at Goshen College. I had no academic training in this field, so I applied for and received an Eli Lilly grant for study in conflict mediation at the University of Colorado. This grant also included mediation training at the Center for Dispute Resolution in Boulder, Colorado. I was looking forward to a very interesting year. Carolyn and I began making plans to move to Boulder. But all of us know about counting chickens, or a bird in the hand, or the best laid plans of mice and men. That is, our plans for study at Boulder almost instantly went on hold as a new opportunity presented itself.

Goshen College asked Carolyn and me to be faculty leaders for twenty-one students going to the People's Republic of China for a five month Study-Service Term. It was an invitation we could not refuse. China presented itself as the adventure of a lifetime. This Study-Service Term was to start in August, 1989, which turned out to be a momentous year in modern Chinese history. As you will recall, the summer of 1989 was when Chinese students staged major political protests at Tiananmen Square in Beijing. CNN provided daily coverage of student activities, the lady liberty statue, and the tanks. On television, we watched that bloody night in June when fighting broke out between the students and the army. We were horrified when we saw students being carried out on bicycles by friends trying to find medical help. We saw the single man standing in front of the column of tanks. It was riveting television. In just a few weeks we would be in Beijing. But was China open to foreign students? Was it safe for Goshen College students to go into that environment? Yet, China's Department of Education said come and the U.S. State Department gave its approval. So in late August of 1989 we, along with twenty-one students, boarded a JAL flight from Chicago to Beijing. I could not begin to imagine what this year would be like.

Our students assisted in teaching English at Sichuan Teachers College in Chengdu. We regularly held "English Corner" on a small campus plaza where we engaged Chinese students and faculty in casual conversation, thus increasing their language skills. The topics were wide ranging:

"Did we know any movie stars? Had we ever met any Indians? Have we ever seen Michael Jordan?" As we talked with these students and professors, they often raised questions about religious faith. China did not forbid religious practice; it simply was not necessary. Most of the population had very little interest in religious practices. For most of our Goshen students, this was their first experience in a country where religious faith was not a dominant presence. These American students were challenged to rethink their own faith and the role it held in their own lives.

Soon after arriving in Chengdu, we learned there was a small group of American Christians who met every Sunday afternoon in the JinJiang Hotel in downtown Chengdu. For several weeks, Carolyn and I made the thirty-minute bus trip to meet with them for worship. It felt good to sing familiar hymns and have a brief meditation. We enjoyed the fellowship of these friendly, generous people. But the relationship gradually became strained. As faculty leaders, we were encouraging our students to learn to know their Chinese student friends, asking them to share their lives, their values, and their dreams. As we, the faculty leaders, kept pushing for more student interaction, these American Evangelical Christians were praying that our students would be kept safe in this heathen land, protected from all pagan Chinese influences. They prayed that we would not get sick eating Chinese food, and that we would convert the Chinese to the true Christian faith. This approach clashed with our educational goals, and our respect for the Chinese people for whom we were developing a lot of appreciation. We gradually withdrew from these Sunday afternoon worship services.

The China adventure forced me to look at my own faith again. I wanted to know if my faith, which was tightly held and correct in its doctrinal beliefs, kept me untouched by the world, especially a "pagan Chinese world." I asked myself some essential questions. What should I be learning from our Chinese friends? Were our Chinese colleagues able to recognize that my Christian faith was not simply an expression of my American identity? Was I able to make that distinction?

An exciting challenge came when two Chinese English professors asked me to give a series of lectures on the Bible as Christian literature. These professors had been in my Biblical Literature class at Goshen College and had seen the frequent use of biblical words in American life. The Chinese university gave their approval for a series of four consecutive Friday evening lectures in a three hundred seat lecture hall. At first I saw this as a sneaky government conspiracy to make sure that no one would come to hear these lectures! Scheduling a series of Bible lectures on Friday evening would never work at Goshen College. But if I didn't follow through, that would insult our hosts, so I began to prepare the lectures.

I hoped that perhaps twenty-five to thirty students might show up that first evening. As I expected, none of our Goshen College students were interested! They had already taken my Biblical Literature class. At 7:00 p.m. I walked into the hall and discovered there were students everywhere. Every seat was taken; students were standing two-deep all around the edges! They were even sitting on the floor in front of the podium!

I quickly dropped what I was planning to do, pulled my Biblical Literature class notes out of my head, adjusted the language, and began talking about the Bible for *ninety minutes*. No one moved. On the third week, still with a full house, I told the story of Jesus. I explained how Jesus taught the way of peace, calling us to love our enemies. I told them, "I hope China and America never, ever go to war against each other. But if they do, I want you to know that no Goshen College student will ever march down the streets of Chengdu with a gun." I was not prepared for the student response. These normally sedate students jumped to their feet with enthusiastic applause and cheering. I hoped that I had not made a promise future Goshen College students would not keep.

I wondered about many things during those five months in China. Here were compassionate people who were not caught up in competitive capitalism. They helped their neighbors; they were concerned about peace in the world; and often they were as provoked with their government as I was with ours. When a colleague was sick, others in the department took over teaching classes until the person recovered. Families worked together planting community gardens and then shared the produce with older colleagues for whom gardening was physically too taxing.

Isn't this what Micah 6:8 means: "What does the Lord require of you but to do justice, love mercy and walk humbly with your God?" These people were quietly doing what they believed was the right thing to do. Could it be that God is an unconscious presence in their lives? They did not identify God as the driving force in what they were doing. I recognize that. Yet does God walk only with those who call God by a certain name? When we see others as heathen sinners doomed for hell unless we save them, it usually means that we feel compelled to preach judgment at them. But if we believe the good news of Jesus is about the presence of a new kingdom (way of living) where we love, care, feed, and help others, then we invite them to join with us, and together we can work at building bridges of peace and love for all humanity.

I asked myself many times, "How does God see these people? How do I see them?" Indeed, does God judge them to be wrong simply because they have not accepted Western Christian ideas? What does Christian faith offer these intelligent people who are far more concerned about a future for their children on this earth than they are about a future existence in heaven after they die? I listened as they told me they could not accept Christian faith because it is too militaristic, too individualistic, and too materialistic. They told me that Christians are far too quick to go to war to protect their own wealth because they feel they are superior to other people. They saw Christians as selfish people who place their own personal rights above the needs of others. How should I respond, since I share those same concerns? But at the same time, is their understanding of Christian faith a fair representation of what Jesus actually did teach?

Being in China forced me into a time of serious theological reflection. I felt tension from our American Evangelical friends at the JinJiang Hotel who worried about my soft stance on the importance of right Christian beliefs. They were clearly honest, sincere people, but they did not approach faith the same way I did. I also felt internal stress when I talked with my Chinese colleagues because they were rejecting Christian faith for what I felt were the wrong reasons. I came home from China feeling caught in the middle of a theological tug of war about how we believe in Jesus. Can people believe in Jesus without being active, open followers of Jesus? Can people follow the way of Jesus without having correct doctrinal beliefs? Little did I know this was only Act 1 in my existential drama of this unusual year. Act 2 was just around the corner.

Carolyn and I returned to Goshen for two weeks before moving to Boulder, Colorado. Once we settled in Boulder, we plunged into six months of Conflict Mediation Studies at the University of Colorado. Our experiences in China gave living intensity to our conflict studies. Almost everything I heard in class I had just experienced in China. We had lived with centuries-old cultural conflicts and mutually exclusive religious conflicts, all of which had strong political overtones. It was though we had done our field work first and now our classroom studies were helping us understand what we had been learning. After five months of stimulating study and internship work at Boulder, we left for Russia and the Ukraine.

As a college history major I was fascinated by Russian Mennonite history. Some Russian Mennonite farmers and business persons had become quite wealthy before the Russian Revolution. Their lands were seized, and they were driven from their homes in the early 1920s. This led to massive migrations from Russia to the U.S. Great Plains, to Canada, and to Paraguay. I wanted to visit the Ukranian colonies of Molotschna and Chortitza where these migrations originated.

Our Eli Lilly education grant specifically included international travel to the Soviet Union. Carolyn and I planned for a week in Moscow and a second week in Kiev. Soviet-American Homestays arranged for us to live with local families, rather than stay in hotels. In Moscow, we were guests of Slava and Natasha Feschenko and their son Alex, a college student. Then in Kiev, we lived with Leon and Natalia Shamhalova and their eight-year-old daughter, Maria.

Our week with the Shamhalovas was a profound spiritual experience in dramatically unexpected ways. Leon was an environmental engineer and a leader in the Kiev Peace Movement. I was amazed to learn that there was such an organization. Natalia was a professor of business at a local Kiev university and was equally committed to peacemaking. They were surprised and delighted to discover our own active commitment to peace, especially since we were Americans.

Natalia's mother was a Christian. When Natalia told her about their American visitors, she casually mentioned that I was a pastor. This brought much delight to her mother. In contrast, Natalia told us of their neighbor who had called the day before we arrived, warning her, "If you have anything valuable that you do not want the Americans to steal, you can keep those things in our apartment until they leave." We were in for a very interesting week.

Natalia and Leon were marvelous hosts, but we were quickly drawn to them by the way they cared for others. One afternoon we came back to the apartment to discover the delicious smell of stew coming from the kitchen. I lifted the lid on the pot only to have Natalia playfully slap my fingers. "That's not for you." She then explained: "Our neighbor down the hall has been taken to the hospital, and everybody knows her husband can't cook a thing. Their three children will starve if they have to depend on him. I've got the whole floor organized, so they will have a hot supper each evening for the next week. Tonight is my turn." I was impressed. I wondered if Natalia knew about the little boy who shared his five loaves and two fishes with Jesus so that others could eat?

On another day, five young children were playing in the apartment. When I asked Natalia about them, she replied: "These children live in this building. They get out of school at 3:30, but their parents don't get home from work until 6:00. They don't have any place to go, and I don't think small children should be running the streets, so they come here two afternoons a week. I give them a snack and help them with their homework. Other families in the building take care of them on the other days. The parents will be here about 6:15 to pick them up. Supper for us will be a little bit late this evening." Without thinking I asked, "Do the parents pay you for doing this?" Natalia turned and looked at me as if I had just dropped in from Mars—or maybe Chicago! "Pay me? Why would they do that? They're children!" Jesus once said, "Allow the little children to come to me and don't chase them away, they are important in the kingdom of God" (Luke 18:16). I wondered if Natalia knew about that Bible verse?

The most energizing times were later each evening when friends dropped in to visit. Natalia's faculty colleagues from the university and Leon's friends from work came for tea and cookies, plus vodka for those who wanted it. All of them spoke fairly good English and they stayed for hours of delightful conversation. We talked about work, about economics, and about family life. Always, the subject of religion came up. They wondered why someone with a PhD would believe in God. Carolyn and I shared how we experience God; how the teachings of Jesus are the foundation of our faith; and how our faith is expressed more in the life we live than in specific doctrines that we believe. Their interest was high, their questions were excellent, and the intensity of the conversation stayed strong. It was always after midnight before the group went home.

On the final evening, a slightly larger than usual group gathered; all of them had been there before. It was an emotional evening as we talked about the stereotypical views that our two nations had of each other. All of us were interested in how we might improve relationships between the American and Russian people. We focused particularly on faculty exchange options that would involve our academic communities.

Late in the evening, the subject of religion came up again. One couple said, "Dr. Blosser, there is a one bedroom apartment open in this building. We will furnish it for you. Why don't you stay here? We'll get a group together each week, and let's talk about God. Would you do that?"

Wow! How do you answer that? I had never been asked to do that before. There was just no way we could stay. We had five children in Goshen. I had a job. We had no work visa for the Ukraine. It was emotionally taxing to say, "Thank you, but we can't!"

I wondered whether Natalia knew the story about Lydia and the early Christians who met at her house where Paul told them about Jesus? I have often wondered whether we could have stayed. Would the Mission Board have approved? Would Goshen College have given me a leave of absence? Would College Mennonite (our home church) have been willing to support us? How would our college-age children respond? Who would pay the mortgage on our house? Was this, like hearing President Burkholder at Mennonite General Assembly in Eureka, Illinois, ten years before, another way that God was nudging us to take a new step of faith? I had always wanted to serve with Mennonite Central Committee (MCC) or with Teachers Abroad, yet now that I was being asked, I had to say I couldn't do it.

It was after 2 a.m. when the group broke up that evening. We were all in tears as we hugged each other, received kisses on both cheeks, and said our good-byes. It was a spiritual, God-present experience that was faith shaping for me. We had gone to the Soviet Union expecting to learn about its culture and people. I was not expecting to be immersed in God's love and presence, especially not with a group of teachers and scientists who were all members of the Ukranian Communist Party. I have often wondered: If we had accepted their gracious invitation, how might life have been different for them and for us?

That experience continues to stay with me. Leon and Natalia cared for children and neighbors simply because they believed it was the right thing to do. My mother did these same things because of her commitment to Jesus as Lord. Is there a difference in how God sees Leon and Natalia as compared with my mother? Are not Leon and Natalia equally loved by God? Or must one be a Christian in order for God to love you? Paul says that when people who don't have the law yet instinctively do what the law requires, it is just as though they have the law written on their hearts (Rom 2:14). Matthew tells us that God welcomes those who feed the hungry, visit the sick, and clothe the naked, even though they are not thinking about God as they do it (Matt 25:37–40). I cannot exclude persons like Leon and Natalia from the family of God simply because they do not confess Jesus as Lord as a theological concept.

It is exciting to note that after twenty-two years, we have reestablished contact with Leon, Natalia, and their daughter Maria through e-mail and Facebook. The recovery of this relationship was instantly positive, and Natalia extended an invitation for us to visit them again. She promised that if we come, she would gather people together to continue our conversation. An invitation like that cannot be ignored. Since we have a daughter living in Germany, it made perfect sense to combine a family visit with a "Kiev-family" visit to relive and reestablish this relationship. We returned to Kiev in 2011, shared a long weekend with Leon, Natalia, Maria (who is now thirty and has two children of her own), and her husband Sasha. The warmth and joy with which we were received had not changed. We continue to have much in common in what we believe and how we choose to live.

Theologian Karl Rahner provides a positive perspective in understanding the Shamhalovas. He has written that membership in the kingdom of God is not identical with denominational allegiance. Drawing from Matthew 25, Rahner properly indicates that orthodox doctrinal beliefs do not always lead to Christlike living. He wants us to recognize the existence of Christlike persons who are not traditional believers. He refers to them as "Anonymous Christians." These persons are near to God but are not consciously aware of it. They are entering the kingdom of God using roads that are not always clearly marked on traditional theological roadmaps. (Rahner, *Rahner in Dialogue*, p. 135.)

My life is enriched by persons like Leon and Natalia. Certainly God's grace and acceptance is much broader than my own limited ability to comprehend it. Is Christian faith best defined by orthodox creedal confessions? Or is faith best expressed in a life of mercy and grace? We are quick to divide the world's population into "sheep vs. goats; us vs. them; friends vs. enemies." But when we establish these arbitrary divisions, we lose sight of the biblical truth that God's love extends to all human beings regardless of political boundaries, social or racial distinctions, or even religious allegiances. How different might the world be if we could see people through the eyes of God, or relate to them with the love of Jesus? We might truly be surprised by the unusual settings in which we find God.

When Did God Become a Christian?

Christians have always been divided over how we should relate to persons who are members of other world religions. Most Christians believe that if you are not Christian, you cannot be saved. Therefore adherents of other religions are on their way to hell unless they convert to faith in Jesus. This assumes that the primary purpose of Christian faith is to provide salvation so that, when persons die, they will be received into heaven to be with God. Without denying the belief that the soul continues on with God after death, I find myself questioning whether this reflects the essence of Christian faith. I see in Paul the assurance that "now is the day of salvation" (2 Cor 6:2). I see in the teachings of Jesus an emphasis upon the kingdom of God as a present reality in which we live as persons committed to the new way of God. And, in so doing, I recognize a connection between how we are "in Christ" right now as we follow Jesus and how this impacts our eternal destiny.

Christianity, for me, has gradually shifted from being a cognitive, doctrinal set of beliefs to being an incarnational, living response. This approach recognizes that God is far more encompassing than any human being can fully comprehend. For me, Jesus is central for my faith. But I no longer insist that Jesus is the only way people can discover the love of God. My commitment is clearly to Jesus as Lord, but I have seen too many situations where persons do not organize their beliefs exactly as I do, yet their lives reflect a desire to be merciful, loving, and caring in their relationships with other people.

Paul faced this same issue at Ephesus. There was a group who believed only they knew the truth about Jesus, and unless people believed exactly as they did, those people had no hope of salvation. They said that only they had the secret knowledge needed to escape from this world and enter into the heavenly realms where God dwells. As we read in Ephesians 1:3–14, Paul reacted with a series of strong "we" and "us" statements declaring that all the blessings of the heavenlies have come to us here in Jesus, and we all have access to them.

If God is all-powerful (something most exclusive believers insist upon), then certainly God has the power and the freedom to reach out to all humanity, using any method that God chooses to use. I would prefer to work alongside these people to bring food, shelter, healing, hope, and peace (plus all the other things that Jesus talked about) to a suffering world, rather than fight among ourselves over who is most loved by God.

Conservative Christians often use John 14:6 as the authoritative text declaring the exclusive nature of Christian faith. I continue to believe that Jesus provides an accurate understanding of the nature of God as he calls us to live as God's people in God's new way right here on earth. In that sense, I continue to proclaim Jesus as the way, the truth, and the life. But these are living expressions and not doctrinal requirements. We have been taught that God is love. Therefore, it would be theologically appropriate for us to also say that wherever love is, God is there, truth is shared, and life is lived fully. This sees the life and teachings of Jesus as being inclusive of all who seek truth and who desire to walk in the ways of wholeness and peace with all humanity.

I know that this is not exactly what my parents taught me. But respectfully, I want to do as Paul suggested: There are many things that I did as a child that I no longer do (or believe) because I have become an adult and I now see God in new ways. We can only go so far with human wisdom, with prophetic ideas, or linguistic utterances. However, love outlasts each of these ways of communicating. Love never ends. I want to share this never-ending love with all humanity, inviting them to join with me in creating a new world where all people experience and share this love with each other.

The Columbus Mennonite Church sits on the edge of the Ohio State University campus. They have a multinational congregation with persons who have strong connections with other world religions. What does it mean to be clear and forthright in our identity as a Christian church in a specific Christian tradition? Can a Christian church retain its faith while reaching out to other people in open, inviting conversation that respects diversity of faith, yet emphasizes and honors Jesus as the center?

This congregation invited me to share a Sunday with them and help them explore a better understanding of the place of Christianity in a multifaith, multicultural setting. What does Jesus call us to be as we share life with persons whose understanding of faith and God is not identical with our own? Can people live faithful, responsive, Godly lives without having us Christians demand that they accept Christian doctrines and structures? Does the recognition that God is far greater than any human understanding mean that we dare to open our minds to new vistas of God's presence and love in our world?

The words of Jesus to the Pharisees have always troubled me: "You travel over land and sea to win a single convert, and when he becomes one, you make him twice as much a son of hell as you are." (Matt 23:15).

Might some of us still be functioning as Pharisees as we attempt to convert people to a religious way of thinking that no longer captures the spirit and message of Jesus?

The following sermon is an attempt to explore the biblical message with a broader, open understanding of God's grace and human responses.

* * *

When Did God Become a Christian?

My mother was truly a delightful person. I would be on my way out the door to catch the school bus when she would grab me by the shoulder. "One more thing," she would say. "Remember, after school, make sure you get your sweater that you forgot to bring home yesterday so that I can wash it." Her final words drove home the importance of what she was saying—"Donny, now don't forget!"

According to Matthew, the last words of Jesus to his disciples were, "All authority in heaven and on earth has been given to me. So, I am telling you to go and make disciples everywhere, baptize them and teach them to do everything I have told you to do. And I will be with you wherever you go."[3] It is interesting to note that the last words of Jesus to the disciples are not about what they are supposed to believe, but rather what Jesus wants them to do.

God's intentions are a constant theme throughout the Scriptures. It starts with the call of Abraham and the formation of a community. This community is called to share with the whole world the good news that God is a God of peace, health, and wholeness. This call does not give Abraham status, it simply entrusts him with this message of God's concern for all humanity.

Throughout the Old Testament, this theme on how humanity might live together appears again and again. Israel had been liberated from slavery in Egypt. As they began reshaping their identity, they were reminded five times in Leviticus 25, "I am the Lord your God who brought you out of Egypt." Each statement of God's grace for Israel is followed by a social, ethical, or economic guideline on how Israel was to organize their life together, and how they were to treat other people.

---

3. See Matthew 28:20.

Over the next several hundred years, Israel began to assume that because God had chosen Abraham, and God had liberated them from Egypt, they must have the most-favored-nation status with God. But Amos offered a corrective to that point of view. "The Cushites are as important to me as you Israelites. Yes I brought you out of Egypt, but I also brought the Philistines out of Caphtor, and Arameans out of the land of Kir."[4] We must note that the Cushites, Arameans, and Philistines were nations who had been tormenting Israel. How could God also save them?

Years later Israel once again found itself in an identity crisis. In exasperation, the people asked the prophet Micah, "What does God expect of us?" They believed that if they could find out what God wanted, they could do it and God would bless them. So Micah told them: "What does the Lord *require* of you? Act with kindness, love mercy, and walk humbly with your God"[5]

Isaiah added his voice: "Nations will say, let us go to the house of the God of Jacob, that we may learn his ways and walk in his paths. Out of Zion will come the Word of the Lord. They shall beat their swords into plowshares and their spears into pruning hooks. Nation will not lift up sword against nation, neither shall they learn war any more."[6]

Consistently, throughout Israel's history, this message of God's love for all nations continues to be at the center of their faith. Whenever the people of Israel asked how they could best serve God, the response was that they were to be a living model of God's salvation, love, and compassion.

In Jesus, salvation is a dynamic experience that is to be shared by all humanity. It is not the blessing of privileged status that is given to a select few. The ministry of Jesus fulfills this vision of God. This dream, found in Abraham, Moses, Isaiah, and Micah, becomes the touchstone for everything Jesus said and did.

The biblical message emphasizes the importance of God's dream for shalom. When the Old Testament prophets called people to be converted, they were not talking about other nations converting to Jewish faith. When the Bible talks about conversion, it is not conversion from one religious faith to another faith. It is the call to leave the ways of sin and walk in the paths of righteousness. The Jesus message of conversion

4. See Amos 9:7.
5. See Micah 6:8.
6. See Isaiah 2:3–4.

does not mean telling Muslims they must stop being Muslim and become Christian. It does not mean that Jewish people must reject their faith and accept our faith. The Jesus call is to be godlike in all that we do—to do justice, love mercy, and walk humbly with our God. That message is directed at Christian people every bit as much as it is aimed at any other religious people.

How then does this theme of salvation fit into the ministry of Jesus? Mark 1:14–15 tells us, "Jesus went into Galilee, proclaiming the good news of God." And how did Jesus define the good news of God? He said, in effect: "The time has come, the kingdom of God is near. Change how you live—repent—and believe this good news." This is what Jesus said as he went about preaching the gospel. "There is a new way of living, right now. We urge you to invite others to join in making this new way of living a reality for all humanity." This is a universal call for peace, caring for the poor, feeding the hungry, setting prisoners free, and thus redeeming all people everywhere.

In the New Testament gospels, Jesus stays firmly with this message. He is not calling us to convert other people to our theological system. Jesus calls us to a new way of living (even within our own religious system). He fed the hungry, he healed the sick, he offered hope to the poor, and he reached out to those who were excluded. He teaches us a whole new way of thinking about war, about wealth and power, about being male and female.

The world's problem with Christianity is not with the message of Jesus—it is with people like us, Christians. The problem is what we do (or don't do) with Jesus. The good news has become God's promise of eternal life, given to us when we die. For millions of people this does not sound like good news. If you are not one of the select, privileged few, this is bad news. It often validates the harsh treatment given to others by people who claim to be saved and blessed by God. The good news of Jesus calls us to reach out (not push away), to knock down walls (not build them), to feed people (not kill them), to give ourselves for others (not sacrifice others to save ourselves).

There are fascinating stories in the New Testament of people who came to Jesus asking about salvation and how they might be saved. This question of personal, spiritual salvation has become a critical focus for much of contemporary Christian thinking. "How can we be saved for heaven when we die?" It is helpful to see how Jesus addressed those questions. The question is similar, but the answers are quite different.

In our world, the answer usually is this: "If you believe that Jesus was the Son of God and that he died for your sins, you will be saved." This puts the focus of Christian faith on correct doctrinal beliefs. There are biblical texts that can be used to support that answer. But that is not the answer Jesus gave. Jesus responded by calling these questioners to love God with enthusiasm, and to love others the way you love yourself. The sixteenth-century Anabaptist leader Hans Landis said: "We believe . . . in what Christ taught and did."[7] I wish we could rediscover a faith that bases our salvation *in Jesus*, rather than in what Rome did *to Jesus*.

Luke 10:25–37 tells the story of an expert in the law who came to Jesus asking about his relationship with God. Jesus asked what he thought. The man quoted the law: "Love God, love your neighbor." The response of Jesus is very important: "You are right. Do this and you will live." Now hear that carefully: It is *not* "do this and when you die, you will have eternal life in heaven." It is simply "you will live." This is the Jesus message of salvation. It is a life we are invited to participate in: experiencing God's grace and affirmation. We are invited to respond with truth, love, grace, and peace for all people.

For years Christians have been taught that God calls us to convert other people to Christian doctrines of faith. Jesus was critical of religious systems that focused on right belief and rigid, separatist ethics as the path to godliness. This put him in almost constant conflict with the Pharisees. Their emphasis upon right doctrinal beliefs and strict separatist behavior denied the emphasis Jesus placed on loving your neighbor, healing the sick, feeding the hungry, or visiting those who are in prison. When we place our hope for salvation in right doctrine and pure separation from sinners, we are rejecting virtually everything Jesus said and did during his ministry. If we are committed to being the people of Jesus, then our call for conversion focuses not on religious identity, but on God's mission of peace, hope, justice, and mercy.

Our local Jewish rabbi is a friend of mine. He comes with his commitment to Torah. I come with my commitment to Jesus. We have become brothers in our common faith in God. We talk together about God, about faith, about caring for people who are hurting, about peace, and forgiveness. We tease each other a bit. He thinks I would make an excellent rabbi. I tell him he would make a good Mennonite scholar. We are

7. Roth, *Beliefs*, pg. 19.

each committed to God. We are also delighted to be friends who see no reason to convert each other.

Does Jesus want us to follow him so that someday the world will be full of Christians? Or is Jesus inviting us to commit ourselves to God, and then join with other people who are also in step with God (even from other traditions) in expressing God's love for all people here on earth? Loving God, and loving your neighbor! Isn't that what salvation and God's love is all about?

What does this do to our assumptions about eternal life? We believe that God is present all around us right now. When a person dies, they continue to be in that comforting presence of God. Death changes how I relate to you and the events of this life, but it does *not* change how I relate to God. When we die, we continue to be in the presence of God. This relationship with God is enriched, heightened, and multiplied because we are freed from the limiting restraints of our humanity. I believe the same God who is with me right now will be with me in that experience also. I am fully prepared to trust God for however and wherever that experience with God takes place for me. In the meantime I want to live my life as fully as possible.

Jesus calls us to live fully, completely, and generously, with excitement in a life that is shared with others. We see this new way of life modeled for us in the life and teachings of Jesus. I want to share the joys of living without first having to check whether others are conservative or progressive Christian, or Muslim, or Jewish. My calling as a Christian is not to judge others who do not believe like I do. My calling is to find ways for us to join together in caring for the poor, the hungry, the widows, and the children of this world.

The meaning of mission for Christian people is not to tell Muslims they have to become Christians or tell Jewish people that they must join a Christian church. Jesus made it clear with the Pharisees that God has no interest in simply creating more children of Abraham. If God wanted that, God could make children of Abraham out of the rocks.[8] What God wants is not more Christians who sit in church, sing hymns, and support the church budget. God wants people who are committed to sharing mercy, grace, and truth with whoever needs it. A familiar quote from the sixteenth-century Anabaptist leader Hans Denck, makes exactly this

8. See Luke 3:8.

point: "No one can truly know Christ except one who follows him in life."[9]

That sounds like Matthew 25. People are standing before the throne of God. Some are invited in, others are turned away. The striking part of this story in Matthew is that their religious identities are never mentioned. The focus is on their acts of mercy and compassion for others. Those who are invited in were not even aware they had doing anything special. They had acted because it felt like the right, human thing to do, and God blessed them for doing it.

In this same spirit, Jesus once told the disciples that he had other sheep who were not of this fold (in other words, not Jewish). The disciples were bewildered, and the Pharisees were furious. This idea that only they could be right was deeply entrenched in their beliefs, just as it is for many Christians today. But this did not seem to be how Jesus saw other people.

What mattered for Jesus was not a distinction that separated religious traditions from each other because only one tradition can be right. The separation that Jesus spoke of grows not out of differences in how we structure our theological identity, but out of faithfulness to God in how we live. It grows out of the compassion we show for the hungry, the lonely, and the sick. Entry into the presence of God is not validated by religious orthodoxy, but by acts of mercy, grace, and compassion—of God for us, and of us for each other.

The call to mercy and compassion throughout the Scriptures is clearly anchored in knowing that God loves us. But we are not the only ones whom God loves. Jesus calls us to trust in God's love for us, and then to share that love with others in transforming acts of mercy, grace, and peace. When we do that, we are showing the world that we truly have experienced the presence of God in our own lives.

What might happen if, instead of seeing others as persons who need to be converted to our religious way of thinking, our days might be filled with acts of mercy, deeds of kindness, and expressions of love so that others can honestly say, "I have felt the presence of God today."

9. Roth, *Beliefs*, pg. 27.

What Kind of Faith Is This, That Offers New Life?

In my childhood home, we had a picture of the two disciples walking on the road to Emmaus. That picture fascinated me. I would sit in the living room and look at that picture. For me, it had a special mystical quality. I often wondered what it was like for these men walking home from Jerusalem. Who were they? What had their life been like? What would it have done to them, to have lived through this last week as persons who were there when Jesus was tried and crucified? Especially when there was nothing they could do about it? What would it be like to have your dreams shattered and have something that you had worked on for several years taken away from you?

This story of Cleopas and his friend (Luke 24) began to grow on me. It has become my favorite story in all the New Testament. If there is anyone that I envy in the biblical narrative, it is Cleopas and his friend, getting a lecture in Old Testament Christology from Jesus himself as they walked along the road.

As a child growing up, I was taught the story of the resurrection and how important it was to believe that it really happened just like it says in the gospels. I remember resurrection was something that happened to Jesus. This made him very special, different from all the rest of humanity. I don't remember ever thinking about whether resurrection could be a possibility for me or anyone else in the world. That was an event reserved only for Jesus.

Dr. Howard H. Charles taught New Testament at Associated Mennonite Biblical Seminary. He was the best teacher I ever had. It was from him that I learned to read the biblical stories in a new way. He taught Inductive Bible Study in a way that allowed the Scriptures to come alive in the classroom—and in those inductive studies that we had to do each week. He challenged us to see people in these biblical stories as real human beings struggling with life much like we do.

He wanted us to see these stories as more than simply historical narratives about ancient events. He urged us to get inside the stories, to explore their reality and to feel what they were feeling so that we could discover what the story means in our own lives. He told us that we could not really preach on a biblical story until we had lived that story in our own lives.

So I went back to Luke 24 and walked with these two on the road to Emmaus, looking over their shoulder, sharing their questions, excited about discovering new answers, and eager to tell others what I had found: Resurrection is more than a doctrine to be believed, it is a way of life to be lived!

* * *

What Kind of Faith Is This, That Offers New Life?[10]

They had reason to be sad. Their best friend, and teacher, was dead. And memories can be emotionally draining. Now there was nothing left to do but go home and try to start over As they walked, they talked about how it had been for them over the past three years. They remembered how Jesus had held the crowds spellbound as he talked about God. They smiled as they remembered how the children would climb all over him, begging for a story. He was the best storyteller they had ever heard. They remembered how for so many people just a few minutes with him seemed to help them discover new hope for the day.

Sadly, their memories brought them back again to last week. It was such a paradox. How could someone committed to loving and caring about people be treated with such hatred? Why do people do that? What's wrong with us?

They remembered how they had seen the storm clouds gathering in the distance. They all had this feeling that something was going to happen. Everyone was hoping that finally, after all these centuries, God was going to establish his reign here on earth. Then, for perhaps the hundredth time, their pace slowed as they thought back, and the sound of the mob started ringing in their ears all over again, "Crucify him—Kill him!" How could people do that? Why wouldn't anybody listen?

And now he is dead. Has been dead for three days. They remembered the sudden surge of hope when, just this morning, several women came to them and told them that the tomb was empty. He was risen, they said, he wasn't dead any more. They had seen an angel at the tomb.

These had been difficult days for everyone. They had all been under terrible strain, and their grief had led these women to have hallucinations. But several men had gone to check it out. What they found only added more pain to an already unbearable situation. The tomb was empty! Now, who would be so cruel that they would steal a dead body? What is this

10. The biblical foundation for this sermon is Luke 24:13–35.

world coming to? He is dead. But not only is he dead, his body is gone, and a new wave of shame and grief swept over them.

Hearing footsteps, they glanced quickly at each other with a look of warning. The Sanhedrin had spies everywhere. You simply could not be too careful about what you said in public. Soon, a stranger caught up and fell in stride with them. They began to visit. There was something familiar about him. Maybe it was the way he walked with a comfortable, easy stride, or the way he seemed to take an honest interest in what they were talking about.

Sensing their sadness, the stranger asked, "What's wrong? We've just come through the feast days; it was a great celebration." And before they knew it, they were pouring their hearts out to this stranger. They were telling him about all the pain and grief they had been through as their world had come crashing down around them. For several miles they talked, until they reached their home. When they invited the stranger to come in and stay with them, he replied that he really couldn't; he had promised to meet some friends in Galilee the next day. But Cleopas urged him to stop at least for supper, so they could continue their conversation. This man had the most amazing grasp of the Scriptures.

As they sat at the table, rather than wait for the host to offer the standard ritual prayer for the evening bread, the stranger prayed a very simple, beautiful prayer—as though God were right there in the room with them. Then he reached for the bread and began to break it, giving each of them a piece. Suddenly, Cleopas knew. He sat there dumbfounded, unable to believe what he was seeing. The way he prayed, the way he broke bread. He had seen that before. It was exactly the way Jesus had done it when he fed the five thousand. The Bible tells us that their eyes were opened, and their most fantastic dreams had come true. They saw that it was Jesus sitting right there across the table from them. But before they could recover and say anything, Jesus was gone and they were alone.

These two men immediately jumped up and ran the seven miles back to Jerusalem to tell the disciples what they had just seen. And as they ran, they remembered how good it felt when he explained what Isaiah meant, and what Moses was talking about, and how the prophets should be understood.

The resurrection, or at least the transformation of life for Cleopas and his friend, is a bit less dramatic than was the resurrection of Jesus—unless of course, you are Cleopas. This event gives us wonderful insight into the meaning of resurrection for ourselves.

Can you image what it must have felt like to be with Cleopas and his friend? They heard this seminar in Old Testament theology, and then discovered that their world had not really fallen apart. So many people are willing to stand around the doorway of the tomb, asking each other, "How did he do that? Where do you suppose he is?" And for them the resurrection becomes a theological concept to talk about, rather than a reality to be lived.

Or are we like Peter? We get word that the tomb is empty, and wanting to know for sure, because we don't trust the women, we go to see for ourselves. We find that it is true. The tomb is empty, so what do we do? We go home and think about it. Or like the twelve, once the excitement wears off, we go back to the old patterns of living. Figuratively speaking, we go fishing, too.

Several years ago I was in Colorado Springs, Colorado, at the Rocky Mountain Conference. One evening, as I was going into the Beth-El Mennonite Church, I was overwhelmed with the beauty of the sun going down behind a snow-covered Pike's Peak in the distance. It was absolutely gorgeous. We don't see that very often in Goshen. I stopped and stared, "Wow! That's fantastic!" A friend, walking beside me, looked at me and asked, "what is?" I just pointed at the mountain, because words to describe that level of creation magnificence didn't come easy. "Oh, that," he said. "Out here we call that a sunset, happens every day. Come on, we're late."

Maybe that is what is happening to each of us. We see the mountain every day, and we watch the sun go down every night. We talk about the empty tomb every Easter, and we no longer think much about it. *Of course the tomb is empty!* What did you expect? It ruins the story if the tomb is not empty!

For Christians, the resurrection of Jesus is more than just a powerful doctrine. It is God's stamp of approval on everything that Jesus said and did. Without the resurrection, Jesus goes down in history as another in a long tradition of great teachers. Have you ever thought about it? Why are you so sure that following Jesus puts us back in relationship with God? How do you know that what Jesus taught is really what God wants you to know? The resurrection! That is our affirmation that Jesus was telling the truth—about himself, about God, and about what God is trying to do in the world.

For the Christian, the resurrection is an invitation to new life. Romans 8:11 tells us "when the Spirit of God who raised up Christ Jesus from the dead lives in you, God will, by that same spirit, bring to your whole being new strength and vitality." Christians often need help in accepting the possibility of new life for themselves. People who hold tenaciously to the doctrine of the resurrection of Jesus sometimes have real difficulty seeing how resurrection happens in their own lives. What a tragedy it is when yesterday's failure is allowed to program our lives for tomorrow!

How much of the ministry of Jesus was used in helping other people find new life? Jesus refused to allow the lame man to continue in the passivity of begging; he called him to a new life of walking. Jesus refused to allow Zacchaeus the luxury of cheating people on their taxes; he invited him into the new world of honesty and generosity, where people are friends and not potential bank accounts. Jesus refused to allow the woman caught in adultery to be judged and condemned by others; he sent her off in the direction of purity and holiness where she could live in dignity with herself and with others. Everywhere Jesus went, he left behind him a trail of persons who had been resurrected to new life.

How can we, living nearly two thousand years later, still meet Jesus and have our own experience of new life and resurrection? Two very simple things show up in this story. The first of these happened to them, and they remembered it as they ran back to Jerusalem. What would have happened if these two persons, when Jesus asked them what they were talking about, they had kept their pain and sorrow to themselves and would have said, "Oh, nothing really, it's just been a long day." Now I am not in favor of having you walk down the street, pouring out your heart to every stranger you meet. But I do believe that God is present with us as we share together, so it is important for us to have persons with whom we can confide. It can be a small group, or a good friend, or another couple who will listen and help us through our times of stress without being judgmental. We are not alone. Each of us needs others who will walk along the way with us. I believe, as that happens, God is with us in special ways.

The second is a reflection on the comment that we often hear: All you have to do is believe." I find it very interesting that the two men recognized Jesus as they shared their bread with him. We talk a lot about how God is present with us as we give food to the hungry, clothes to the naked, and shelter to the homeless. It is so easy to look for the presence of Jesus in the glamorous places on earth; but for these two persons, they discovered Jesus when they sat down at a kitchen table. Maybe that will be where others find Jesus with you as well.

Don't ever let the resurrection become just another theological doctrine that you are supposed to believe. Allow the resurrection to become a way of life, experienced as the power of God's love flowing through you to others. I want to suggest three very simple ways in which the resurrection of Jesus can put meaning and hope into our own lives:

1. Because of the resurrection, let's remember that God loves us—even when we are not very lovable.[11] In the death of Jesus we see that kind of love being demonstrated. Let's renew our pledge to be people of the resurrection. Let's become God's reconcilers in a world that is far too eager to get involved in war, hatred, hostility, and violence as methods of controlling other people. In Jesus, we discover God's way of love, so let's be people of peace. We can do this because, in Christ, we have discovered the power of loving another person so much that you would give yourself for them.

2. Because of the resurrection, let's intentionally be more aware of the many ways in which God comes to us, talking with us, sharing with us, and accepting us. Let's look for the presence of God in the very common daily experiences of life. Let's start every encounter by expecting to experience God's spirit in this conversation, in this time together, in this person. That will help us be more open, more accepting, and more understanding of others as we share this planet, and this community. This means that we will slow down just a bit. We will become more willing to put aside our hurried pace of important tasks. We will listen, cry, celebrate, or just be a friend to someone who would love to be listened to, and cared for, or held—if only for a moment or two.

3. Because of the resurrection, let's each commit ourselves to be more conscious of God's love for us. Then we can respect and honor our own lives, our own opportunities, our own dreams. If we do that, I believe we will be more open to share with others, and to ask for help from others. We will do better at listening to others, and we will be more open with others. If we trust that God is with us, we might do better at believing God is also with you.

Recently, a volunteer church worker from Western Scotland burst upon the world through the British TV program *Britain's Got Talent*. Susan Boyle, a most unpretentious forty-seven-year-old woman, impressed

11. See Romans 5:10.

no one as she walked out on stage. But then she began to sing. And as Susan sang, an unexpected change came over the judges. Their mouths dropped, their eyes got big, and the whole audience erupted with joyful amazement and enthusiasm. Even notoriously tough, hostile Simon Cowell leaned back, began to smile, and slowly shook his head in wonder. I saw in that moment a model of resurrection power. Can we see beyond initial outward appearances and experience the depths of one's spirit and the joy of God's presence coming at us in ways we had never expected.

It might just be that the resurrection will burst in upon us, and this discovery will open us up to others so that we will delight in walking together, sharing life, knowing that God is on the road with us. And because of that, we just may never be the same again either.

The Futile Walls of History: "Great—Hadrian—Berlin—Theology"

Assembly Mennonite Church was planning a series on the book of Romans. They invited me to introduce this study with a series of sermons. As I read Romans again I was reminded of a series of problems that Paul spoke to because they were dividing the congregation. This is to say, I was reminded of Paul's counsel in its context, which is a specific set of instructions for a particular congregation. In order to understand Paul's message in this way, we must understand the history and the first-century experience of this small congregation at Rome. We must do this because only then can we apply Paul's message to our own situation.

I recognize that this approach gives more authority to Paul as writer and does not emphasize the literal "eternal voice of God" in the text as much as some might prefer. Yet orthodox Christian faith has always viewed God's role in the inspiration of Scripture as being in and through the writer. If we place a writing of Paul's alongside a writing of Peter's, a careful reader will quickly recognize which writer belongs with which writing. To separate the writer and the first-century life of the congregation from the counsel that is given does significant damage to the message.

As I focused on these ideas, I was fascinated to discover that the issues Paul saw in the congregation at Rome are still present with us today, and they are as divisive now as they were then. Thus, it was not difficult to apply the counsel of Paul for the first-century church at Rome to this twenty-first-century congregation in Goshen, Indiana. The times have changed, but the issues remain the same.

Assembly Mennonite Church has a significant number of college and seminary students (plus teachers from all across the educational spectrum), so this audience quickly understood the themes presented in the following sermon. Nonetheless, some members were surprised at the ease with which twenty-first-century applications were found in a first-century text. The sermon did serve as a springboard for a lively follow-up discussion of what a faithful, ethical response to the gospel would look like. There were questions about how we got to where we are today. People wondered how we might continue to move forward when it is so commonly accepted that our current position is the correct, most faithful one for the church. In the same way, readers might wonder how we help the church look at itself, and its walls, without raising undue fears and concerns that any change from where we are might mean a loss of what is right and true.

* * *

The Futile Walls of History: "Great—Hadrian—Berlin—Theology"[12]

There have been many times in history when people have felt threatened by other nations or by other cultures within their own nation. People frequently responded to these threats by building a wall. I have walked the Great Wall of China. It was an impressive experience. This wall is a magnificent structure that stretches for miles over the hills and mountains of northern China. This wall claims to be wide enough that a four horse team can be driven on it. Having walked this wall with its narrow steps, I do not see how any horse could handle it. But this wall is, nonetheless, an impressive structure. By contrast, Hadrian's Wall in the north of England is significantly less impressive. Our children took great delight in jumping over this famous wall that was built to protect England from the dreaded infidels of Scotland. This wall shares a certain kinship with the Berlin Wall, which was a hurriedly constructed, ugly cement block wall that for a short time effectively defined people as being either in or out.

These walls, different in appearance and location, were all built with the same objective: to save one set of humans from another set. When you look at them today, they appear to be an exercise in futility. Their only lasting value is as a tourist attraction. But don't be too hard on those historic cultures for their commitment to wall building. We are still building walls—in Israel, in Northern Ireland, and in Arizona. Each wall is intended to protect us from persons who are, in some perceived way, different from us.

That brings us to the theological walls of history. I wonder if these theological walls are any more effective than those physical walls? We invest great energy in building them. They work for a while, some longer than others. But, someday, will people look at these walls and wonder what our world view was? Will they ask what it was that we were so afraid of?

---

12. The biblical foundation for this sermon is Romans 1:1–6; 5:1–11.

From Robert Frost: "Before I built a wall I'd ask to know what I was walling in or walling out, and to whom I was likely to give offence. Something there is that doesn't love a wall."[13]

But when we are builders of the wall, wall building makes great sense. This wall is going to save us from danger and protect us and our way of thinking from the evils that lurk just outside our wall. If we only have this wall, certainly we will sleep better at night.

Usually, we read Paul's letters to find God's counsel for us. We focus on the words and pay little attention to the person of Paul or the culture of the church in Rome. How did the events in Rome shape what Paul wrote? How might what is happening in our lives today affect the way we read what Paul wrote two thousand years ago? What would happen if we read Romans as a letter to a specific congregation, rather than as a theological treatise for all Christians living in all places throughout all history?

Christianity had spread to Rome at least a decade before Paul got there. We know that in the year 49, Claudius expelled the Jews from Rome, including Jewish Christians. Five years later, Claudius was dead. These Christians were now returning to Rome, only to discover a religious community that was very different from the one they had left only five or six years before. This new group had no pastor that we know of. They had no creed, no New Testament, no Sunday school, no special places of worship. They returned to moral and religious values that had slipped quite badly. Paul knew only a few of them, whom he identified by name, in what is now chapter 16 of the book of Romans.

We also need to remember that Paul was doing theology as he wrote. There were no gospel accounts for him to cite as supporting authority for what he said. Instead, Paul brought his Pharisaic background—shaped by events in the Roman Empire, heavily influenced by his theological training with Gamaliel, and turned upside down by his encounter with Jesus on the road to Damascus. Given all that, what does he say? His thesis is found in Romans 1:16–18: "I am not ashamed of the gospel, for it is the power of God bringing salvation to both Jews and Gentiles in exactly the same way—through faith in Jesus. For God's view of righteousness is seen through faith: the one who is righteous will live by faith."

Martin Luther has been a dominant influence, so that now we tend to read this text as saying that the individual person is saved by faith in

13. Untermeyer, *Enlarged Anthology of Robert Frost's Poems*, p. 94.

Jesus, not by the good works that we do. Without denying that theological concept, would it help clarify Paul's original message if we knew a little more about church life in first-century Rome? Shouldn't we recognize that Paul's concern was not simply the salvation of the individual, but also the spiritual condition of the believing community? Paul had heard of some things happening within the church that were destructive to other members of the church.

John H. Yoder once said, "Whenever the church accepts new members, we have to take some time to rethink who we are as a people because we are no longer exactly the same people."[14] But in most cases, joining the church is like hopping on a moving train. You run alongside and then jump on board. The train keeps on going down the track and you ride it without any thought about going anywhere other than where the tracks lead. We who are already on board quietly absorb you into our life. Not much changes except that we have a few new paying passengers on the train. These new passengers might be on the train with us, but they still know there are theological or social walls that limit their input in guiding the direction the train is going. Yet we keep right on doing it.

I'd like to suggest some walls that Paul saw in Rome and then ask a few questions about what we see today.

The wall of declaring spiritual privilege

Paul sees both Jew and Gentile in the same situation before God. Since it is by grace that all humanity experiences their salvation (wholeness), there is no basis for anyone to claim special status within the community. We all know this. We have no such thing as birthright Christians versus. conversion Christians. But the birthright folks ought to ask the conversion folks whether they sense a different level of acceptance! The challenge to the church is to find how we can create a faith community where there are no status levels for membership. Can we allow the Spirit of God to create a faith community where loving each other is more important than making theological statements about why God loves us?

We know about this because of our theology of the priesthood of all believers. We resist the temptation to make leaders special people with status the rest of us don't have. But can we do better at integrating new persons into the fellowship? Are we prepared to risk being changed by

14. Used from personal class notes from seminary lecture given by John H. Yoder.

them, rather than simply absorbing them into our group. Is it right for us to assume that over time they will become just like us and they will be grateful that we did that to them?

The wall of defining sexual practice

Paul sees trouble in how Rome was defining sexual practice. Remember, some members have come to a Jesus-centered faith without any background in Jewish morality. They brought with them some economically abusive sexual practices that in Paul's Jewish culture would have been repulsive. Today these practices would be criminalized as sexual abuse of children. We have laws that discourage people from doing these things, because they are equally repulsive to us. But because we don't know much about the Greco-Roman sexual practices of Paul's day, traditional scholarship has decided to apply Paul's language to specific sexual practices in our own culture. We do not recognize that Paul would have had no basis for defining sexuality as we do. He knew nothing about genetic or psychological factors in the formation of sexual identity. In Paul's day, one's sexuality was identified almost exclusively by the attributes of one's physical body.

There are references in first-century literature that describe sexual abuse of adolescent children for adult pleasure and economic gain. Paul knew about this and was clearly opposed to it. Thus, the sexual identity wall that we build excluding gay and lesbian people today does not represent the reality that Paul was facing in Rome. We are not being faithful to Paul's concern about abusive sexual practices in his day even though similar practices of sexual slavery still happen to young children in Southeast Asia and in some of our own Western cities right now. We have built a very substantial wall, based on an inappropriate fear of "the other." By misapplying the biblical text in this way, we have turned our attention away from the sexual abuse of children, leaving them to suffer miserably at the hands of adults. We then mistakenly apply Paul's message to same-gendered persons today, causing them to suffer in a different, but equally miserable way. I do not believe that Paul or Jesus would approve of our treatment of these persons. It is way past time that we tear down this wall.

The wall of divine parentage

How do we determine "who is a child of God"? When we ask this question, Paul hears it as a Jew–Gentile wall. For us it might be a Christian–Muslim wall, or even a Fundamentalist–Progressive wall. Paul attacks this wall by redefining divine parentage. He uses inclusive language that says God sees all people in the same way. Paul talks about people who try to separate what you believe from who you are; and who you are from what you do. However, today we believe we are intricate human beings shaped by nature, by belief, and by deeds. When we dissect persons like cadavers, we do enormous damage to them, and to ourselves.

Paul insists that God does not show favoritism. So, what about us? Can we walk alongside persons who do not believe certain things exactly as we do, or engage in some ethical behaviors based on values that are different from our own? You see, salvation (wholeness in relationship with God and ourselves) is not an achievement that we accomplish by working hard. Salvation is a lifelong relationship with God as experienced in Jesus, empowered by the Spirit, and put into practice right here, right now, every day of our lives.

We are helped by revisiting the words of Jesus about the kingdom of God. If it truly is something that Jesus declared is already present wherever people give expression to the grace of God, then we have to look at other persons in a new way. Do we really believe that only Christians can be born again or live in positive relationship with God? Is it possible that the universal love of God for all humanity can be seen, experienced, and accepted by people in many different ways—and still be valid?

How do we define what it means to be a child of God? How do we understand "godliness" or "righteousness"? How do we respond to people who live with compassion and mercy; who speak the truth with integrity; who forgive others and work for peace; but whose religious beliefs don't always match our own interpretation of traditional Christian orthodoxy?

Welcome to Paul's dilemma in Romans 2:14–15. Paul says, "When Gentiles [that's us] who do not have the law, do by nature what the law teaches, they show that the teachings of the law are written on their hearts." In Romans 3:29 Paul says that the good news is "God is God of the Gentiles, too."

This leads me to ask a few more questions of us—about ourselves:

Do we have the courage, or perhaps the trust in God, to revisit our own walls of faith?

Karl Barth once said: "When you expand the circle of light, you also expand your encounter with the circle of darkness."[15] What does he mean? When we share the gospel message of justice and integrity, we uncover new areas wherein injustice and oppression are still in control and these forces fight back against the gospel with new intensity. Paul urged the Christians at Rome to be aware of how God's grace is being experienced all around them. There is so much good that needs to be done in the world, and it helps to remember that when we expand the circle of light, we are going to encounter new and even more vigorous challenges to that light. We might even run into some new walls! Paul would admonish us for trying to protect ourselves from the darkness by building new walls, when in fact we should be knocking down the walls of darkness by sharing the light of God's truth and love.

How do we see our faith?

There are places in Romans 3 where Paul talks about believing the right stuff. But Paul is critical of people who think that believing the right stuff is what saves them. Christian faith is not a doctrinal exam. It is an experience of grace that we want to share with others because we have discovered how much that grace means to us. When we focus more on faith *content* than we do on faith *living*, we risk losing the experience of faith that liberates us to be people of love and grace. Remember what Jesus told his disciples: "There are other people who are part of my group, even though you don't accept them as part of your group" (John 10:16). How big is our circle of faith? How high are the walls that we have built?

How do we best do church?

Paul tells the Christians at Rome, in effect: "Don't allow these futile walls to be built among you. Build upon your experience of grace so that you can be effective witnesses to that grace." Can we do better at reaching out and changing the world, rather than trying to protect ourselves from it? Can we be living expressions of who Jesus was and what Jesus taught, so

15. O'Neill, "Karl Barth's Doctrine of Election."

that others can experience that reality and rejoice in their discovery? This Jesus-message brings hope, love, peace, and that is good news for us, for our neighbors, and also for those who we are told should be our enemies. We no longer need to waste time or energy in sorting out exactly who is in and who is out, because we have discovered that in God: "There is something that doesn't love a wall." Instead, God loves everyone, including us! When we recognize that, we no longer need the walls. *And that is truly good news.*

6

Making Friends with God

The effect of righteousness will be peace,
And the result of righteousness is quietness and trust forever
Isaiah 32:17

I have loved you with the same love my Father has for me.
Make yourselves at home in my love.
I have told you these things so that my joy will be your joy,
and that your joy will be complete.
This is what I am asking of you:
Love one another the way I have loved you.
This is the best way to love; give yourself for others.
You are my friends when you do the things I have asked you to do.
I am not calling you servants any more
because servants do not understand what their master is thinking.
I am calling you friends
because I have told you everything that I have heard from God.
—Jesus
John 15:9–16

The tragedy in life doesn't lie in not reaching your goal.
The tragedy lies in having no goal to reach.
It isn't a calamity to die with dreams unfulfilled,
but it is a calamity not to dream. . . .
It is not a disgrace not to reach the stars,
but it is a disgrace to have no stars to reach for.
Not failure, but low aim is sin.[1]

—Dr. Benjamin Mayes

1. Mayes. Online: www.morehouse.edu/about/chapel/mays_wisdom.html.

Making Friends with God

Following graduation from Goshen College in 1959, I was accepted at Associated Mennonite Biblical Seminary (AMBS) in Elkhart, Indiana. This transition was made all the better because of the excitement of an emerging relationship with Carolyn Brooks. We had an active courtship of less than six months before I asked her to marry me. It was only after we were married in April 1960 that I learned we had broken some rules. Nothing immoral or anything like that! There was an obscure rule somewhere in AMBS policy that stated if you were planning to marry during your seminary years, you were expected to clear this with Seminary Dean Harold Bender before you actually got married. We didn't know that, and I'm not sure we would have complied even if we had known it. I grew up in a family where rules were temporary guidelines to be applied only when necessary, and usually to others. Because my marriage with Carolyn was certainly not a problem for us, I saw no reason to involve the seminary in any problem solving.

Not long after our marriage, Dean Bender called me into his office and recommended that I consider a summer internship at the Freeport Mennonite Church in Freeport, Illinois. This was a rural congregation that would provide excellent training for a young pastor. The previous pastor had resigned to accept a new pastorate, and the congregation was not facing any internal turmoil. It was well known among seminary students that one did not question Dean Bender's advice. Two months after our marriage, Carolyn and I moved to Freeport where I began work as a pastor, and we started learning how to live together.

At the end of the summer, we returned to Goshen. Once again I was a seminary student, but I kept the relationship with the Freeport congregation. Twice a month, I would attend Friday classes and then make the five hour drive to Freeport. Saturday was used to visit with members of the congregation and to finish up the Sunday morning sermon. On Sunday afternoon I would prepare another sermon, which was preached on Sunday evening. After the service I would make the long drive back to Goshen. This meant that during the first year of our marriage, Carolyn was alone for three days every other weekend. She handled it very well. But sadly, I did not have the sensitivity to be aware of how she felt about these long weekends with an absent husband. I simply assumed that since I was "serving God" she would gladly adjust to my life as full-time student and quarter-time pastor with very little time left for family. In June, after completing my second year of seminary, Carolyn and I moved back to Freeport with our newborn daughter, Lois. We were eager to start living like a normal family.

The Freeport congregation did not have a formal pastoral job description. They assumed I would know what pastors do and that I would do it. It was a half-time job, so I also drove a school bus and did some substitute teaching in the local high school. These two part-time jobs meshed very comfortably with my pastoral work. I especially enjoyed the experience of being a substitute teacher, although I had no formal academic credentials for that job. The school bus and the classroom gave me regular interaction with students. It provided an interesting diversion from the normal pastoral work, plus many nonpastoral contacts with the local community.

It was at Freeport that I learned about preaching. For my first six months as a pastor I was far too nervous to eat breakfast on Sunday morning. Each week began with the stressful search for a topic around which I could build a sermon. Preparation for the sermon itself usually took at least two days of study and reading. On occasion, the Sunday evening program committee would ask me to preach a second sermon for the evening worship service. After dinner on Sunday, I would play with the children for a few hours, then head down to my church office to work on the evening sermon for three or four hours. I never understood why, but people often commented positively about the Sunday evening sermon. As I think back, my guess is that these evening sermons were more conversational in style and more life centered in content. It was at Freeport that I learned to thoroughly enjoy preaching.

I learned about small groups from Phyllis Rogers. One Saturday morning the phone rang and a woman with a marvelously lyrical British accent identified herself. She asked about coming to church the next morning. She had learned about Mennonites from a small booklet that she and her husband, Gil, had picked up at a stop on the Pennsylvania Turnpike. She came, and she kept coming. It was not long before the whole congregation fell in love with Phyllis. She was so not-like-us, but in many ways she had become one-with-us.

Phyllis had a strong personality. She was convinced that spiritual growth happens best when people meet in small groups where they talk about their faith, pray together, share their concerns and questions, and offer support to each other. I was intrigued, but not easily convinced. At that point in my life, I still believed that faith was best described as knowing the truth so that we would do the right thing.

Phyllis wanted to nurture faith through relationships where people could be more open, accepting, and supportive of each other. The most persuasive thing about Phyllis was that she was a living expression of this approach to faith in her own life. She cared about people. She wanted to know about your faith and what life was like for you. She was candid in talking about her own life, freely admitting her need for others who would walk with her. She often asked, with honest interest, about how things were going for Carolyn and me with our children. I wasn't ready to admit it yet, but I was coming to understand that perhaps small groups might be a good thing. I began to believe that Phyllis might be right when she said we do our best work in coping with life when we share together, not when we function as isolated individuals who keep other people at arm's length.

Phyllis gave new meaning to the theological concept of "community." She challenged my strong, traditional beliefs about an individualistic, internalized, and private faith. She urged me to be more human and vulnerable with the congregation, sharing from my own life experiences as I shared from the Scriptures. Phyllis believed that it was appropriate to experience God as a friend who was always present with us. I was not quite there yet, but the door was quietly being opened for a new approach to faith that would reshape my views about God. I did not know it, but this understanding of faith would become a core belief for how Carolyn and I would nurture our faith and share more openly with others.

After nine good learning years at Freeport, I began receiving exploratory invitations from other congregations who were looking for new pastoral leadership. Our response to each of these requests was very simple: "Thank you, but not at this time." But then one day we received a letter from the Akron Mennonite Church in Akron, Pennsylvania. I am not sure why, but both Carolyn and I were instantly fascinated by this invitation. Other than being in the heart of Lancaster County, everything we knew about this congregation was appealing, and it seemed like the right time for us to make a change. So we responded, met with the congregation, and then accepted their invitation. In June 1969, Carolyn and I, with our four children, moved to Akron, where I became solo pastor of the Akron Mennonite Church.

In many ways it was a dream position. I felt Akron was the most exciting Mennonite church in the denomination. I was thirty-two years old;

I felt that I had shown I was a good pastor. I was climbing my mountain and a wonderful future was ahead of me.

"George" was the chair of the pastoral search committee that invited me to Akron. He was a very competent, respected professional leader. In my first week on the job, he invited me to his office where he told me, "You are young, you've got a lot to learn. You will make mistakes. When you do, I will be watching. I am going to hold you accountable. I've got a lot invested in you, and I am not going to let you fail. Don't let me down." I was not bothered. Failure had never been part of my vocabulary.

The first year went very well. We were getting acquainted, the church was growing, response to sermons was positive, and the church seemed to be upbeat. I loved what I was doing, and life in general was going well. We had built a new house and our fifth child, Miriam, was born.

Near the end of that first year, there was a pastoral review. The plan was that we would have a conversation to provide guidance on areas where things could be done better. I was assured it was not a big deal. The chair of the Church Advisory Council told me that they had asked George to lead this conversation. He was a professional, and they wanted to be sure that it would be done right. That was fine with me. I was quite satisfied with how things were going and was expecting a positive evening with perhaps a few minor adjustments.

The review was scheduled for Wednesday evening. On Monday, George called and asked me to meet with him to talk about the review. At this meeting, George did virtually all the talking. His evaluation was as follows: My theology was bad, my preaching was shallow, my administrative skills were abysmal, and my relationships with members were manipulative. I was not open and honest. I was not dependable in getting tasks completed. "Frankly," he said, "you are not the person you portrayed yourself to be when you met with the search committee. You are a hypocrite, and if you want to keep your job, you had better grow up fast." With that, George walked out.

No one had ever talked to me that way in my life. I was stunned. I couldn't breathe. I couldn't move. I finally went back to my office, shut the door and just sat there for several hours. This was how my family had taught me to handle conflict and anger: go off by yourself and sit on it. Finally, I went home. Carolyn casually asked me how the meeting with George went. I shrugged and said, "Okay, I guess." I was unable to share with her the shock and hollowness I felt.

Wednesday evening, George reported to the Church Advisory Council that we had met. He told them what he had said to me, and that I had agreed with his analysis. (I did not recall my having agreed to any such thing.) He then recommended that they require I get psychiatric help. That was another shock. In our family, psychiatry was for mental hospitals and crazy people. Asking for help, or even admitting you needed help, was simply not part of my family system. We helped others, we did not need help ourselves, and certainly *not* psychiatric help.

How could I process this? For ten years I had been a pastor who assured people that God is our help, if we just ask for it. But now, when I desperately needed help, God was nowhere to be found. I was experiencing none of the supportive presence of God that I had promised others would be there for them. What do you do when you have told people that something works, and you have built your life on it, only to discover that, in fact, it doesn't work? Add the assumption that pastors aren't supposed to have problems. They are servants of God who are always available to help others. Everything I claimed to believe was all crashing down right around me.

Other members of the Advisory Council had sat in stunned silence. I later learned that they were as surprised as I was, yet they accepted George's analysis because "he was a professional."

I remember going home that evening, telling Carolyn what had happened and that I was going to resign immediately, and we would be leaving Akron. Nobody treats me this way and gets away with it. I had no idea where we would go or what I would do. We would just leave. I was still living out my family pattern of running away from conflict. Carolyn quietly urged me to wait at least a week. A decision of this magnitude had to be talked about.

The following Sunday George talked with Carolyn giving his explanation of the meeting and telling her that I needed help. Carolyn's love and support during these awful days was absolute, even though she did not fully understand what was going on inside me. In the weeks ahead she had to face a totally new marriage relationship. I did not want to get out of bed in the morning, I avoided people whenever I could, which is difficult to do when you are the pastor. I did not play with the children. I ate very little. I was virtually nonresponsive at home, yet I managed to function passably well at church. But Carolyn stayed with me. She gave leadership for the family, and she took care of me. She accepted a lot of undeserved behavior (silent treatment, emotional and physical distance, short temper, constant irritability, and complete withdrawal of any help around the house). I was an exhausting, emotional drain on her life.

One day she said to me, "Honey, why don't you go see Abe Hostetter. Talk to him. I'll bet Abe could help you prove George wrong." I had never thought of that rationale for getting help. She touched my competitive drive by presenting a challenge. So I made an appointment with Dr. Abe Hostetter, a psychiatrist at Philhaven Hospital, near Hershey, Pennsylvania.

I liked Abe immediately. He wasn't shocked, and it seemed as though he understood. He asked what I wanted to do. I told him that I wanted to prove to George that he was wrong in his evaluation of me. Abe wondered how I would do that. I didn't know. I expected him to tell me how to do it. All Abe said was, "I really don't care whether George is right or wrong. Can we talk about you and what you would like to do?" I developed a strong professional relationship with Abe. But Abe kept reminding me he wasn't into doing miracles.

I looked forward each week to my hour with Abe. But I worked hard to make sure no one else knew about it. I did not know what people would think, and I was afraid of what might happen if they found out. How do you trust a pastor who needs psychiatric help?

Each week I would walk into the reception area at Abe's office and immediately check out the room. Is there anyone here who might know me? One day, just after I sat down, a local Mennonite church leader walked in, saw me, came over and sat down beside me. Oh God. *No!* Panic!

He asked, "Good to see you Don; how are you doing these days?" (I am sitting in a psychiatrist's office and he wants to know how I am doing!)

I lied. "I'm doing fine."

His response, "It is good to have persons like Abe who can help us get through tough times."

My answer was another lie—well, not exactly a lie, I just made a technically accurate statement that communicated something quite false. "I'm okay; I have an appointment with Abe to get some help with some problems we are having at church." (I was not ready to be totally honest just yet. I was still running away!)

In my hour with Abe, we talked about how ashamed I was of myself for what I had just done. Pastors are supposed to tell the truth. Abe wondered whether God had a different set of rules for pastors than for ordinary people. He wondered why "what other people think" was so important to me. It was a tough hour.

The low point came about six to eight months into my meetings with Abe. I did not feel that we were getting anywhere. I knew every day was going to be awful, that yesterday was probably better than today would be, and that the rest of my life would get progressively worse on a daily basis. I didn't want to get up in the morning because I knew that today would simply be a repeat of yesterday, only worse. Seeing myself as the appointed channel of God's grace for the congregation simply made it all too much to handle. I could see no way out.

It was at about this time that two things happened within one week. I was driving home from an appointment with Abe. It had not gone well. I had no idea if what I was experiencing would ever end. If this is how it was going to be for the rest of my life, it just wasn't worth it. I came to the intersection of US 322 and PA 72 that goes down to the Pennsylvania Turnpike. I pulled off the road and just sat there. Did I really want to go back to Akron and continue being a failure? Why not just get on the Turnpike and go—I had no idea where—just go. I had no thought about how far I could go. I had maybe three dollars in my pocket.

As I sat there, images of Carolyn started going through my head. I could not do this to her. I couldn't leave her; she was the one who was holding my life together. The images of Carolyn were as powerful as if she were actually sitting beside me in the car. I turned east on 322 and went home—to Carolyn. And in a crazy way that I had not felt for a long time, I actually looked forward to getting home.

Carolyn was in the kitchen when I walked in the house. I put my arms around her and held her—and cried. It was the first time I had held her, or touched her, or let her touch me in months. Carolyn did exactly the right thing. She put her arms around me and cried with me.

But life does not let you get by that easily. A couple of days later an older member of the church came into my office. "Don," he said, "there is a terrible rumor going round town about you. People are saying that you are seeing a psychiatrist. *It's not true, is it?*" I couldn't think of anything worse that he could have said. It confirmed my worst fears. Seeing a psychiatrist meant I was crazy. I certainly was not spiritually in touch with God. Worse yet, everyone in town knew about it. How could I ever go out in public again?

I quickly decided I had nothing more to lose. "Yes, I am," I said. "I have been going through a lot of stress lately, and I wanted help in knowing how to handle it." The man sat there for a moment, said nothing, and then walked out. What did I do after he left? I laughed! That might seem trivial, but I had just experienced two emotions in one week. That is a lot for a depressed person.

The next week I told Abe about this. I could sense the excitement beneath his professional restraint. That week started the beginning of gradual one-degree shifts in direction for me. I had made a decision to go home. I had accepted an emotion that was bottled up inside of me by crying. I had publicly owned up to who I was. And who cares what the town of Akron thinks.

I continued to see Abe for over a year, gradually moving from weekly to biweekly to once a month. It had been eighteen months. What had Abe done? I really don't know. He listened, and he asked questions: "Where did you learn that?"; "How does that feeling help you?"; and "What would you like to do with that?" One day, I told Abe, "You know, I don't think I have to come back any more." Abe smiled, "I think you are right."

Am I cured? In a way, maybe; but I don't use that language anymore. In some ways, none of us is ever totally cured; we simply learn how to be fully human. When things pile up on me, and I feel overwhelmed or frustrated, I still want to go into my study, shut the door and sit by myself for a while. Sometimes creating a little space for a short time of personal reflection is a good thing.

Two stories give new meaning to this very painful period. About five years later, we were living in Scotland where I was working on my PhD. Margaret, the school teacher for one of our children, was hospitalized for stress and depression. About a month later, I walked past her home and saw her sitting in the backyard. We knew each other in a casual way, so I went in, and asked if I might visit for a few minutes. She simply nodded without looking up. I talked with her about the garden, and then I took about twenty minutes to share my story with her. As I left, I asked if I could stop by again. One week later I saw her on her knees working in her flower garden. I sat down on the grass beside her. She looked at me, sat back, and smiled. "You know what it feels like. Without knowing it, you told me I was not crazy. You told me there was hope. You were living proof that life could be different. I decided if you could do it, I could do it." Two months later she was back singing with us in the community choir. She continued to have struggles, but in her words, she was back on a good path again.

More recently, a very dear friend of ours was overwhelmed by some things that had happened in her life. Carolyn and I visited her one day. She was functional, but overwhelmed by feelings of depression she had never had before. She was convinced her future would be dismal, and that there was nothing she could do about it. We were sitting in her kitchen, and I said, "Mary, when you wake up in the morning, you feel like you just don't have the energy to get out of bed, much less get breakfast. Sometimes the children demand attention and you don't even want to see them. It makes you feel like you are an awful person, and you hate yourself. When you see other people enjoying life, you know you will never feel that way yourself. And some days you aren't even sure you will make it through the day." She looked at me with a blank stare. "How do you know that? That is exactly how I feel."

I quietly said, "I have been there, and I know that life does not have to be this way. Find a good counselor. Let someone help you. They won't tell you what to do, but they will help you figure it out." In her case it was a chemical imbalance that was quickly diagnosed, and within weeks she had turned her life around. Now, ten years later, she is a vibrant, caring mother and devoted wife with an excellent professional career.

For these two people, my year and a half journey through the valley of the shadow was worth it. I am grateful to God, to the Akron Mennonite Church, to Abe Hostetter, and most of all to Carolyn. There is hope, there is help. Like Abe, I am not into miracles. But I do believe in the healing power of God experienced through caring, compassionate, and professional people. Finding healing takes work, and sometimes it is not fun, but it is worth it.

A few people have asked whether I have made peace with George's actions. It took a while, but I am at peace. He did what he felt he had to do. I even accept that he thought he was doing the right thing. I disagree with his methods, but I learned a great deal about myself and about life by living through my own valley of the shadow of death. I am much more comfortable with myself, and with others. That is a good feeling. I would not wish this kind of experience on anyone, and I certainly would not want to repeat it for myself; but looking back, I see good things that have come from it. I am not responsible for what others do to me. I can only control how I choose to respond.

Without having survived this experience, I am not sure I would have lasted very long as a pastor. Others would need to verify this, but I feel that I transitioned from having an intellectual and very critical belief system to being a person of compassion and understanding. I think I began to actually like God, rather than afraid of this powerful being whom I could never fully satisfy.

I am skeptical of people who make promises that God cannot keep. I no longer accept the idea that whatever happens must be God's will. People who say that simply have not been there. They either don't know or they live in denial. I believe that, among other places, God is found within the faith community. So I turn to other people for God's help, believing that God is present with us right now. In the process, I have come to see God as a friend, one who cares about me and all humanity. God is with me as a caring presence who does not harm or destroy innocent people in order to teach me a lesson. God is a life-giving presence who wants to draw from me the very best that life has to offer.

Our challenge is to be a faith community that encourages healing, promotes hope, and walks with people who are afraid or lonely. I hope that this path has made me a more compassionate, patient person who is a better listener, more willing to walk alongside others with caring, supportive love. I hope that I am less judgmental, more flexible, and a better friend with those who are experiencing difficult days. But that is a judgment call that others make about me, not one that I can declare for myself. I feel, in a strange way, that I have made friends with God. That is a good thing, because it has helped me learn to be a good friend with myself. Certainly, that is what happens when God is at work in and through us.

The Embracing Face of God

Christmas 2009 was a difficult time for many people. The economy was suffering, people were losing their jobs, and those who had jobs were not sure how long they would keep them. The housing bubble had burst, and people were facing the awful anxiety of losing their homes in foreclosure. We learned a new meaning for the phrase "under water" as it was applied to home mortgages. Members of both political parties were blaming each other, but positive answers were hard to come by. Many Christians were tempted to blame God. But because they believed that blaming God was not permitted, they had to somehow find ways within themselves to reconcile their anger and make it through each day.

It was my impression that few churches were offering much help. Political commentary was not acceptable, sermons tended to stick with the standard Christmas themes of hope and celebration. There was a kind of oblivious awareness that people had little hope and almost nothing to celebrate. There was a pervasive sadness in the air.

I was living in Elkhart County, Indiana. We had the highest unemployment rate in the state. The president had even visited twice, trying to offer hope. None of us knew how long this downturn was going to last.

I was asked to preach in a small congregation in a nearby town where the recession had hit especially hard. Where is the Christmas joy for this congregation? Where is the hope that we usually associate with this season of the year? How does the gospel deal with hard times?

I decided to take on the unidentified elephant that all of us knew was there. I have never been a good Pollyanna-type person. I hoped a bit of honest reality would be helpful. The pastor agreed, and we worked together on the following sermon.

* * *

The Embracing Face of God[2]

For many people, this has been a difficult year. All around us people are experiencing the stress of an economy in severe turmoil, forcing them to adjust how they live, how they think, and how they plan for the future. Some folks are wondering if life will ever again be as good as the way they remember it used to be.

2. The biblical foundation for this sermon is Luke 2:22–40.

This situation today is very much the way it was when Jesus was born. Roman military control was present everywhere, taxes were brutally high, more and more working people were just one step away from a life of poverty with its hunger, disease, homelessness, and despair. Religious people were crying out to God because this was not what they believed God had promised them in the land of milk and honey. They were pleading with God to deliver them. It certainly is not an identical experience, but for many people today it is vaguely familiar. We never intended for life to be this way for us.

So where is the embracing face of God to be seen today? What is the message of the gospel for people who are discouraged by what is happening right now, and even more afraid of what might happen tomorrow?

How can Christians bring a word of hope without sounding like we are totally out of touch with the reality facing so many people? The Christian story is filled with people who were desperately longing to see the face of God. They longed for security for today, hope for tomorrow, friends whom they could trust, stability and food for their family, and peace in the world. The message of Christmas speaks to that desire. But is that the message the church is sharing with the world right now?

It is so easy and so tempting to look for the embracing face of God in the clean, the magnificent, the miraculous. While I certainly do not want to deny any of that, in the biblical story the face of God becomes most real in the lives of suffering people. Our assumptions about God and how God works are deeply affected by the secular religious themes that are so prevalent in our world. We are as confused as were the wise men. You want to find God? Like them, we are told to head for the places of power, or the sacred sanctuaries of the professionally religious. And so you wind up in Herod's palace. But virtually every Jewish person in Palestine could have told these seekers, "Herod's palace is the last place to go to find God." Eventually, the wise men actually did find God—in the hope and joy of two parents holding their newborn child in a stable behind an inn in the tiny little town of Bethlehem. That certainly was not what they were expecting to find when they started their search.

Perhaps the challenge for us this Christmas is to reaffirm where we find God. Can we return to the biblical model of embracing our neighbor, and every other human being with whom we share life? The joy of Christmas is the biblical message that God has come to us, to be one with us, and to live among us, so that together we can survive in difficult times.

Certainly, Christmas is about the birth of the Christ child. But the message that gives us today is found in what that birth means, and what that birth tells us about God. Yes, we tell people that in Jesus, who is the Christ, we see the face of God. But we also say, "This is what it means for us when we see the face of God in this way." We do much more than just tell a story. We share what that story means, and we live out the hope that this story gives us in our own lives.

Let's look at this story, which we all know so very well, and see how this event gives us life, and peace, and joy. Perhaps we will also find the courage to affirm again that in this story we see the face of God.

First, this story revolves around the birth of a baby. Those of you who have ever cared for a newborn baby know the energy and time that a baby takes. But think beyond that: the birth of a child is a profound statement about our hope for the future. Babies aren't about the past, they help us look ahead, to dream about what this child might become. They challenge us to hope for a world and a life where this child can be safe, and to pray for God's love and presence to be with this child.

But think also, there is a commitment that parents make. They accept the challenge to protect, train, teach, feed, and guide their new baby. Now think about what this means. We believe that, in the baby Jesus, God has come to us in a wonderful new way. But we also believe that God is fully present in every newborn child, so that in the birth of every child we experience the hope for new life. And with that hope comes the awareness that God is entrusting us with the message of hope for a new world. If God had come into the world as a powerful military hero, which is exactly what most of Israel was praying for, God would be telling us, "I do not trust you; I will have to take charge and change the world for you."

God did not come as King David but in the form of a very vulnerable infant. God is saying rather clearly, "I trust you to provide what this child—what every child throughout history—will need." What are we doing with this message of hope seen in the birth of Jesus to be sure that every child born on this earth has the opportunity to experience the love, peace, and life that God wishes for every human being?

Second, this story is liberally sprinkled with very ordinary people. Yes, I know there are the rich wise men and the powerful King Herod, but they are on the edges of the story. You would not pick Mary or Joseph as being two persons who would be remembered two thousand years later for what they did. And you certainly would not trust a bunch of shepherds huddled on a hillside to explain the theological importance of the story.

(Imagine, if you had a major breaking news story today, would you want CNN to cover it or would one of the supermarket tabloids be okay?) Can you imagine what it was like to have angels interrupt your peaceful night, telling you, "I've got good news. There will be peace on earth because the savior has been born? Glory be to God." I've never much wanted to be a cowboy or a shepherd, but I certainly would have loved to have been one of those shepherds that night outside Bethlehem.

But what does this tell us? The good news is that God honors the poor, the simple, and the commonplace. God uses them to proclaim the message of peace, of hope, and of salvation for the world because they are the ones for whom the gospel message is most critical. Most of us are in the category of being pretty average people. What an honor it is to know that God trusts us to share this message with the world. It is ordinary people who make themselves available to do the will of God. It is simply amazing what happens when we do that.

Third, is the star over Bethlehem. This symbolized a light in the darkness that will guide us if we are willing to follow. The Bible often talks about God's truth guiding us along the path of life and of God's word being a light. Now connect that with the three wise men who, by no stretch of the imagination, can be seen as traditional, Bible-believing, God-fearing people. Dare we believe that God's truth can be seen in fresh, creative ways that cause people who aren't part of our religious history to do very unusual things in their own search for truth? Can we allow God to reveal the divine message of peace, love, and salvation to people who don't think, look, or act like we do? Can we rejoice that God got through to them, or do we want to argue about whether they really deserved to get the message that we value so much for ourselves?

Fourth, we all know the gospel is about the love of God for all humanity. But note how it is shown in this story. It is not simply a profound theological statement. It is actually seen in the human expression of love between a man and a woman—for each other and for their child.

Imagine with me what this experience must have been like for Mary and Joseph. Imagine the emotional impact upon Mary over the early rejection of Joseph (and what life would have been like for Mary as a single mother in that first-century culture). Imagine the grief and anguish of Joseph when he first learned that his fiancé had been unfaithful to him— even though she had a very different story about how it actually had happened. Live with Joseph for a few weeks or months while he wrestles with what to do.

I've been a pastor, and I have seen what can happen in a family when this kind of crisis explodes. What does it say about love and commitment when God chooses a young, unmarried woman and a struggling young carpenter to be the persons who will nurture, train, and raise an infant who will become the savior of the world? How do we handle the crisis events that come upon us, events that upset our plans for what we hoped our world would be?

I wonder about Joseph, but at the same time he is one of my biblical heroes. He wrestles with God, with Mary, and with himself, and he stays in the story. I wish more of us had that kind of courage, that kind of commitment to swallow hard and plunge ahead not knowing what tomorrow is going to be like. Can you imagine what it meant to Mary when Joseph finally told her, "I don't know if I fully understand what is going on here, but it doesn't change anything for me. Let's be a family and raise this child together." Can you imagine what that simple statement did for Mary? Can you feel the relief, the liberation, and the salvation that swept over her? Her world had not come to an end; there was hope, and there would be a new day for her and the child. That is love. That is commitment. That is seeing and embracing the face of God in a way that most of us would never have expected.

This is much more than simple, symbolic imagery. It is the living reality of the love of God for each of us. This story is saturated with events and emotions that demonstrate for us how God works in human experience; how profoundly God loves and cares for us in difficult times; how God does not leave us when tragedy strikes; and how God reaches into our lives and invites us to experience—then share—this good news of hope, of love, and of a new world in which salvation becomes the norm, not the rare exception to how life is.

But the story is not without the horrible, painful intervention of human reality. How does Herod, leader of the local Roman state, respond to this good news? He has a very different way of thinking about life and the importance of his own role in this part of the world. He launches a violent display of military force. He invades a small town and kills every baby boy who might possibly grow up to be a threat to his throne.

We learn from Herod's part of the story that the gospel is not a wonderful fairy tale where everyone loves everyone else, where there is prosperity, peace, and sunny days forever. This is a reality story. God's love invades the world in a very unusual and dramatic way. But the world fights back because the powers of the world don't want to give up control.

Even yet today, though these powers may have changed names, the policies have not. How do we solve human problems so that we can live together in peace? How do we treat the hungry, the homeless, and those who are different from us? The powers of the world and the followers of Jesus have two very different solutions to these human problems.

The way of Herod still doesn't work, but the governments of the world still use it. The way of God does work, but we are afraid to trust the power of God's Spirit and the truth of God's message. God's way is seen in this story. This Jesus, whom we call Lord, grows up to be an adult. He is the one who teaches us how God is and how we should be.

Perhaps the challenge for us today is not so much whether we see the embracing face of God in Jesus who was born in Bethlehem (and I certainly hope that we do). But perhaps the crucial question is this: do people around us see and experience the embracing face of God in us? And again, I certainly hope that they do. Because when the birth of Jesus happens again in the lives of human beings, then we move another step closer to the message of the angels: "I've got good news: the savior has come to you. A child is born in Bethlehem. Glory to God in the Highest and on earth peace for all people."[3]

That, truly, is still good news.

3. See Luke 2:10–14.

When the Right Answer Is Wrong[4]

The biblical writers tell the story about God's interaction with people in human history. In the gospels, Jesus is given the primary focus. It is helpful to put these stories together, because when we see them in sequence we see things that might otherwise slide by us.

Several years ago I was leading a weekend series of Bible studies in a congregation. After one of the studies, a member of the congregation asked me, "Why do you Bible teachers and preachers think you have to make everything so complicated? The church didn't have that problem when Jesus was here. He made it all really simple so common people could understand him." Okay, what do you do with that? Indeed, there was no church when Jesus was here. That didn't happen until after Pentecost. And, was it really that simple?

You remember John the Baptist. He baptized Jesus and it was a dramatic experience. The Bible tells us the heavens opened and there was a voice that gave affirmation to the ministry of Jesus. I would think that should be pretty convincing. It was not long after this that John made some very strong statements about the ethical behavior of the ruling Roman authorities, and so he was arrested. While he was in prison, some of John's friends came to Jesus with a very interesting question on behalf of John: "Are you the Messiah, or should we be looking for someone else?"[5] In effect, they are asking him, "Jesus, who are you?"

If John the Baptist was there at the baptism of Jesus, and if John heard the voice from heaven, why should John have any question about who Jesus was? Certainly he would remember that. Maybe it wasn't really that simple.

How would you answer the question, "Who is Jesus?" Where would you go to find evidence for your answer? Listen to what Jesus told these friends from John the Baptist: "You go back and tell John what you have seen and heard. The blind receive their sight, the lame walk, those who have leprosy are cured, the deaf hear, the dead are raised, and the good news is preached to the poor."[6] Evidently, Jesus thought that would answer the question. But, then, Jesus adds an interesting comment: "Blessed are those who are not offended by this answer."[7]

4. The biblical foundation for this sermon is Mark 8:27–38.
5. See Luke 7:21.
6. See Luke 7:22.
7. See Luke 7:23.

In case you are wondering what Jesus is talking about, go down a few verses in Luke: "And all the people, even the tax collectors, when they heard what Jesus said, acknowledged that God's way is right. But the Pharisees and experts in the law were offended and they rejected God's purposes for themselves."[8] What did the common people hear when Jesus spoke? Why didn't the religious leaders hear the same thing? Maybe the answers weren't quite as simple as we think they should have been.

This is early in the ministry of Jesus, so it is understandable that people might not catch on to what Jesus is doing. But today, for us, it is clear. We believe that we know. Let's go to John 6 where it is later in the life of Jesus, and his ministry had just hit a rough spot. People are drifting off, saying the message of Jesus is just too radical. Jesus sat down beside the road, looked at the disciples and asked, in effect, "Do you guys want to leave too? Everybody else is." Peter is quick with his answer, "Where would we go? You are the only one telling the truth. We know who you are."

Aha, the truth is finally getting through. The crowds may not understand, but Peter certainly does. There is no question about Peter and what he believes.

Now with that background, we come back to Mark 8. We discover there is still confusion among the disciples. The Pharisees are back again, asking Jesus to prove himself by their standards. "Give us a sign from heaven and we will believe." And Jesus said, "No!" Once again, he sat down along the road and asked the disciples, "Do people understand what we are doing?"[9] Clearly the Pharisees did not. Is anybody getting the message? Who do people say that I am?

The disciples quickly came up with the traditional answers: John the Baptist, Elijah, one of the prophets. These are all pretty good people, by the way, and so these aren't bad answers. But where did they get those answers? They certainly did not come from Jesus.

In first-century Judaism, there were a variety of images used to describe the coming Messiah. We know of six persons within fifty years before Jesus who publicly announced that they were the Messiah. Literally, tens of thousands of people died following these false Messiahs.

For three hundred years before Jesus, Israel had been dominated by foreign nations, and the Israelites were praying for a Messiah who would

8. See Luke 7:29–33.
9. See Mark 8:27

lead them in a military revolt against these foreign powers. In Jesus' lifetime that power was Rome, and the people hoped that, like King David, the Messiah would come and restore Israel to the grandeur it had enjoyed a thousand years before. They quoted Old Testament texts to justify their beliefs. King David, the military liberator, was a very popular Messianic hope.

But there were others who said, "No, no. That is not how it will be. The Messiah will come sweeping down from heaven with a host of angels, and we will just watch as God delivers us." These people also had Old Testament verses that they quoted to prove their point.

There was yet a third image that was much less popular. In fact, it had been pretty well rejected by virtually all the Jewish leaders, so it was almost totally unknown by the common people. This image came out of Isaiah, saying that the Messiah would be a spiritual presence calling for a restoration of the law and renewal of the people.[10] When Jesus asked the disciples about what people were saying, the answers were not surprising. The disciples simply gave a summary of the popular positions of the day. Jesus rather casually dismissed these popular notions with, "Okay, I hear you, but what do *you* say?"

Peter quickly blurts out the right answer: "You are the Christ!"[11] That is a really good answer, but it doesn't end the conversation quite yet. Jesus warned them, "Don't tell anyone." That sounds ominous. Why did Jesus say that? Certainly he would want everyone to know he is the Messiah. Jesus knew that if he had said to Peter, "Great answer Peter, your job now is to make sure everybody knows who I am," Israel would have heard, "King David is here" and they would have grabbed their swords and started a military revolution. You see, Peter's answer was right, but his right answer would have communicated the wrong message.

Jesus took Peter's confession and began to explain what being the Messiah meant. This gives a very interesting twist to the story, because Jesus talks about suffering, rejection, and death, followed by resurrection.[12]

Carolyn and I have been married for fifty-two years. Over those years I have developed some bad listening habits. Carolyn starts a sentence and I listen—at least to the first half. Then I think I know where she is going, so I sort of stop listening and drift off into another world.

10. See Isaiah 61:1–11.

11. See Mark 8:29.

12. See Mark 8:31.

But Carolyn changes the last half of the sentence, comes out at a different place, and I am lost, because I am not listening. (And Carolyn is upset with me for not paying attention.) I think some of you recognize that annoying "husband habit."

I think that is what happened to Peter. When Jesus started talking about suffering and death, Peter stopped listening because he knew that was not going to happen to the Messiah. The Messiah will lead us to victory over our enemies.

Now don't be too hard on Peter. He is not alone. Just a week later, the disciples got into an argument about who was going to be, in essence, Prime Minister and who would be Secretary of the Interior in the new kingdom that Jesus was talking about (see Mark 9:34). Wouldn't you know it, King David and his political empire was still hanging around in their minds.

So, Peter starts to lecture Jesus about his bad theology. That is an interesting image, Peter arguing with Jesus about what it means to be the Messiah. That makes even less sense than arguing with Bobby Knight about how to set a screen in basketball. But Jesus does not let Peter challenge God's methods of redemption. Jesus even says that Peter's way of thinking about how God works in human redemption is not of God, it is demonic. Now that is awfully strong language, even for Jesus. Maybe we need to hear that too!

Is it possible that the dominant "right answers" proclaimed so loudly in our day are actually the wrong answers because they are based on the wrong assumptions about Jesus? Maybe we need to listen more carefully when Jesus gathers the crowd and explains what it means to be a follower of Jesus, because here is where we get involved.

Jesus said, "If you want to follow me you need to see salvation as God sees it."[13] Salvation is not just about where you end up; meaning that how you live until that day comes doesn't really matter. Rather, God's salvation is shaped by the process you use to get it. Ungodly methods do not lead to godly solutions.

The image that Jesus uses gets pretty intense. Let me paraphrase: "If you are in this only for what you can get out of it for yourself, you are going to be very disappointed, because it doesn't work that way. You will end up losing everything because what you think you want will not do

13. See Mark 8:33.

what you expect it to do, and you will discover that is not the way God does it."

But, if you are willing to get out of the world's mad rush for power, prestige, and domination over everyone else; if you are willing to invest your life in service and care for other people; if you can see through the foolishness of the world's philosophy that says your happiness is found in having more things that anyone else, then you will discover an excitement in life and a personal fulfillment that is beyond your wildest imagination. You will find contentment and satisfaction in life that you never even dreamed of having.

You see, this is the call of the gospel, and this is why it is really important how we answer the question "Who is Jesus for you?" We are heading toward Easter, and in the death and resurrection of Jesus we see a clear vision of how God works in human experience. I pray that we might have the wisdom and the courage to say *yes* to this Jesus. I hope we can allow this vision and this awareness of God in our midst to dramatically impact our lives so that we join with Jesus and the people of God all around the world, calling for new life and new hope. I pray that we might become the living presence of God in this church, in this community, in this nation, and in this world. God's love for all humanity, as seen in Jesus, will not let us be satisfied with anything less.

Allow me to ask the question one more time in a slightly different way. Like Peter, we still face the temptation to shape Jesus so that he fits the cultural patterns of our day. But there is another option—to give our lives to the Jesus who calls us to be a living expression of God's love and truth and hope.

So perhaps the question is "When people meet you, which Jesus do they see?"

Let us pray: Dear Jesus, it is in you that we find our hope. Open our eyes, clear our minds, and live in our midst in a way that helps us to say, Yes Lord, you are the Christ. May we then find in that confession the anticipation and the fulfillment of all that you wish would be in our lives here this day and forever. Lord, we are grateful beyond expression. Thank you so much. It is in the name of Jesus that we pray. Amen.

The Humanity of God[14]

The humanity of God! I suppose that on the surface this must seem like an impossibility for some and, perhaps, even heresy for others. Certainly it did make some persons with whom Paul spoke furious to the point that they wanted to kill him. How dare he say anything like that? Everyone simply knows that God is not human, and we humans are not God. When a person talks about the humanity of God, it does a number of things. For one, it brings God out of the misty vastness of the heavens and places God here among us so we can see and understand God in new ways.

John speaks of this when he writes, "We write to you about the word of life, which existed from the beginning of the world. We have heard it, and we have seen it with our eyes; yes we have seen it and our hands have even touched it. When this life became visible, we saw it. So we speak of it and tell you, so that you will join us in the fellowship we have with the Father and with Jesus Christ, God's son" (1 John 1:1–4).

The humanity of God? Is it so strange that even yet today it sounds a bit absurd? It is so much simpler to hang on to the divinity of God. That sounds so much better, so godlike! But the mystery of the incarnation is precisely that. God did something very ungodlike for the human mind. God came to us, so that God could get around some of the communication barriers we set up every time we try to think about God.

Today, Christmas is one of the most popular of all Christian holidays. But it wasn't always this way. Easter, Pentecost, Ascension—all have more history than Christmas. It wasn't until about the year 400 that Christmas became a holiday of significant importance for Christians.

The message of the early church focused on the living ministry of Jesus climaxing in the death and resurrection experiences. The message of the early biblical evangelists was not "He is born" but rather, "He is risen." In Mark's gospel, the earliest of the four accounts of the life of Jesus in the New Testament, his birth, is not even mentioned. Instead, Mark gives half of his gospel to report on the events happening in the last week of Jesus' life. In ancient times, birth records were seldom kept except for royal families. And because birthday celebrations were reserved for kings, most Christians felt that to mimic this practice would have pagan overtones. Throughout Christian history, we have regularly remembered the faithful saints on the dates of their martyrdom—not the date of their birth.

14. The biblical foundation for this sermon is 1 John 1:1–4, 4:7–12.

I am suggesting that if we understood how Christmas came to be such an important holiday in the life of the church, it might help us in our understanding of it for our own time. The celebration of Christ's birth developed over the years—even centuries—because it answered a basic evangelical theology need. Second- and third-century preachers had to make the gospel understandable to people whose thinking had been shaped by the Roman and Greek cultures.

As the church moved out into the world with the message that God had come to earth in human form in the person of Jesus, a skeptical, disbelieving world began to fire questions. The account in Acts shows how Paul handled some of these questions at Athens. The idea that God became a human being seemed totally absurd to them. For some, it was even blasphemous! In their view, the home of the gods was as far away from earth as the traditional East is from the West. By telling the story of the birth of Jesus, they were trying to explain how the humanity of God becomes real for us in the person of Jesus.

For these early Christians, Christmas became the "Festival of the Incarnation," a Latin term meaning "to be made flesh." It comes directly from the Bible: "And the Word became flesh and dwelt among us, full of grace and truth."[15]

Drawing on the Matthew and Luke stories of the birth of Jesus, the early church summarized the meaning of the incarnation in two phrases in the Apostles' Creed: "conceived of the Holy Spirit, born of the Virgin Mary." These words were intended to affirm that God was fully present in Jesus while at the same time say that Jesus was the human presence of God, born of a natural, physical mother just like everyone else.

In Jesus of Nazareth, the early Christian believers encountered the activity of God. As they heard his teachings, learned of his ministry and his death, and saw his followers resurrected to new life, they could only identify it as the presence of God. They believed that only the indwelling presence of God could explain Jesus' single-minded concern for others. They saw it in his absolute trust in the goodness of life. They experienced it in his own self-understanding, which enabled him to live among friends and enemies alike without being swayed by praise or threatened by hostility.

When the church looked at Jesus, it knew that it was looking into the ultimate depths of God's eternal purposes for the world. The humanity of

---

15. See John 1:14.

God had come to us in Jesus, and in Jesus they could see God's highest intentions for humanity.

We ought to stop here for just a moment. If the church believes and affirms that God was present in Jesus, then it can also be affirmed that the attributes we saw in Jesus are the very same attributes that God would also wish might be seen in our lives. This tells us that God was present in Jesus and shows us, and all humanity, what God intended we should become in our own lives and our own maturity.

Therefore, it becomes the mission of the church, reaffirmed in the celebration of the incarnation, to be Jesus people. When this happens, God comes alive in our world through us, just as visibly as God came into the first-century world in Jesus. In the incarnation, God has placed the divine stamp of blessing on *humanness* and has called all people to give of themselves for others just as Jesus did. There is a great deal we can learn from Jesus about living among both friends and enemies while maintaining our loyalty to God. Because of the humanity of God seen in Jesus, we are given a glimpse of the possibilities for our own humanity. From this we also learn about the goodness of life for all people.

The humanity of God—the Festival of the Incarnation—the attempt of the church to affirm that God is not to be found in some far off, secluded paradise carries a profound promise for us today. It is the promise that God is knowable, God is touchable, that we can even be so blunt as to say that God in Jesus has become one of us—a human being.

"Conceived of the Holy Spirit, born of the Virgin Mary" are the words used in the Apostles' Creed. When the church tells its story, the unbelieving world asks, "Was there ever a real person such as the one you talk about?" And the church replies, "Yes there was such a person. He lived in Palestine, he was born in Bethlehem during the reign of Tiberius, and his mother was a young Jewish woman named Mary." Unlike the Greek gods who visited the earth only in the form of thunderbolts, or through showers of golden rain, our God has become known among us as a human being, in a form that we could identify with and understand.

For many Christian people today, "born of the Virgin Mary" has become a way to focus on Christ's divinity as we emphasize "virgin." But in its original setting, the focus was on "born." It was intended to affirm for a pagan world the human aspects of Christ's birth, focusing on that humanness that unites us, not the divinity that divides or separates us.

We have trouble with Christmas today. Maybe it is because we are not talking about the same things any more. In the incarnation, God was talking to us in human terms and was doing it in our human, earthly settings. But today, we focus on the divine. A friend of mine commented recently that he is fed up with the Christmas manger scenes that so many people set up these days. He does not like them because they are way too clean and spiritual. They just aren't dirty enough. Growing up on a farm, where Christmas vacation from college was always spent cleaning out the stables, I understand what he means. While we keep emphasizing the spiritual and the divine, God is still trying to get through to us in human form, in a life that is lived right in front of our eyes.

It is so easy to look in the wrong places to find God. We still want to gaze up into the heavens and worship the king. But the humanity of God in Jesus tells us that now we should be looking around us and seeing God in the poor, the sick, the hungry, and the homeless. But it is so much cleaner to look for God in nicely decorated churches, in Christmas pageants, and around Christmas dinner tables with our loved ones. So, in a very legitimate way, Christmas does become a problem, for it is a mixture of the divine and the human that is still difficult for us to comprehend.

We believe that Christ dwells in the hearts and lives of God's people. But it is hard to practice that belief, for it is a belief that says God still comes to us in very human form. It says that God still reaches out to people in ways that even we can comprehend. That is because it is exactly the way we reach out to those whom we love. The celebration of the incarnation is all about God's love for us.

You see, the "humanity of God"—Jesus—having come in human form, reverses a lot of our ideas about God. God is not primarily experienced as the ruling monarch of the Old Testament. Now, God is to be experienced as the loving, caring servant of people who are hungry, hurting, and homeless. God is no longer described as a distant deity robed in splendor and majesty far out somewhere in the heavens above. Now, God is to be experienced as a presence among us, loving, caring, and walking alongside us.

And that says a lot about the stance Christians should be taking in their lives. The humanity of God changes the relationship of God and humanity—although I don't want to push this too far. It is changed from the sheep-shepherd concept of Psalm 23 to the brother-sister-family relationship. The Festival of the Incarnation is the celebration of God's action inviting us to join the family of Jesus.

Now, what does all this mean?

In 1957, Helmut Gollwitzer, a German theologian, was asked to preach a Christmas sermon at a refugee center in Europe. The essence of the sermon can be summarized as follows: Where are we if God lets himself be laid as a refugee child in a manger and be nailed to the cross and buried in a grave? One thing is certain, everything has changed. There are no longer any holes where there is no light. There is no place we can go where we are alone and totally dependent upon ourselves. Even in the worst loneliness, there is one who takes his place beside us and is there in an indefinable, yet strength-giving way. That God lay so humbly there in that stall means that God shies away from no place in our lives. God is present in every night and in every situation of poverty. No place is so dark or so distant that God cannot find it—or find us in it. It is not that God has ceased to be God, but rather God has come to us in new and unusual ways.

In the earthly existence of Jesus, the power and presence of God have been experienced in our world and in our lives. God does not stay away in some distant heavenly realm, but has come to dwell in the world in which we live. Because God lived in the flesh, facing the insecurities and tensions of human existence and bringing new meaning and potential for living, we can find courage to live through the stress and pressures of our own lives. Humanity has been cleansed, blessed, and redeemed—for God is now Emmanuel, "God with us." And for that we should give thanks, we should celebrate, for indeed, we are a people who are very deeply loved by God just as we are.

7

Follow Your Heart

Don't let life make you frantic.
Has anyone ever gotten even one inch taller by standing
on their tiptoes in front of a mirror?
If fussing about life can't do that, then why fuss at all?
Walk out in the fields and look at the wildflowers.
They don't fuss about how they look,
but have you ever seen such color and design?
If God gives such careful attention to the wildflowers,
and most of them are never even seen by anyone,
don't you think God will take pride in you?
What I am trying to tell you is to relax.
Don't be so pre-occupied with *getting*
that you forget how to respond to God's *giving*.
Don't be afraid of missing out on anything.
You are my dearest friends.
God wants to give you the very best of all that God has.

—Paraphrase of Jesus' words from Luke 12 and John 14

Keep sharing your good thoughts.
Don't be afraid to dream, because every good idea began as a dream.
When you dream, that idea can become real.
Follow your dreams because they will take you places
that other people neither see nor understand.
Dreams are God's invitation to experience today
what the future will bring tomorrow.

—Howard Brembeck
Personal letter

Follow Your Heart

I was a young pastor in my first congregation. Two years of seminary had prepared me for this work, but suddenly I was doing things I had never done before. Preaching two sermons over five months in a homiletics class is quite different from preparing a new sermon every seven days. Church members were living with concerns that were not included in the syllabus from my Pastoral Care class. They were asking questions for which I had been given no answers. I was facing issues that my seminary professors had never introduced in the classroom, and we students had never talked about over coffee. It was exciting and terrifying at the same time because I was on my own.

Back in the seminary classroom I was confident that I knew how to do a lot of things. Now I had this uneasy feeling that I knew almost nothing that these people assumed I would know. If I had been asked about my vision for the church, I would have said something about hoping that in ten years the church membership list would be longer than it was right now. I began in ministry with a stable, cautious vision based more on sustaining the life of the church than on any concept of growth in mission.

As a new young pastor in Illinois Conference, I received numerous invitations to preach in other congregations. These people were legitimately curious about the new pastor at Freeport. After preaching in one congregation, an older member of the church said to me, "Wouldn't it be wonderful if we could just return to the spirituality that the first-century church had? How I wish the church could be filled with the Spirit like the church at Corinth."

I didn't know what to say. But I thought, "If that's what people believe, I'd better think about it." Where do we go to find our spiritual base? Is the early church described in Acts the best model of how church should be today? Is it really true that our best days are behind us, so the most we can hope for is to slow down the rate of an inevitable spiritual decline in the church? Should we be focusing on the past in order to discover what God would have us do in the future?

There was something inside me that would not let me accept the belief that our future has to be a repetition of the past. I had a deep appreciation for Associated Mennonite Biblical Seminaries (AMBS) New Testament professor Dr. Howard Charles. One day I was in a meeting at the seminary, so I stopped by his office and talked with him about how he saw spirituality in the early church. He smiled and gave that little chuckle that was so characteristic of him. He asked me to define what I meant by "spirituality." He suggested that I go back and reread the Acts of the Apostles more carefully. He also suggested that I take a long look at the church in Corinth before deciding whether I wanted that to be my model for spirituality in the church today.

This wasn't the answer I was expecting, but I agreed to do it. I read the Acts of the Apostles again, this time focusing on the quality of life, the depth of relationships, and the nature of faith within the early church as the story is related by Luke. I wanted to get inside those wonderful stories of God's saving acts to see what was going on in these spiritual congregations that my contemporaries were wishing the church would emulate.

In order to force myself to slow down and read more carefully, I offered to teach a Sunday school class on the Acts of the Apostles. I knew this would demand that I wrestle with the text more carefully as I prepared to share with others what I was finding.

As I studied the text and then taught the class, I began to see that there is a powerful mythology surrounding the life of the early church. The imagery that many people have about first-century spirituality simply does not match the reality I found just below the casual reading most of us give the Bible. Certainly, the story includes numerous dramatic experiences, but I wondered whether these dramatic stories reflected the norm for church or if they were radical exceptions to how most people were experiencing church life.

Over the next weeks I developed a growing conviction that I certainly did not want to return to the first-century church with their conflicts, theological disagreements, and interpersonal tensions among the church leaders. Some leaders of this very young movement dared to challenge the religious-cultural values "that had always been true." (Whether they had actually been true or not is another issue).

Church life was constantly being disrupted by tensions over who could be a member of this new faith community. What was the proper way to conduct worship? What practices should be permitted in, or excluded from, worship? How could they convince people living in city A to give generously in support of people who lived far away in city B because these people whom they had never met were facing a severe hunger crisis? How did the faith community function when among them were people who believed they were far more spiritual than, and thus superior to, other followers of Jesus who did not believe exactly as they did?

Being the pastor of the "First Church of Jesus" in Corinth was a clear invitation to criticism, serious misunderstandings, and severe social clashes with the surrounding community. Just ask Paul how that congregation treated its leaders! The church at Ephesus (Paul's favorite congregation) was equally difficult because of the differing understandings of spirituality among its membership. Depending upon your theological point of view, it would have been either very exciting or terribly discouraging to have attended the first major church conference reported in Acts 15. Was this new, more inclusive faith that Paul was advocating, which allowed people who were not like us to be full members, a departure from the historic faith (as many felt it was), or was it an exciting sign of the Spirit's leading (as others thought it was)? How would you report that decision to your home congregation when you knew they were not of one mind on this, or any other, religious practice?

I could no longer hold to a vision that wanted to return to a spirituality of the past. In seminary I had studied these periods of biblical and post-biblical history, and while they were certainly intriguing, they did not provide many compelling reasons for using that history as the glorious model for positive church life in our own time. Is God best seen as a power from the past that needs to be protected from the new ideas of our own age? Wouldn't it be better to think of God as a force drawing us into the future, giving us the freedom to explore fresh ways of following Jesus that take seriously the message of Jesus as we face the events of our own day?

I do not know exactly when it started, but I began to be increasingly excited by the belief that God is calling us to new life, to new expressions of faith that neither deny nor reject the past, but that build upon it. We are constantly adjusting and making course corrections as we learn new things about God's presence with us. I wondered whether we will ever reach the place where we know all that we need to know in order to be faithful followers of Jesus.

How would life be different if we would visualize the church as a people on a journey? How would it be if we were excited about trying to keep up with what God is doing, always anticipating what new experiences might be just over the hill, or around the corner, or in the new year just ahead of us? Is there a way for us to honor the past without having to repeat it? Episcopal priest Wes Seeliger wrote and illustrated a fascinating book, *Western Theology*. In this work he argues with the image of church as the city courthouse protecting the past. Seeliger prefers the image of a wagon train that is always looking for new adventures in the road ahead. This image of a wagon train exploring the future was tremendously exciting for me.

I was quite young in this new task of leading a congregation. Suddenly it hit me how much there was that I had to learn. How could I best be a pastor for those members who wanted to commit themselves to the excitement of discovering new ways of living and sharing their faith? Our historic faith is filled with spine-tingling stories of danger, hostility, and persecution of people who literally gave their lives for what they believed. Could that faith provide a foundation that allows us to move into the future with confidence and without being defensive? Is there a way that we can be open to new discoveries without having to reject the answers that were meaningful to our grandparents? Are there new languages and visual images that catch the imagination of younger contemporary minds without sacrificing the reality that gave such vitality to the images and language of our parents?

The call seemed so clear and so obvious. But I wasn't sure I knew how this would happen. Could we experience faith in Jesus as tugging us toward the future with all its unknown possibilities? Or does faith have to be the brakes that occasionally lock up and throw us into the ditch, making us unable or unwilling to move while the world passes us by? Is it possible to develop a faith that is oriented toward the future, a faith that continues to be filled with hope and excitement, rather than becoming more and more irrelevant and outdated?

I wanted to be part of a faith community that has the courage to explore new trails and find new ways of experiencing faith that provides integrity for people right now. I wanted a faith that encourages us to ask questions (without having to know the answers in advance). A faith like this would be willing to take risks, because we believe that God's presence is with us in everything we do, even when we fail.

Not everyone shares this excitement about the future. Some are frightened by almost anything new because they are convinced God is best seen in the past. My belief in God tells me that God is not only with us here, but is already in our future—long before we ever get there—urging us to keep up and to discover the promise that is waiting for us as the sun comes up on each new day.

My experience has been that this new vision does not protect me from all things painful, nor does it stop me from making mistakes when I should know better. But it does allow me to continue on a journey that is exciting, fulfilling, and full of surprises. I am comfortable believing that this commitment to the future as a way of living in the present is a good one. I still become a bit uncomfortable at times when people tell me about all the terrible things that they are afraid of in this unknown future, but I am encouraged by the knowledge that God is out there ahead of me, and so it is appropriate for me to take another step forward.

How Do You Tell the Story of Jesus?

In the early 1970s, Uganda was fighting a civil war. Refugees were fleeing for their lives. Mennonite Central Committee urged congregations in the United States to become sponsors for refugee families.

The Akron Mennonite Church accepted an extended family of three siblings with their spouses and children. These families were of Muslim faith. We helped them get settled in good housing, find jobs, and adjust to American life. We also found empty space right next door to the church offices in downtown Akron where they set up their own worship center.

Rather early in our relationship these families asked if they might visit our worship service as a way of saying "thank you" for helping them get settled. They indicated that this would be a new experience for them. They knew very little about Christian faith and had never attended a Christian service before. I gave them a warm welcome. I also explained what happens in worship, and that they should feel comfortable simply observing or participating as it felt appropriate.

But now, the challenge was mine. What should I do in the morning sermon? I wanted to help them understand the central principles of Christian faith while being respectful of their own Muslim faith. I was also in the process of rethinking my own faith and how I understood the message of Jesus. I was having serious questions about whether Christian faith was best described as telling people how to get to heaven (something only Christian people will do) or whether it was a call to live as children of God right here on earth (something all people can do).

I remember a conversation with John H. Yoder years before. He told me, "Don't expect that everything Jesus said was absolutely brand new and had never been said before. This is exactly what we should be doing with this message in our own day. We should rediscover its truth and apply it to our own time."

I decided to tell the story of God's interaction with humanity beginning with Abraham. I would include the Old Testament prophets and then present Jesus as the continuation of God's original intention of calling a people who would be God's witness to truth, justice, and peace here on earth. Working on this sermon helped me develop my own emerging understanding of faith in Jesus. This sermon moved the focus away from what we get from Jesus to what it means to follow Jesus.

As I told the Jesus story within the context of *heilsgeschichte* (God's salvation history), I wanted to show that Jesus was a continuation of

God's activity all throughout history. Jesus had to be seen in his own first-century context, while still calling us to be faithful people living out God's message in our own experience. From this Sunday on, saying "Jesus is Lord" took on new meaning for me.

I gave this sermon and it was well received. However, sermons often generate unexpected responses. The next morning, a young mother stopped by my office to express her deep appreciation for the previous day's sermon. She had always seen Jesus as a special figure that just dropped out of heaven with very little connection to anything else. She had felt a lot of guilt about her uncertainty over what to do with Jesus. The sermon gave Jesus a place in biblical history. For her, this made so much good sense in a very healthy way.

In the months that followed, this sermon opened a lot of good conversation with the Muslim families. Because their worship center was right next door to my office, we had many opportunities to talk about faith. Their knowledge of the Koran was only average (much like the level of biblical knowledge that most Christians have). Together, we discovered that the Koran and the Bible each have some texts that we wish were not there and are not sure what to do with them. We also discovered that both the Bible and the Koran have a rather solid peace theme that is, for the most part, ignored by both religious communities. They had always seen Christianity as a very violent, war-driven faith; and for them, this particular sermon, and our ongoing conversation, was very helpful. These conversations were equally helpful for me because they greatly improved my understanding of and appreciation for Muslim faith and the Koran.

Through these conversations we developed a good friendship and mutual understanding that I wish might happen far more often between Muslim and Christian people. Perhaps finding settings where we can simply share what we believe without implying that our listeners must believe as we do, and listening to others tell their stories, is an effective step toward interfaith dialogue and improved human relationships. Sharing our faith with persons, rather than preaching it at them as dogma, might facilitate conversations within our own Christian congregations over the differing faith ideas held by many members. Doing this affirms that it is possible to hold firmly to one's own religious beliefs while accepting others who hold equally firmly to their own beliefs—even when at times those beliefs appear to be in total conflict. My work with these Ugandan refugees was one of my first extended experiences with persons of a different world religion. Over the next few years, I learned many good things about Muslim faith. I learned, as well, that there are some areas where we hold quite different beliefs. But being able to talk about our personal faith, including those areas where we differed, made it much easier for us to visit together and develop a friendship that was enriching to us all.

The particular sermon that follows is a later version that was adapted to include more recent references to national history and our own personal experience. Some illustrations or references have changed, but the core content remains the same. Most pastors don't want to admit that they preach old sermons. But I have used versions of this sermon often and now, nearly forty years later, this sermon still speaks to me. It is still well received in congregations across the Mennonite Church, and it represents the theology that was becoming the foundation of my faith.

* * *

How Do You Tell the Story of Jesus?[1]

Peter and John have a problem. A lame man has been healed and the authorities have arrested them. Note, however, that it was not the miracle of healing that led to their arrest. It was the explanation they gave. They dared to say it had been done in the name of Jesus. The religious authorities were not happy with this explanation. They had just crucified Jesus a couple of months ago. They thought they were done with him. To hear that he was still doing miracles made them very nervous. And, even worse, Peter and John used this situation to tell everyone why they should also follow Jesus.

Storytelling is a great way to communicate. Christians should always be ready to tell the story of Jesus. But how do we do that? Most of us believe we already know the story, so what's to tell? Like these religious leaders, we think we know what God is doing. But the way Peter and John tell the story challenged people to rethink what they believed about Jesus. After all, the evidence was jumping up and down right there in front of them. By inserting new information into an old story, people were confronted with God in a new way.

Today, when people tell the story of Jesus, they usually start with themselves and their need for forgiveness, salvation, and inner peace.

1. The biblical foundation for this sermon is Acts 3:1—4:4.

They then work their way out from their own story to the Jesus story, and finally to the God story. But that is not how the biblical writers tell the story. They began the salvation story with God's love for all humanity. Into that God-story the biblical writers insert Jesus, and only then do they include you and me in the great sweep of God's redemptive activity in history.

When the Bible tells the story of Jesus, it starts in a place that is currently called Iraq (today our government tells us that this is enemy territory). The story starts with Abraham hearing the call of God to leave the security and stability of Ur, a town just north of Baghdad (and already, for Americans today, the story has a different tone). God's call of Abraham includes the challenge of living in an open relationship with God so that *other people* get healed, *other people* find life, and *other people* discover hope. The story of God is about mission: letting God's grace that means so much to us flow through us to others so that they might discover this same grace and mercy in their own lives.

In the time of Abraham, every nation had their own gods. Much like today, they asked their god to protect them from their enemies and cause them to prosper. As Abraham travelled from place to place, he came to believe that there is just one God who is over all people and all nations. That was a dramatic discovery, far ahead of the traditional god-thinking of his day. He came to believe that God is not confined within the geo-political boundaries that nations create to identify themselves and their territory.

Not long ago, Carolyn and I attended a Smothers Brothers concert. Some of you will remember their famous argument about how "mom always liked you best." Using that same logic, Israel began to think that since God is God over all nations, and because God chose us, that must mean that God likes us best. Now before we get too critical of this logic, just listen to the political and religious voices of our own day where virtually every public speech ends by asking God to bless us. National religious leaders tell us that our prosperity and success proves that God is on our side, not on theirs.

There were prophets in Israel who saw what was happening. These prophets had the annoying habit of identifying very specific things that needed attention. They believed that God had given them the land, and that they were to share it so that all people could eat. Sadly, by the time of Amos, some people were seizing land and becoming fantastically rich while forcing their neighbors into poverty. Amos had some very harsh words for people who used pious language to support their greedy self-ishness that defied the central purposes of God.

Israel gradually adopted a confusing mix of nationalistic God-language and a self-centered view of God's presence in the world. Hosea drew upon his own painful experience of a broken marriage to tell Israel that God is a forgiving God, but they cannot keep expecting God to save them when they keep wandering off into sin. The prophet Isaiah pleaded with Israel to trust in God, rather than relying on military might for their salvation.

The biblical writers tell us that God saw what was happening and decided to take direct, radical action. In Jesus of Nazareth, God's message came alive in a new, very human way.

Now the obvious question is "Why would God do that?" Jesus himself said that he came to live among us so that other people could experience the grace and love of God in their own lives. We believe that we are called to continue the work begun by Jesus. We are to help people in need, to feed the hungry, to work for peace and justice in the world, and to bring hope to anyone who is giving up on life.

Where do we find the confidence that doing what Jesus taught actually puts us in harmony with God? Here we come to another of the radical beliefs of Christian faith. Jesus talked about dramatic new ways of responding to God in our lives. What he said and did threatened both the Roman authorities and the Jewish religious leaders. These leaders realized if Jesus was right in what he was saying, they were in danger of losing the base of their power. None of us like to admit that we are wrong. These political-religious leaders were faced with a choice. Either they could reach out and embrace this new thing that God was doing or they could dig in their heels to protect their own definitions of what God was doing.

These leaders took the easy way out. They decided to get rid of Jesus. Today, we fire people to get rid of them or we vote them out of office when we don't agree with what they are doing. These first-century leaders twisted the Mosaic law. They told lies about Jesus. They fabricated a case against Jesus by hiring paid informers. They put political pressure on the judge, and they got away with it. They collaborated with Rome to solve their problem by killing their enemy. That approach to problem solving is still very common today. But God does not quit that easily. Three days after Jesus was crucified, the Bible reports that he was raised from the dead. This radical belief that God is a God of resurrection is at the heart of faith for those who say *Jesus is Lord*. This confirms for us the belief that Jesus was telling the truth about God, and how God would have us live.

This radical faith is still present in our world, but it struggles today much like it did in the first century. It is still dangerous to challenge people in power when they defy God's will for humanity. It is even more dangerous to tell religious people that the way they think and act is not of God. Jesus told us it would be this way. When God reaches across the lines that we draw, in order to maintain our own security, we often respond by building walls to protect these lines. The result is that the persons who most desperately need the love of God find themselves walled out. The really tragic thing is that we feel okay doing it!

What does this say to us this morning? The first word comes from the prophet Hosea as he explores the imagery of God being a God of love. This theme literally comes to life in the person of Jesus. The apostle John puts it this way: "Beloved, let us love one another, for love is of God and anyone who loves is born of God and knows God."[2] Jesus said, "Love your enemies, do good to those who hate you, bless those who persecute you."[3]

One of the exciting things being rediscovered in Christian faith today is the call to share the depth of God's love. I don't mean God's love for us. I mean God's love for others, even our enemies. If we are serious in our claim to be followers of Jesus, that means we must make a conscious decision to center our lives in Jesus. This often places us in direct conflict with the pressures of our world as it calls us to join in hating, and killing, our enemies. Today, we are bombarded with religious language from both religious and political leaders, but the thunder we hear loudest is the voice of Mars, the ancient Roman god of war.

The second voice comes from Amos as he went to Bethel and was confronted with the contrast of wealth and power in his day. Jesus made this a theme for his own ministry: "Don't lay up for yourselves treasure on earth, where moth or rust can ruin it, and thieves break in and steal it, for your values and your character are all wrapped up together."[4] Where do we find our security? Is it in military might? Is it in the collection of material resources for our own use? Or do we find our security in people working together for peace and justice? In every generation God has been calling people to live simply and responsibly. We have not done very

2. See 1 John 4:7.
3. See Matthew 5:44.
4. See Matthew 6:19.

well at that. Right now we are caught in an economy that is making life very painful for many of us. Where do we find our security these days? Is church a place where people find food for today and hope for tomorrow?

The third voice comes from Ezekiel as he looked out over an old cemetery in Babylon wondering if there was any hope for new life. Jesus took the words of Ezekiel and called for a radically new way of looking at life. Jesus called it "being born again." The problem today is that this language is so commonplace that it has lost its meaning. "Born again" language today means little more than rearranging our theological ideas to include going to church on Sunday morning. We assume that being born again speaks only to how you think about God. We separate the love of God from how you treat your enemies, how you spend your money, how you use your own body, or how you use God's creation.

You see, the story of Jesus takes on new life when we discover that God consistently does things among us. But we keep trying to use the same old answers to explain a story that is dynamic and creative. When we say "we alone have all the truth" we assume there is nothing new for us to learn. When that happens our energy goes into defending and protecting that truth. As we define and protect, the walls keep getting higher and higher. Tragically, inside these walls, we feel less and less secure, so we fight harder and harder. We restate our old definitions about the grace of God and then decide who else is worthy to receive that grace. We even tell God whom God dares to love.

I suggest that we dare not assume that we are already doing all the right things, so that all we need to do is more of what we are already doing. We dare not think that we just need to hold more meetings, preach more sermons, pray more prayers, give more money so that we can make more people become just like we are. That is exactly the criticism that Jesus leveled at the Pharisees. When you believe that you have the right answers, you keep doing the same things, and nothing new happens in your life.

When we risk doing new things, like loving enemies or reaching out to the oppressed, tension often increases. The challenge given by Jesus is to find new language, new avenues of expression, and new vehicles for engaging people in conversation. We are challenged to learn together about God, reaching out to others where they are and not simply expecting them to come to where we are.

Our challenge is to find new life in the confession *Jesus is Lord*. As followers of Jesus, instead of fighting other people, we become peacemakers in the name of Jesus. Instead of pushing to get into positions of power so that we can control things, we serve so that others may live. Instead of letting the world define what it means to be human, we see in every human being the presence of God yearning to burst out into new life. Instead of building walls to protect ourselves, we trust the Spirit of God to give us new life, and through us to others, so that together we celebrate God's presence with all humanity.

It is my prayer this morning that, myself included, we might open our hearts to the truth that comes to us in Jesus, to the living God who yearns to share life with us, and to the Spirit of God who empowers us to make all things new. When we do this, the story of Jesus becomes our story. We become new persons, and the world will be better because of it. *Prayer:* We open ourselves to you Lord, and we pray for the courage to entrust our lives into your hands. May we be loving expressions of your grace, agents of healing and hope for all whom we meet, that your name might be glorified in all that we do. Amen.

Who Stole the Tent?[5]

Sherlock Holmes is my favorite detective. One weekend, Holmes and Dr. Watson took a short vacation to go camping on the moors of England. After an evening of conversation, they crawled into their tent and went to sleep. Several hours later, Holmes nudged Watson and asked, "Look up at the stars and tell me what you see." Watson replied, "I see millions and millions of stars." "I know, but what does that tell you?" asked Holmes. Watson thought for a moment, "Astronomically, I observe that Saturn is in Leo. Horologically, I estimate it is about 3 a.m, and theologically, I conclude that compared with God in the heavens, we are very small and insignificant. And I think we will have a beautiful day tomorrow. What do you see, Holmes?" "Watson," Holmes replied, "As usual, you have missed the obvious. Some dodger has stolen our tent!"

I think that once in a while, as we study the Bible and examine words (looking for mismatched pronouns and exegete phrases) and as we do research in ancient cultures, we forget to notice that someone has stolen the tent. Churches today, us included, are living with growing tension. We read the Bible differently, we experience our faith differently, but nobody thinks to ask—"Who stole the tent?"

The book of Acts is the story of a rapidly growing church in which people are being saved. Some of these people had met Jesus personally. Others had never met Jesus in person but were hearing the Jesus story from Paul. As these people heard about Jesus, they liked what they heard, but they didn't have the same religious history or foundations. These new believers, simply by their presence, were causing tension with the older, more traditional folks. They had a few practices that were hard to accept. They had the audacity to ask "why" questions that don't have easy answers. And the older folks kept thinking "somebody is stealing our tent."

So the church called a meeting. They prayed together, they talked together, and quickly found that the Holy Spirit had a solution for the problem. They rejoiced, sang a few hymns, wrote down the Spirit-directed solution, shared it with the larger church, and everyone was happy with the way God had led them.

Now that would be nice, and we even wish it would happen to us, but that is not the way the Bible tells the story. In our eagerness to protect the tent (the unity of the church), we don't see the process, the anxiety, the differences of opinion, and the tension that this church meeting in

5. The biblical foundation for this sermon is Acts 15:1–21.

Jerusalem caused. The faith community was going through tremendous upheaval, facing issues they had never dreamed would hit them, and they survived.

When I read the book of Acts, I see the church fighting over organization, over how to include persons from other cultures, and over how to handle racial and sexual prejudice. They struggled with blatant immorality among members, they faced division over how they served communion, and they argued over who gets to speak in worship or how a person gets to be a member—all while simply trying to survive in a very hostile environment.

The book of Acts warns us that if we want to avoid tension in the church, then we need to find an effective way to keep other people out. Unfortunately, there are churches who still think that is the way to do it. But Acts 15 tells us that if we want to be a dynamic community of faith, we need to reach out to new people, share the grace of God with them, receive them as sisters and brothers, and, along the way, listen to their concerns, their questions, and their ideas.

So maybe we could learn something by looking at how the early church managed to pull it off. This Jerusalem conference was led by the Spirit. It resulted in a startling conclusion, one that most of the group was not expecting. How God led them to it can be very helpful to us, because the church today is facing similar issues. It revolves around the nature and experience of salvation. Who is saved, and how does it happen?

In that day, circumcision was mandatory in order to be part of God's people. It had always been that way, and people knew that is the way it would always be. Everyone was expected to believe this because it was obvious that is what the Scriptures taught. But the problem was that some of the new people simply did not believe it.

It is easy for us to look back on that issue and think that it was a pretty simple problem. "We know where God stands," we might imagine them saying. "So, why the fuss? Of course uncircumcised people can be saved. They just have to be circumcised. Ever since the time of Moses, over twelve hundred years ago, this is the way it has been, and a lot of people are wondering why we are even talking about it."

But this was not an easy problem for them to solve. They called a meeting to discuss what a person had to do to be saved. The text says they had "much debate." That tells me that people did not all agree, but at least they let each other talk. There is an interesting point made in verse 12. Paul and Barnabas got up to report on their experiences among the

Gentiles. The text says "the whole assembly became quiet." Now, I wonder if maybe during the earlier debate there might have been some times when the people weren't silent, where they interrupted each other, shouted at each other, perhaps even quoted Scripture at each other. It might even have been the case that, once in a while, the discussion spilled over into heated argument. After all, this is not just a decision about black-topping the parking lot; this was *salvation* they were talking about. This silence doesn't sound like the quiet silence of God miraculously changing people's hearts. It sounds more like the hostile silence of persons who want to object because they do not like what is being said, but in that moment they simply can't think of anything to say.

When we get into conflict situations, we often fight over secondary issues. In Acts 15, circumcision was the presented issue, but it wasn't the real issue. The primary issue was "Who can be saved? Who can be a member of the church?" The church members wanted to talk about doctrine, about history, and about circumcision. But Paul and Barnabas wanted to talk about what God was doing and how people were experiencing salvation. Very quickly the secondary issue took center stage: "These people have to be circumcised and keep the law." I find it interesting that when circumcision was the topic, there was confusion. But when they started talking about salvation, the place became silent and people listened.

Any church that is growing spiritually is going to have conflict and will face difficult issues. When that happens, we must be clear among ourselves on what the issue really is. For the early church, the confusion revolved around ideas like "Can Gentiles be saved?" versus "Do saved people have to be circumcised?" Behind that discussion was an unspoken fear. "Will the church be ruined by these uncircumcised people who probably don't have any moral standards either?"

Might this be a bit like the dilemmas we face today? Perhaps we are confusing "Who is saved?" with "How do saved people worship?" Or put another way, "What is the conformity level that we expect of persons before they can join us in worship?" As for the debate described in Acts 15, one group insisted upon a high level of maturity and achievement, while the other group affirmed the salvation experience without insisting on an identical understanding of every related issue.

There is another significant event that often gets overlooked as we read Acts. After Paul and Barnabas reported on their experiences, James got up, quoted an Old Testament text, and then said that this verse verified that inviting Gentles to be among the congregation was the will of

God. And we agree with what James said. But I wonder. That Old Testament text James quoted had been a part of their worship experiences for centuries. They had read it often, but no one ever thought to quote it as the solution for this particular situation. It was only after Paul and Barnabas reported on the activity of God that James said, "That is what this verse is talking about. This is not something new that God is doing. Way back in the Old Testament, God was telling us this and we just didn't see it." That is truly a major step forward in sensing the guidance of the Holy Spirit as we read the Scriptures.

Do we honestly believe that God has a solution for the issues that are creating tension among us? Some of us tend to say, "Yes, and God has shown me what the solution is!" But when I say that, other persons respond with their own "godly solution"—and now we have simply added another layer of tension to the discussion. For if I know that my solution is a godly one, and your solution does not agree with my solution, then it is perfectly obvious that you are not a godly person. And that is a very ungodly conclusion!

There are several observations about the experiences described in Acts 15 that I think might be helpful for us today. We need to recognize that we have differences in how we look at faithfulness to God. For some, it is keeping up with what God is doing, reaching out, sharing love, and accepting new ideas—for that is where God is. But for others, it is being faithful, holding fast to what God has been doing in history, and being faithful to the long-standing beliefs of the church—because that is where God has always been. And because both answers are right (for God is there, and God is here, and God is also in the future), we have opened the door for tension over what appropriate faith is all about. So what can we do?

First, let's start by rejoicing that all of us care deeply about our faith, and that is a good thing. It is important to us, and we do want to be faithful to God. If we accept the truth that we all care deeply about faith, then we might not be quite so quick to condemn others who believe differently about certain issues or experiences. Can we see past our human theological differences and reach out to each other with acceptance? If we can do that, then we can also reach out to others with food, peace, justice, and the call of salvation for all humanity.

Second, let's meet together to pray and study the Scriptures. Let's meet together in small groups to share and pray for each other. It is easy to pray that God will reveal God's truth to us and give us "the answer."

That is a content prayer. The problem with content prayers is that when we pray content prayers, we often have a pretty good idea of what the answer should be before giving God the time and space to share it with us. So in effect, we are praying at people in order to get them to hear the answer we think God has already given to us.

May I suggest that in times of conflict and tension we should be praying process prayers that ask God to help us create a community of faith where God's voice can be heard by all and God's truth can be experienced with one Spirit.

Third, we need to listen better. I know that sometimes I don't listen very well. When another is speaking, and I am not talking, as often as not all I am doing is politely waiting for the speaker to stop talking so that I can start. Perhaps you do this, too. And while you are talking, I am thinking about what I am going to say, which by the way, is much more important than what you are saying! Perhaps you also do this.

If we believe that God is active in our lives, then we need to hear the testimony of others in whom God is also active. And as we listen, we may discover that what God is doing is far more encompassing than our perceptions of what God is doing. It is hard to listen when you already know what the truth is. And please hear this. This is not a call to give up your truth, but a call to allow God to expand our common understandings of truth.

Fourth, we must talk together. Real talking means that I share my ideas with you and that I listen to your ideas. When we share with others, we invite them into God's circle of love, and that helps all of us grow. Thus, how we talk to each other can be very important. When I hear how you have experienced God in your life, then my knowledge of God is increased. When I hear only my own voice telling you about my experience, then I am learning nothing. I am only reinforcing that which I already know, and that may have nothing whatever to do with learning.

We have not always done very well at talking and listening. Sometimes we have silenced others by intimidation or ridicule. Sometimes we have ignored them or expelled them from the circle in order to keep peace in the congregation.

As I look back at Acts 15, I imagine there were a few people who thought that other individuals near to them had a lot to learn, and unless they changed, they would be unacceptable. But these people listened, they shared what they believed, and together, as a group, they came to a conclusion they could all live with: to be faithful to what God was doing in their midst. As I look at the Acts 15 story, I see the same kind of emotions that we experience today—fear, stress, deep conviction, frustration, and a bit of anger. Like them, we feel what we feel in the moment. The experience is intense because it is what we are feeling—right now—and we don't know what the future is going to be like. I am convinced that on the day before the Jerusalem conference, the participants did not know how the conference was going to end, any more than we can know how such a meeting might end in our time. Such a conversation, regardless of location or era, is an act of faith—profound faith in God.

We should not be afraid in times of change; but rather, we must trust that God is present with us. Can we affirm the spirituality of those with whom we differ so that we can talk together, pray together, worship together, eat together, and actually enjoy doing it? When we cut each other off and refuse to listen or participate in fellowship together, we lose touch with some of the channels of God's grace that are being extended to us.

I recognize that it is sometimes hard to feel God's presence in people with whom we differ. But until we learn to feel God's presence in such circumstances, we really don't have much hope for restoration of a caring community within the church. Dare we believe that the same God who is at work among us offering healing and hope was also at work in that tension-filled gathering of Christians some two centuries ago? And might it be possible that this same God is calling us to a new level of spirituality that will deepen our faith, broaden our horizons, and strengthen our congregation?

In the movie *The Poseidon Adventure*, Maureen McGovern sings a tantalizing song that may actually speak to us even though our situation is very different. "There's got to be a morning after, if we can hold on through the night. We have a chance to find the sunshine, let's keep on looking for the light." Does God have a new morning for us? I think there is, and in the meantime, let's worry less about who stole the tent, and simply enjoy the beauty of the heavens above us, because the handiwork of God truly is marvelous to behold.

How Can This Be?

Several years ago, I heard Dr. Marcus Borg speak at a conference in Portland, Oregon. He described a Native American storyteller who often began a story about an event from his tribe's history by saying, "Now, I don't know if it happened exactly this way or not, but I do know this story is true." This sounded very much like Hebrew storytelling, which focused on communicating the central message, rather than dwelling on the technical details used to tell the story. Thus, ancient biblical stories were more theological narratives than historical chronicles.

With that said, Christmas has always made me uncomfortable. Not just the commercialism (that annoys me a great deal), but also the mythology that so many people have about the story. I was recently in a worship service where the children of the congregation told the Christmas story as a pageant. They did a delightful job of storytelling, except the scriptwriter inserted twenty-first century theology into the mouth of Joseph. At the stable, as he reflected on the future significance of this child who had just been born, did Joseph really wonder about how this one-day-old son would someday give his life as a ransom for the sins of the world?

A much more fascinating telling of the story happened one year at the Akron Mennonite Church. One of the church members, Doris Longacre, came to me with a children's story about a Central American immigrant family who had come to the United States. The mother was pregnant. They had no friends and virtually no money. They had no place to stay and no access to a hospital. Their baby was born in their old car in the parking lot behind a Walmart store. A young nurse saw the car and asked if everything was alright. When she saw what was happening, she stayed and helped with the delivery. Several store employees brought clean diapers and a blanket. One shopper, seeing the activity, invited the family to come stay in her home for a few days.

That story really stuck with me. Would this be an accurate modern Mary and Joseph story? It is such a contrast to the beautiful biblical story as we tell it in Christmas carols and church pageants. Was the actual birth really as beautiful and sanitary as it seems when you surround Mary and Joseph with rich foreign royalty bearing gifts, and a choir of angels singing four-part harmony?

For many years, I never did anything with Doris's immigrant story. But I never forgot it. One Christmas, many years later, I was scheduled to preach the Christmas Sunday sermon. Although I was sure everyone knew the story, I decided to tell it as Joseph experienced it. After all, what father wants his first born child to come into this world in a barn? I tried to imagine the anger, the anxiety, and the feelings of dismal failure that Joseph must have had. This simply was not how he had wanted it to be. I wanted the congregation to feel the humanity of Mary and Joseph in this experience. I wanted the meaning of the story to have priority over the technical details of how the story is told. What does this story tell us?

In the sermon itself, my wife Carolyn was the voice of Mary in the conversations that took place. I still remember an older woman in the congregation who came up to me immediately following the service. "Do you really think that is how it happened? You made everything so human." She was followed a few minutes later by a young mother, holding her own infant child. She was on the verge of tears as she said, "Finally, a Christmas story I can believe. Mary and Joseph became real people for me this morning. I think I know what it felt like for her."

But there were also a few people who were not happy with the sermon because it took away the majesty and the miraculous glory of God coming into the world. They made almost the same comment in reverse: "You don't really think it happened that way, do you?"

Perhaps this is what biblical stories do for us. Each of us sees them differently, depending on what we want to find there. But is it not important to see biblical persons as real human beings? To do otherwise is to lose the integrity of the story. If these persons are perfect saints, how can we relate to them, or learn from them? We do serious damage to the Christmas story, and any biblical story, when we feel we have to dress it up, making it clean and pure. None of us are that way. If we believe when God works in a person's life that events fall into place, nothing ever gets dirty, and everyone has a smile on their face, we have lost the meaning of the incarnation.

I still don't know how many of the details are historically precise in every way, and I don't really worry about that. But I do know the story. When we tell it with all its human anxiety and pain, it tells me a lot more about how God works in the lives of young people just getting started, as well as older people who are starting to slow down. Just maybe that theological insight is more important than the historical accuracy of every detail.

* * *

How Can This Be?

They were tired. They had good reason, because the day had been long and the trip was not easy. Joseph walked along the dusty road muttering to himself in anger. No one likes to pay taxes, and the Romans can be so stubborn. It didn't matter if you were poor and it didn't matter whether you could afford the trip. It didn't even matter when you asked if your wife could stay home because she was pregnant. "No Exceptions!" they said. "Everyone has to go!"

"How can this be!" Joseph muttered to himself as he worried about Mary having to ride on a donkey in her condition. He worried about the money. It was hard enough just paying the taxes. How would they pay for this trip, especially now that there would be a new baby to support? Joseph grumbled about the unfairness of life, in general, until Mary tried to calm him by reminding him, "Joseph, please don't worry, God has promised to take care of us."

The registration didn't take long. It mainly consisted of giving your name, local address, what property you owned, and how you made your living. The soldier who took the information seemed like a nice man. Joseph was glad for that, because some Roman soldiers made you stand in line for hours for no reason at all. But this soldier had pulled them out of line and took care of them right away. He had actually smiled at Mary. Maybe he had a wife and family back home, too. Maybe God hadn't forgotten about them after all.

"Now," Joseph told Mary, "let's find a room so you can rest. There's an inn just down the street; it doesn't look too expensive. Let's go there." Joseph helped Mary off the donkey; they went up to the door and knocked.

"We'd like a room for the night, please," Joseph said as the door opened.

"Oooh, I'm sorry sir; I don't have a thing. You might try down the street." The man pointed to a small building about a block away. "They usually have room."

So Mary climbed back on the donkey, and they started down the street. Joseph breathed a quiet prayer to Yahweh as he knocked on the door and asked the same question. "Sorry," the innkeeper said, "we're full."

"Could you suggest someplace for us?" Joseph asked.

"Why, yes, just go up the street to that place; he's a friend of mine, good place."

"We've already been there; he sent us here."

"Oh, well, let's see, there's another place about two streets away. It's a little out of the way, they'll probably have room."

So they went there, only this time Mary decided to stay on the donkey, rather than go with Joseph to the door. Joseph wondered about that, but then was glad she had stayed behind because the owner just swore at him and told him to "get out of here, go bother somebody else. A lot of nerve you have trying to get a room at this hour."

Trying not to show the discouragement he felt, Joseph simply reported, "They don't have any room either." He started to apologize to Mary, telling her this was no way to treat a wife, and he felt just awful about what she was going through. But Mary interrupted him: "I understand, Joseph, it isn't your fault. You are doing all you can, and I appreciate that. We'll get a room, I know we will. Only, we'd better hurry."

Joseph suddenly knew what Mary meant as he saw her eyes go shut and her whole body go tense. He started down the street, determined to find an inn, any inn, at any price. For almost an hour, they tried. At every door the answer was the same, and every time the door went shut in his face Joseph felt even worse . . . *how can this be?*

At about the sixth or seventh place (Joseph had stopped counting), he knocked on the door, and pleaded, "Please sir, can you help us; we need a room?"

And once more his heart dropped as he got the now familiar answer, "Sorry, we're full!"

"But you don't understand," Joseph cried, "my wife is having a baby; you've got to have something!"

"Look my friend, I am truly sorry, but the only empty place I've got is a corner stall in the barn."

With that Joseph exploded, "The barn! You don't think I would take my wife to the barn!" But just then he heard Mary's voice, "Joseph, we'd better take it."

So they did. But all the way down the path, Joseph was fighting back tears, feeling like a complete failure, miserably and inexpressibly sick at heart. He wanted to cry out, to shake his fist at God, to do something—anything—to express the frustration and anger he felt welling up inside him. "*How can this be—a barn!* Where is God? What is God doing to us!"

Actually, when he saw it, he had to admit it wasn't all that bad. It was dry and warm, and they were off by themselves. It was a lot better than being out on the street with those drunken Roman soldiers. The innkeeper's wife had come out with some hot soup, a lantern, and some blankets. She even offered to stay and help. But when Joseph saw Mary putting some clean straw into one of the feed troughs, then folding a clean blanket over it, he just could not restrain himself. He went off in the corner, pounding his fist on the side of stall. *How can this be—why?!*

It wasn't long before he heard Mary's exhausted voice calling him, "Joseph, come, it's a boy; aren't you proud?" Joseph was proud. Proud of Mary, proud of his little son, proud of everyone but himself. Their first child, born in a stable. But as he sat down beside Mary and held her in his arms as she held the baby, suddenly it didn't seem so bad. Mary was fine; the baby was here; it was healthy, and gradually his words of anger turned to quiet prayers of thanksgiving to God.

Soon Mary and the baby were asleep. As they slept, Joseph heard the quiet creak of the barn door opening. In came some shepherds who whispered the strangest story. They said some angels had told them about this baby, and they had come to see. Mary heard their excited whispering and woke up, carefully lifting a corner of the baby's blanket so they could get a glimpse. Mary smiled as one of the elderly shepherds, with tears streaming down his cheeks, knelt beside her, kissed her on the forehead and began to pray: "Lord God, Father of Abraham, Isaac, and Jacob, we bless you for this night and for this child." Joseph couldn't remember the rest, except that it was a beautiful prayer and he felt strangely moved by it. *How could this be?*

That's how the Bible tells the story . . . the wonderful story of God coming to earth to be one with us in a new and very personal way. It is a familiar story, only we tend to forget that Mary and Joseph were real people with real feelings, real dreams, and real hopes just like us. But let's not forget, this is the way the Bible tells the story, and may I suggest that this just might be the way God comes to us yet today. For you see, when God comes to us in a stable, we suddenly discover that God really does care about the dark, painful places in our lives. Those places where things do not always work out like we had hoped; and we also wonder, *How can this be?*

The exciting message of Christmas is God's answer to Joseph's "How Can This Be?" In the story of Christmas we discover again a God who comes to us, a God who stays with us when all doors slam shut in our face, and a God who is there with us when life becomes lonely, harsh, and unfair. The God who came to us in a stable two thousand years ago still comes to us in the human, the common, and the lowly places of our lives, often in the very places we wish we could avoid.

The good news is that God loves us. God loves us so much that God comes to us. The good news of Christmas is that God is right here—in our world, in our joy (and our pain), in our celebrations (and our sorrows), bringing light into the darkness, and hope into the world.

You know what the second bit of good news is? That God has loved us so much that he trusts us to share that good news of love and of hope with each other and with all the world. Can we truly comprehend the God-message of Christmas: As God dwells in us, we become the light of the world, the word of forgiveness, the message of hope, and the expression of God's love.

It is not that God is no longer God, nor that God has ceased to function—not at all. Rather, it is the amazing promise that the power of God has come to us, to rejoice and celebrate with us, to walk down the dusty roads of our lives, and to sit with us on a hay bale in the dark stable corners of our lives. God is with us in those times when we also wonder: *How can this be?* Because that is when God says to us "I know how it feels, I know how it hurts, and you are not alone."

And guess what happens? The neighbor's wife comes out with a blanket, a friend stops by and joins you for a cup of coffee, a colleague gives you a word of affirmation, and we begin to think, "Maybe we can make it, maybe there is hope for us, maybe there really is a God."

The Scriptures tell us that God was in Christ, and that by looking at Jesus we have a much clearer vision of God. This is what we celebrate at Christmas—the coming of light into our lives. The only problem is that God does not always do it the way we expect. We don't quite know what to do with that. So we keep pushing God away, trying to keep God at a distance, and making sure that God stays divine and holy, fitting the saintly, spiritual image the world has created for God.

But when we do that we miss the whole point. For in Jesus, God comes into our world and brings light. Through Jesus, God calls us to go out into our world with that light, out into a world where lots of people will try to blow out your candle.

Christmas is such beautiful mixture of faith—and the insecurity of trying to find a room; of angels—and the distinctive smells of a stable; of majesty and splendor—and a young family struggling to pay their taxes. It's a glorious picture. It shows us a God who knows us because God has come to us—up close and personal—and yet God loves us. That's the Christmas story's image of God, and *that truly is good news.*

Does God Permit "Do-Overs"?[6]

It was one of those beautiful days in July. My long-time golfing com-
panions, Del, Duane, and John were with me on the ninth hole at Black
Squirrel golf course. The ninth hole runs right alongside state route 119.
I was having a really good day, but on number nine I hit a truly horrible shot. It started right and just kept getting worse and worse as it
flew over the trees, across the road, hitting the bike path, and bouncing
over the fence into the cornfield. Not a good shot. I pounded my driver
on the ground in disgust, muttering to myself about being an idiot, and
demanding answers to questions like, when am I going to learn to play
golf, what am I doing hitting a ball out there, and what in the world was
I thinking? Duane merely said, "Come on Blosser, you can do better than
that, hit another one."

In fact, that is what the rules of golf say you have to do: If you hit a
ball out of bounds you take a two-stroke penalty and hit another one. But
that's not the point. Duane's comment brought me back from dwelling
on the awful shot I had just hit. He quietly told me I could do better on
the next one, and I did. At least I kept it in the fairway. In my childhood,
we called those "do-overs." But our culture doesn't like "do-overs." If you
make a mistake, you have to pay for it. But I wonder this morning: Does
God permit "do-overs"—the chance for us to start over in our lives?

Zechariah was a minor prophet who lived at the time when Israel's
seventy years of Babylonian captivity was ending. He was in Jerusalem as
the temple was being rebuilt. The label "minor" refers only to the length
of his writing and says nothing about the importance of his message.

Zechariah believed that God's original dream for humanity had not
changed. He knew that it still included a vision of shalom, a new creation. Thus, this morning let us consider how we understand the vision of
God for humanity. We often wrap this vision in wispy, mystical language
that focuses on the distant future—with images of angels, streets of gold,
beautiful clouds—things that you see on Hallmark greeting cards. Zechariah uses some of this vivid imagery, but most of the time he describes
God's vision in more homey, even earthy language.

Zechariah uses images that we know very well. He describes places
that resemble retirement villages—communities where older folks are
cared for, where they are honored for their wisdom, where they sit in
comfort and visit together. He describes a city park where grandchildren

6. The biblical foundation for this sermon is Zechariah 8:1–16.

play tag and run around with no fear of harm or danger from predators. His images describe a place where children and grandparents (plus everybody in between) know they are at home in a safe place. In this place, they will not be abused, malnourished, or forgotten. For Zechariah, God's community (of how Jerusalem should be) is a place that takes care of its children and its elderly, the two groups who are most often vulnerable to abuse and neglect. This is a place where the truth is told and where peace is the pattern for the day.

You see, Old Testament prophets were not driven by a vision of a future place prepared for us by God. Their focus was on what can be done by God's people right now. Zechariah wants God's people to live in the present and do what they can do *right now*, because God is with them *right now*, even though Israel was having a hard time seeing that presence of God.

Zechariah gives us a hint at how the people of Israel were reacting to the pressing issues of their day: "We can't pull this off, it's impossible—we can't bring peace in the world, we can't feed the hungry, we'll never make the streets safe for children, we can't provide health care so that the elderly are cared for." Zechariah's response? "This is what the Lord says: It may seem impossible to you, but does that mean it is impossible for me?"

And then the Lord (through Zechariah) launches into the original "do-over." Through Zechariah the Lord says, "I know you folks have just experienced a time when you had no money, and the streets weren't safe for people or animals. I know all that—but I am giving you a chance to start over again because the vision hasn't changed. We will plow the fields; we will sow the seeds of peace. It will rain; we will harvest grapes on the vine, and you will once again be a blessing to the peoples of the world. Don't be afraid—let your hands be strong."

And then Zechariah adds an amazing comment . . . "People from all languages and nations will come to you, and grab the hem of your garment, and beg of you, saying let us go with you because we see that God is with you." That is a wonderfully profound statement that we still have to learn. Zechariah is saying, "If you become a faithful people of God, and if you create among yourselves a community where peace is found, where the elderly are cared for, where the children play freely, where people tell the truth, and where justice is found at the city gate—then the nations will come to you and will say, that is what we want. That is how we want to live, too. Can we join with you in building this community? Can we also share in this new life?"

The message is not just for us. It is not even our message. It is the message of God's intentions for all humanity—not just us.

How might it be if we could get off the detour we have been on for several centuries? This detour says that we have to tell other nations how they must believe in God—and they must believe like we do. At the same time, we are exporting war and destruction in the name of God. We are forcing our political and religious will upon these nations, creating enemies rather than disciples, *killing* civilians rather than *feeding* them, and building prisons rather than schools and parks. And we wonder why it is not working. Is it any wonder that more and more often Christianity is not seen as the hope for humanity but as a people of power imposing their will upon others through military might?

It is important that our vision restores the original purposes of God for all humanity. It is a vision that is seen in God's call of Abraham to be a blessing to the nations; in the proclamation of Moses outlining new life for Israel that rejected the slavery, brutality, and poverty of Egypt; in the pleading of Isaiah that the people of God would not forsake the safety of God's presence for the false security of military weapons; and in the voice of Zechariah calling the people of God to start over, and this time—do it right. It is seen in Jesus who calls us to recognize that in his teachings we see God's new way of living for all people; in Paul as he urges us to pick up this ministry of reconciliation given by Jesus; in the writings of Menno Simons, Martin Luther King, Brian McLaren; and in the lives of Gayle Gerber Koontz at AMBS, Dee Schwartz working with the elderly at Greencroft, Andrew Murray with Anabaptist Network in England, Peter and Jenna Martin doing reconciliation ministry in Ireland—and the list goes on and on. As Hebrews 12 says, we really are surrounded by a great cloud of witnesses! Can we hear their voices? Can we hear God's voice coming to us through them? Can others see the vision of the kingdom of God—that community of God's peace being built right here in Goshen—right now. It might seem like an impossible task, but Zechariah is right, unless our hands are strong it will never get done. Bishop Desmond Tutu puts it very well: "Without God, we cannot—without us, God will not."[7]

The message of Zechariah restates God's original vision for humanity and how the people of God should live together. Hear the prophet again: "These are the things that you shall do: Speak the truth to one another, render judgments that are true and make for peace; do not think

---

7. This phrase is often attributed to St. Augustine.

evil in your hearts against another person, and don't make false statements. These are things that I hate, says the Lord."[8]

I dream of the day when God's vision will become a reality in our own experience. I dream of the day when children will play freely in the park and when our older folks will sit and visit in comfort without having to worry about outliving their retirement savings. I dream of a day when people in authority will tell the truth, rather than spin it for their own political gain. I dream of a day when courts will give justice to the poor, not simply to those who can hire the best lawyers. I dream of a day when our leaders will search for ways to make peace by being peacemakers; and when people from all nations, speaking all languages, will discover we are not trying to make them believe just like we do, but that we simply want to live together as people loved by God, for the good of all of us. Then the community of peace that Zechariah says is the vision of God might just become a reality.

Several months ago, I told the men's fellowship that I have never been so excited about the possibilities and challenges of being a follower of Jesus than I am right now. But I also said that I have never been so frustrated and disappointed with how comfortable we have become with the distortions of the Jesus message that are being proclaimed as truth. Can we once again become a light in the darkness, a sign along the path, and a clear voice in the cacophony of voices that are constantly ringing in our ears?

For us today, the concern of Zechariah is the same, and the situation really isn't very different. Political figures loudly proclaim that their message comes from God. But unfortunately, it does not sound like the Jesus message of the New Testament. Let's listen with discernment. Throughout history, kings and politicians have used the Jesus message to rally support for their own political and military ambitions. It was the challenge of the Old Testament prophets, and it is now the challenge of the New Testament followers of Jesus, to define and clarify the vision of God for humanity. If the church remains silent, the world around us will fill our silence with its own message and will claim it is of God.

Thirty years ago, Carolyn and I were living in a small town just outside St. Andrews, Scotland. We attended the local Church of Scotland congregation. We enjoyed the friendship of the people, but worship had a slightly different feel. Sometimes, after listening to Pastor Miller's sermon,

8. See Zechariah 8:16–17.

parishioners would comment: "That was a good sermon" or "That was a good worship service." I wondered—what was it that made it a good sermon or a good worship service? I discovered that, for that congregation, a good sermon made people feel guilty. They were reminded how sinful they were and how much they needed God's forgiveness. But even sermons about God's forgiveness had a bit of "What? You're back—asking for forgiveness again. How dare you? Don't you think God gets weary of your constant need of forgiveness?" So in addition to feeling guilty for what they had done, they were being taught to feel guilty about bothering God by asking for forgiveness for what they had done. I hope that was not typical of all churches in Scotland, but it happened pretty often in that congregation.

I just don't get that image about God from Zechariah. In Zechariah, I sense an understanding God who deals with guilt by freeing us from it, rather than by punishing us for having it. Zechariah shows me God as a welcoming presence who opens up our future to new possibilities and dreams for how life could be. This welcoming presence is right here with us, where we see what could be, and we are urged to reach out for it and to move toward a better life that more closely reflects what God has always wanted for all humanity.

First John 2:7–8 says, "Dear friends, I am not saying anything new. This is an old command. You have had this message from the beginning. This is what God has always wanted for us; it only sounds new because it is not what you are hearing all around you. Its truth is seen in him, and now in you because the darkness is passing away and the true light is already shining."

I wish I could find the words needed to share with you the gratitude I feel in my own heart when God offers me a "do-over," because I need them. When God says to me, "I know that wasn't your best. Let's do it again; and this time, let's learn from it and do it better. It may seem impossible to you right now, Don—but you don't have to do by yourself. If we work together, we can do it, and the world will be more like I always dreamed it would be."

Just maybe, as we team up with God in that way, people from all over the world will see what we are doing, and they will recognize that God is in our midst, and they will know that God is with them, too. As they see that, we can join together in building a world that is safe for us all, where their children play in our yards, and our children play in theirs. Together we will grow old in peace and experience God's love that encompasses every human being. God has offered us an opportunity to "do it over"—to start again, to redo our theology, to recover God's vision for humanity and how we live together. God is pleading with us—to do it better this time.

It is called forgiveness. It is called grace. It is called hope. It is called "the joy of God still being God." It is called being followers of Jesus and members of the worldwide community of God's people doing God's will. What more could we ask for?

Lord: May our eyes be opened; may our hearts overflow; may our hands reach out to receive and offer hope and help to all those who share this world with us. May your vision for peace, for health, and for safety for all your children everywhere be our vision and our message also. Amen.

Epilogue

Back to the Home Place

I am not saying that I have this all neatly put together,
or that I have it made.
But I am on my way, reaching out for Christ
who has so wondrously reached out to me.
Friends, don't get me wrong;
by no means do I count myself to be an expert in all this,
but refusing to let the past hold me back,
I keep reaching forward for that divine calling
which God has given us in Jesus Christ, my Lord.[1]
—Paul
Philippians 3:12–14

Does your theology stop at the cross . . .
or does it start there?
—Shirley Showalter
President of Goshen College, 1997–2004

Bible study that does not lead to more faithful
and creative discipleship is inadequate.[2]
—Stuart Murray

---

1. Peterson, *The Message.*
2. Murray, *The Naked Anabaptist*, p. 65.

And the Road Goes On

Recently I went back to that farmhouse on the country road where I grew up. I wanted to feel again what it was like to go home. But it just wasn't the same. The bumpy gravel road is now smooth blacktop. And the house! When I got to the house, I just sat there and stared. I thought to myself, "Is that really the house I grew up in?" It was almost unrecognizable. The clean paint job that Dad and I had given it hadn't been touched in fifty years. The house still has the same wood siding, but now it is dirty, badly faded, and a few pieces are missing. Dad would never have permitted that. The side yard where Dad used to play ball with us is now cluttered with broken down farm equipment and an old beat up car. The stone veneer that Dad put around the front door is gone. Unpainted plywood panels give a cold welcome to what I remember as a warm, friendly, fun-filled place for children.

Is that what happens with our faith as well? Faith that is not nurtured has a way of deteriorating. It can become unwelcoming for others and unsatisfying for ourselves unless we let it grow with us, making improvements as life presents new challenges. There is a part of me that wishes the old house would always stay the way I remember it. In the same way, many people want to reach old age with the same innocent security they had with their childhood faith. This old house that I was now looking at had served me very well as a place of nurture, support, and safety. Even though I have grown and changed, there is a part of me that wishes life could always be the way it was back then.

I had intended to knock on the door and ask if I could go upstairs to see my old bedroom. Now, I really don't want to do that. That warm, friendly kitchen where we sat at the table, did our homework, and swapped stories with mom wouldn't be like it was for me as a child. This reminds me that even though I might wish I could, I cannot rewrite my own history as though it never happened.

That is how life is. In this old house, we had one radio that picked up WKBN Youngstown news, most of the time. It faded in and out, depending on the weather. But we assumed that was how it was for everybody. We didn't have TV, a phone, or a toilet in the house. Now I have a 46" HDTV that beams live pictures into our house from all over the world. We have three bathrooms. I have a cell phone that takes pictures, sends text messages, and allows me to get on the web. Do I really want to go back to that old Zenith radio? I certainly don't want to ride in that paint splattered 1935 Plymouth again, so why do I wish my faith could be the way it was when I was a child? Would the faith I had as an elementary school student (although it served me well then) still have integrity for me as a retired college professor?

Perhaps it is even more important to ask where this road is taking me. My life has been far more exciting, satisfying, and yet more difficult than I ever imagined it would be when I was a child. I would not have it any different. I understand the apostle Paul (Phil 4:12), in that I know what it feels like to be in need, and I know what it is to have plenty. I have learned the secret of being content in any and every situation. I have laughed at parties with friends, cried at the funerals of my parents and several siblings, suffered painful defeats, and celebrated exciting victories. I have eaten fried mush or peanut butter sandwiches because there was not much else in the house. I also have been an honored guest for a nineteen course government authorized royal banquet in China. In the midst of all these things, I felt secure in my faith, yet I held it lightly because I did not know what might lie ahead, just over the next hill.

Gradually, the enlightened fundamentalism of my childhood began to develop cracks. As I grew up, I became increasingly uncomfortable with the well-defined and carefully protected spiritual focus of the Christianity I had known as a boy. This discomfort was exacerbated even more by the political nationalism, the militarism, and the diminishing importance of peace, justice, and concern for the poor contained in this domesticated gospel message.

I can no longer wrap my mind around a vision that advocates returning to a spirituality of the past. Is God really best seen as a power from the past who needs to be protected from new ideas? If only we could conceive of God as a dynamic force drawing us into the future. This spiritual God-force would give us the freedom to explore fresh ways of following Jesus in a world of complex issues that the faith community of the first century could never have imagined.

I have strong convictions about God, but I have never had the absolute certainty that some other pastors seem to have in knowing precisely where God dwells. Nor have I ever had the confidence to declare with absolute certainty what God was, or is, doing. God is a reality that has always been just beyond my ability to fully comprehend in the definitive way that TV evangelists seem to have. I remember attending a planetarium program at Franklin and Marshall College in Lancaster, Pennsylvania, that focused on the size of the universe with all its galaxies and light years of space. If God is "up there" or "out there" somewhere in the unbelievably extreme vastness of space, where exactly is that dwelling place we call heaven?

Because I was a pastor, I felt I had to keep these troubling thoughts to myself. Yet, at the same time, I enjoyed every chance I had to challenge the comfortable certainties that other adults simply seemed to know had to be true. Was there a way to be open to new discoveries without blatantly rejecting the answers that were meaningful for others? Could I find better language and visual images that would catch the imagination of the contemporary mind without sacrificing the reality that gave life to old images and language?

I was not sure how it could be done, but I believed that we should experience faith in Jesus as tugging us toward the future with all its unknown possibilities. To my way of thinking, that kind of searching, exploring faith would fill our lives with hope and excitement.

The call seemed so clear and obvious. I wanted to be part of a faith community that had the courage to explore new trails. I wanted to find new ways of experiencing faith that encouraged the asking of questions without having to know the answers in advance. This new faith community would not be afraid of taking risks, because it would believe that God's presence is with us in everything we do, even when we fail—as we most certainly will once in a while.

Not everyone shared my excitement about the future. There were those who were frightened by almost everything new because they were convinced that God is best known in the past. My emerging faith in God was telling me that God is not only with us here, but is already in our future, long before we ever get there. The challenge for us is to keep up, to discover the promises that are waiting for us as the sun comes up each new day.

Thus, for me, graduate school seemed to be a very logical next step in my faith journey. In spite of this emerging faith, I still believed there had to be answers out there, if I could only find them. I still held firm to the old paradigm, trying to pour new wine into an old wineskin; and like the parable of Jesus, it was not working.

My graduate studies on the Jewish year of Jubilee (Lev 25 and Luke 4) helped clarify for me how the ancient people of God experienced the presence and working of this power they called *YHWH* (Jehovah). Their concept of the world placed an external God somewhere just above the sky. Over time, they began to believe that this external deity came into their world and took specific actions that delivered them from danger or blessed them with good things. These Old Testament people used God as an explanation for things unexplainable, both good and bad. It was a very simple next step for them to use this same God as the justification for things, both good and bad, that they were doing to other people. I began to wonder whether God had, in fact, really told them to do these truly awful things that they were doing. Might it be true that they were projecting onto God their strong desire to punish or destroy other nations? They then validated their actions by saying God had told them to do it. This possibility was confirmed for me as I saw my own nation doing exactly the same thing. We still use God as validation to rally national support as we declare war on other less powerful, but very troublesome, nations.

When I moved into the classroom as Professor of New Testament, I was increasingly uncomfortable with the sermons I was hearing in church. These sermons assured me that God would do wonderful things for me if I "only believed." I knew of too many instances in which people had professed a profound faith, and had lived exemplary lives in mission, yet they had not received these promised blessings. I wondered whether we were creating a God who would serve and care for us, rather than experiencing God as a *presence* who is always with us even when really bad things are happening to us. Yet I was cautious about expressing these theological concerns because I knew most students, and their parents, expect professors to have the answers, not the questions. Also, I did not feel it was appropriate for me to work out my own theological musings in front of undergraduate students who did not have the same history or developmental education that I had. In church, I winced at things that were said and promises that were made. While in the classroom, I tried to help students develop positive, holistic concepts of God, and faith for themselves that would give them integrity as they moved forward into their own future.

After more than twenty years of college teaching, I retired. Carolyn and I chose to remain in Goshen and retain our membership at College Mennonite Church. I would preach once or twice a year and was almost always involved in leading a Sunday school class. I was delighted when the pastoral team asked if I would meet with a small group of young adults who were reading *A New Christianity for a New World* by Bishop John Shelby Spong. This group wanted a safe place to explore the edges of their faith, where any question was valid and no one's faith (or lack thereof) would be ridiculed. Within six months, the original group of eight had become twenty. Couples joined us from other congregations as they learned about this group that emphasized openness and honesty, where it was okay to ask unorthodox questions, and where you would not be given simplistic clichés as answers.

This group was a challenge for me: although I found Bishop Spong's vision for faith to be exciting, I did not agree with his methodology or biblical exegesis. Things that I believed to be true were rejected far too quickly by Bishop Spong as simply Midrash (interpretative stories growing out of Old Testament texts). Likewise, I had to listen especially carefully to the members of the class and accept answers that were different from my own, because they had meaning for that person.

This group grew in number, and these new members began asking serious questions. It was clear that once-obvious answers were no longer helpful. They wondered whether they could remain Christians if the old answers are the only possible answers. Without knowing it, these persons were actually verbalizing many of the internal rumblings that I, too, was experiencing. I found myself being pulled into open discussions that danced around the edges of my own faith. I was no longer "the teacher" who led the class; rather, I became a group member with them as we searched for answers. When the group was asked to name itself so the church would know how to refer to us, *Borderlands* emerged as the group name. Group members wanted to continue being Christians, but they knew they were on the edges of their faith and they felt it was important to redefine the content and expression of their faith.

Information about what we were doing, some of it inaccurate, began to circulate within the congregation. Some persons were concerned that we had given up on faith. Others were finding new courage to give voice to their own questions. I was seen as a safe, respected person they could share their troubling questions with. They knew I loved the church, cared deeply about the Scriptures, and would not reject them. But this did not remove all the questions and concerns that others in the church had about what we were doing.

As the months passed, I sensed within myself that this was a new passion or mission for me as a member of the church. This had started years before in the Akron congregation. That church felt called to be in ministry with people who were close to giving up on both church and faith. The Akron church had the strength and security to allow diversity. They wanted a faith that would encourage unorthodox questions. They believed that growth comes by searching together after hearing the question, rather than offering answers before the questions were even asked.

This approach seemed to ring true with the teaching style of Jesus. I was sensing that many people were holding on to traditional answers, even though these answers were no longer meaningful to them. They were doing this because these were the only answers they knew. They wanted someone who could understand the struggle behind the questions and then walk with them in finding answers without fearing rejection. What most of them did not know, however, was that for me, this was also a journey into new territory. I had become quite comfortable having an open-minded, radical faith commitment that led to an active social conscience. But now I was sharing faith with persons who were stretching my own comfort zone with their unconventional questions.

For example, I was finding new meaning in the reality of God, yet I had never challenged the standard theistic beliefs that saw God as a powerful entity off somewhere detached from the world. I was not satisfied with this theistic God concept, but I knew of no other way to talk about God. For all my life, this had been how God is, and all that was left to be done was to learn how we could best serve humanity in the name of this all-powerful, distant God.

I continued to be a bit uncomfortable with most of the prayers that my fellow Christians were praying. They seemed to be quite free to casually tell God to do specific things, such as, be with us in this meeting, or to guide us as we make decisions, or bless us in this time of worship.

These prayers work as long as you don't do second-step thinking about what this says about God. Do we need to ask God to do something that God has already been doing for thousands of years (be with us)? Do we have to ask God to do what God has always wanted to do (be with us in worship)? What is needed in prayer is not asking God to come be with us, for God is already here. The real concern is whether or not we are sensitive to the God who is here. It is not that we tell God to do our decision making for us, but that we might be open to sensing the spirit of God who is present in our lives as we talk together about these decisions.

I found a lecture by Bishop Spong to be revolutionarily helpful. This lecture, titled "God Beyond Theism?"[3] presented ways for me to think about God that were not locked into the old distant, detached, and pow-

3. Spong, John Shelby. "Beyond Theism" was a lecture on given at Depauw University. A three-minute excerpt is available on the Internet. In his book *Why Christianity Must Change or Die*, he develops this concept in several chapters, including "In Search of God" and "Beyond Theism to New God Images." These are not lectures, but the theology is spelled out in these chapters.

erful being images of my childhood. While no one image of God is so complete as to totally capture all possible meanings, these new images helped me become aware of God's daily presence and comfort in my life.

This gave me the opportunity to do some serious reflection on what it means to be spiritual. For most of my life, I understood that being spiritual meant daily Bible study and prayer as a method of staying in contact with the God of the universe who is way up there in heaven. It involved trying to separate myself from the pressures, noise, and tensions of life on this earth while I focused on an internal, spiritual relationship between myself and God. This was difficult for me. I do not have any attention deficits except when I focus on God while praying or meditating. I have never been able to retain focus for more than a few minutes; then I feel guilty for the rest of the devotional time because my mind wanders away so quickly.

This new understanding changed many things in my life. With the help of friends and colleagues, I am learning to be more conscious of God's spirit that is all around me all of the time. I am learning to be more fully human, walking in relationship with the God who has come to me in Jesus, and who now comes to me daily in the form of people with whom I share life quite openly. As I share time with persons who are also sensitive to God's life-giving presence in the simple, beautiful things of life, such as, nature, peaceful silence, or an energizing sharing of human experiences, God has become a newer, living reality. Now I fully expect to sense the presence of God as I visit with an older couple who are facing the realities of aging, or as I meet together with another pastor to be a colleague in thinking through the Sunday sermon, or as I prepare for my own Sunday school lesson.

I have read almost everything Bishop Spong has written, and a group of us from Borderlands once met with the bishop and his wife for supper. I have also widely read the works of Marcus Borg and John Dominic Crossan. These two scholars gave language and integrity to the faith that was becoming the driving force in my life. So it was with great excitement that I attended a Borg-Crossan seminar on radical discipleship. I heard solid Anabaptist theology coming from this Episcopal-Catholic team that resonated with everything I was trying to live out in my own life. These two men urged us to discover a more radical faith in Jesus. This message was not new to me, but it was energizing and wonderfully refreshing. All around me in the Portland, Oregon, Trinity Episcopal Cathedral, pastors and lay leaders were saying to each other, "Why haven't we heard this before? This is a gospel we can believe in. This gives us hope. This will change our lives and our ministry." It was a God moment that energized my soul. First John 2:7–8 was becoming reality: "I am not telling you something new. This is an old teaching that you have had from the beginning. It sounds like a new teaching, but its truth is seen in him and in you, because the darkness is passing away and the true light is already shining."

A few months later, College Mennonite Church asked me to preach on Reformation Sunday. I wanted to draw from Martin Luther's Wittenberg church door experience and share some areas of faith that I wished we could talk about together. I titled the sermon, "Let's Talk About It," and I hoped that it might encourage more of the kind of faith discussions that we were already having in our Borderlands class. The text of this sermon is located in chapter 2 of this book.

Some persons were very excited about what they heard that Sunday morning. They asked the church leadership to create a setting where, in fact, we could "talk about it." Others responded quite differently. Several persons told the pastoral team, "If Don ever preaches again at College Mennonite Church, we will withdraw our membership. The Church Board must make it clear that what we heard him say on Sunday morning does not represent what this church believes!"

I was surprised to learn of these rather harsh and hurtful threats, because they were in stark contrast with the excitement and affirmation that I was experiencing via the Borderlands class for the past two years. It was more than three years (and several pastoral changes) before College Mennonite Church asked me to preach again.

This experience raised personal faith questions for me. What is the role of the Sunday morning sermon? For many people it feels best to have the sermon affirm what they already believe, so hearing new ideas is stressful for them. Should the sermon identify with those who want their faith to be affirmed, or with those who want their faith to be challenged? Is there a prophetic role for preaching that calls for new ways of thinking as well as new ways of living?

I have always lived in the tension between the traditional beliefs of my younger days and the challenging call of new understandings in my adult years. The institutional church tends to gravitate toward the middle, and not without legitimate reasons. That is where security is for the pastor. That kind of safe thinking invites people to return each week for continued affirmation. But if the pastor does not reach out to those on the edges of faith, then who does? We pastors are not always aware of these persons on the edges because they are not always there. Even when they are there, we pastors assume they will be content with the more traditional language and content of sermons intended for "people at the center." Should we expect people on the edges to change and become more "centered" so that those of us in the middle can remain the way we are? I doubt whether that will ever work. Can we pastors insist that those at the center become more accepting by allowing people on the edges to remain who they are? I doubt whether that will ever happen.

I have always loved the church, and my life has been lived in service of the church. And yet the sharpest criticism has always come from within the church itself. What price should one be willing to pay to remain in conversation with those on the more progressive end of the church who feel that the traditional answers are no longer helpful? How will they find answers for their new questions? The answers to these questions are revealed in the people who want to live their lives as followers of Jesus with integrity as honest, caring people. This continues to be my mission as a follower of Jesus.

Years ago our family went hill walking in Scotland. With our five children, we parked our VW van and start up the path toward the top, only to discover that when we reached the visible top, the ground was level for a few hundred feet but then a new summit appeared not far ahead. This process of walking up the hill, finding level ground, only to have a new hill to climb would repeat itself again and again. After awhile our children got tired of me telling them, "just one more to go, that really is the top this time," especially when I had said it three or four times already.

That is the story of my faith. There have been numerous times when I was convinced that I had reached a hilltop in my faith and I had matured. I thought I knew what the questions were and what the right answers should be. This confidence seldom lasted for long, however. No sooner had I found firm footing on that hilltop, I saw that there was a new hill, or a new set of challenges ahead that I had not expected and for which I had given little thought.

My traditional faith background tells me that Jesus gave his life to save me from my sins. Surely I can risk reputation and community acceptance for him, because there really is no comparison in cost. This belief also urges me to retreat into the safer theology and life of my childhood in order to regain the acceptance and trust that I enjoyed as a pastor and college Bible teacher. However, my more progressive side tells me that this mission venture of walking alongside persons on the edges of their faith is valuable for them. Often people in church shy away from their questions and from the steep hills in their faith pilgrimage. Who else is taking the risk of sharing the journey with those who want to follow Jesus but need new ways of understanding and living their faith?

This journey of wrestling with my own faith is not over, although sometimes I wish it would end. On occasion it is lonely, yet it includes frequent unexpected moments that are truly exhilarating. At this stage in my life, I see in the Scriptures that challenging the religious institutions was a significant factor leading to the crucifixion of Jesus. The traditional majority will always be cared for by the traditional pastoral approaches and the preaching of traditional sermons. Who will take care of the others? Indeed, are there enough of us who care about them to make a difference?

My experience has been that this new vision has not protected me from all things painful, nor from making mistakes when I should have known better. But it has allowed me to be on a journey that has been exciting, rewarding, and full of surprises far beyond anything I ever dreamed of. I am comfortable believing that this commitment to the future as a way of living in the present is good for me. I still get frightened at times by what may be just over the next hill, but I am comfortable in the assurance that God is already there ahead of me. Thus, it is important for me to keep taking one more step forward. With Paul as my inspiration, "I do not consider that I have attained, but I am committed to doing this one thing, forgetting what lies behind, and pushing forward to what lies ahead, I press on toward the prize of the high calling of God in Christ Jesus" (Phil 3:13–14).

My passion for the call of Jesus to kingdom living; my commitment to the way of peace; my pain that does not go away when people are excluded or rejected for sexual, racial, or religious reasons; and my pastoral concern for persons no matter where they are on the theological spectrum, will not let me be silent. To turn away from them would imply giving up my own faith, and that would mean walking away from those who are searching for a faith that has meaning and integrity. That would make life quite difficult because I have discovered that, in fact, I am one with them in the search, and I need them every bit as much as they need me.

Postscript

Be thou my vision, O lord of my heart;
naught be all else to me save that thou art.
Thou my best thought, by day or by night,
waking or sleeping, thy presence my light.

Be thou my wisdom, be thou my true word;
I ever with thee, and thou with me Lord.
thou my great Father, thy child may I be,
thou in me dwelling, and I one with thee. [4]

This is my prayer.

4. Sixth-century Irish poem by Dallan Forgail, trans.by Mary Byrne. *Hymnal: A Worship Book 1992*, Hymn 545, Mennonite Publishing House, Scottdale, PA.

Bibliography

Most of us learned our best new ideas by talking with people or by reading books. These ideas then get modified or intensified by the experiences that we have. Included in this bibliography list are books that I read on my journey that had formative impact on my thinking. Many of these are books I have read, reread, marked up, and made summaries of to help me find things quickly. The list is far from complete, but it provides books that I would recommend for others on their journey. The list also includes books and articles mentioned in this volume.

Arendt, Hannah. *The Human Condition*. Chicago: University of Chicago Press, 1958.

Augsburger, David. *Dissident Discipleship: A Spirituality of Self-Surrender, Love of God, and Love of Neighbor*. Grand Rapids, MI: Brazos, 2006.

Barclay, William, *The Mind of Jesus*. New York: Harper & Row, 1960.

Borg, Marcus. *The God We Never Knew*. San Francisco: HarperCollins, 1997.

———. *The Heart of Christianity*. San Francisco: HarperCollins, 2003.

———. *Reading the Bible Again For the First Time*. San Francisco: HarperCollins, 2001.

Brueggemann, Walter. *The Bible Makes Sense*. Cincinnati: St. Anthony Messenger, 2003.

Crossan, John Dominic. *God and Empire: Jesus Against Rome, Then and Now*. San Francisco: HarperCollins, 2007.

Grimsrud, Ted. *Theology as if Jesus Matters*. Telford, PA: Cascadia, 2009.

———. *God's Healing Strategy*. Telford, PA: Cascadia, 2000.

Gulley, Philip. *If the Church Were Christian*. New York: HarperOne, 2010.

Jefford, Clayton N. "Letter to Diognetus" in *Reading the Apostolic Fathers*. Peabody, MA: Hendrickson, 1996.

Keck, Leander. "'The Premodern Bible in the Postmodern World." In *Interpretation* v. 50 #2, April 1996, pp. 130–41.

Kern, Kathleen. *We Are The Pharisees*. Scottdale, PA: Herald, 1995.

Kraybill, Don. *The Upside Down Kingdom*. Scottdale, PA: Herald, rev. 2003.

Lamott, Anne. *Travelling Mercies*. New York: Pantheon, 1999.

Mayes, Benjamin. Online: http://www.morehouse.edu/about/chapel/mays_wisdom. html

McGrath, Alister. *Christian Theology*. Malden, MA: Blackwell, 2007.

McLaren, Brian. *A New Kind of Christianity: Ten Questions That Are Transforming the Faith*. New York: HarperOne, 2010.

Murray, Stuart. *The Naked Anabaptist: The Bare Essentials of a Radical Faith*. Scottdale, PA: Herald, 2010.

Oldham John. H. *Life Is Commitment*. New York: Harper & Bros, 1953.

Bibliography

O'Neill, Michael. "Karl Barth's Doctrine of Election." In *Evangelical Quarterly* 76:4, 2004.

Rahner, Karl. *Karl Rahner in Dialogue.* Effingham, IL: Crossroads, 1986.

Roth, John D. *Beliefs: Mennonite Faith and Practice.* Scottdale, PA: Herald, 2005.

Schrock-Shenk, Carolyn, and Lawrence Ressler. *Making Peace With Conflict.* Scottdale, PA: Herald, 1999.

Seeliger, Wes. *Western Theology.* Atlanta: Forum, 1973.

Sider, Ron. *Christ and Violence.* Scottdale, PA: Herald, 1979.

Spong, John Shelby. "Beyond Theism." Online: www.youtube.com/watch?v=9XL8Lv aJ9Rc.

———. *A New Christianity for a New World: Why Traditional Faith Is Dying and How a New Faith Is Being Born.* San Francisco: HarperCollins, 2001.

———. *Why Christianity Must Change or Die.* San Francisco: HarperCollins, 1998.

Thompson, Marianne Maye. *1–3 John (IVP New Testament Commentary Series).* Downers Grove, IL: InterVarsity, 1946.

Tillich, Paul. *Theology of Culture.* New York: Oxford University Press, 1959.

Trocmé, André. *Jesus and the Nonviolent Revolution.* Scottdale, PA: Herald, 1973.

Untermeyer, Louis. *Enlarged Anthology of Robert Frost's Poems.* New York: Pocket, 1971.

Wenger, J. C., ed. *The Complete Writings of Menno Simons.* Scottdale, PA: Herald, 1956.

Yancey, Philip. *The Jesus I Never Knew.* San Francisco: HarperCollins, 1995.

———. *What's So Amazing About Grace.* Grand Rapids, MI: Zondervan, 1997.

Yoder, John H. *The Original Revolution: Essays on Christian Pacifism.* Scottdale, PA: Herald, 1971.

———. *The Politics of Jesus.* Grand Rapids, MI: Eerdmans, 1972.

Yoder, June A. "Preaching as an Agent for Change." In *Vision,* Vol. 2. Elkhart, IN: Institute of Mennonite Studies, 2001.